"Stephen Seligman's new book is a valuable contribution to the psychoanalytic dialogue concerning developmental theory and its implications for analytic practice. His discussion of 'relational-developmental psychoanalysis' is without parallel. It seems to me to pick up where Greenberg and Mitchell's 1983 classic, *Object Relations in Psychoanalytic Theory*, leaves off. He presents in a highly readable way a multi-disciplinary approach that includes direct infant observation, experience with patients in psychoanalysis, as well as social, historical and biological contributions. The result is a compelling study of twenty-first century psychoanalysis, which will enrich the perspectives of psychoanalysts and infant observers, as well as students of any field that takes as its object of study the human condition in all of its complexity."

Thomas H. Ogden, author most recently of *What Alive Means* and
Coming to Life in the Consulting Room

"This is an outstanding book. It provides a masterly account of developments in psychoanalysis particularly in relation to its theories of childhood and development. The account leads toward relational analysis yet takes off in highly original directions in its discussion of the importance of puzzled and open attention and the implications for the development of the sense of time and of the future in patients filled with a sense of futility. The chapters on the link between temporality and intentionality are fascinating and need urgently to be read by all clinicians. The whole book is wonderfully clear in the way it links infant observation and psychoanalysis. It is also a great read."

Anne Alvarez, *Consultant Child and Adolescent Psychotherapist;
retired Co-Convener of the
Autism Service, Child and Family Dept.,
Tavistock Clinic, London, UK*

"This profoundly integrative work is a remarkable journey through psychoanalysis from the point of view of infancy and child development. Weaving together past and present, directly informing our clinical work with immediacy and energy, this book is superb."

Beatrice Beebe, *Clinical Professor,
Columbia University Medical Center*

Relationships in Development

Relationships in Development is both a clinical resource and a vital intellectual history—a clear account of how research about infancy transforms psychotherapy practice *and* an authoritative survey of the place of child development in psychoanalysis.

It updates developmental psychoanalysis by integrating it with trauma theory, neuroscience, nonlinear dynamic systems theories, and infant mental health work. "Executive summaries" of attachment, intersubjectivity, and "the relational baby" are offered, leading to an open and flexible approach to psychodynamic therapy in varied socioeconomic and cultural situations. This Classic Edition includes a new introduction assessing the current state of developmental thinking in the psychotherapy world.

Relationships in Development will appeal to psychoanalysts, psychoanalytic psychotherapists, and graduate students in psychology, social work, and psychotherapy, as well as to all those interested in psychotherapy and child development.

Stephen Seligman is Clinical Professor at the University of California, San Francisco and the New York University Postdoctoral Program in Psychoanalysis, and Training and Supervising Analyst at the San Francisco Center for Psychoanalysis.

Relationships in Development

Infancy, Intersubjectivity, and Attachment

Classic Edition

Stephen Seligman

Routledge
Taylor & Francis Group

LONDON AND NEW YORK

Designed cover image: Getty Image ©StockPlanets

Classic edition published 2026
by Routledge
4 Park Square, Milton Park, Abingdon, Oxon, OX14 4RN

and by Routledge
605 Third Avenue, New York, NY 10158

Routledge is an imprint of the Taylor & Francis Group, an informa business

First edition published by Routledge 2018

Classic edition published by Routledge 2026

British Library Cataloguing-in-Publication Data
A catalogue record for this book is available from the British Library

ISBN: 978-1-003-86345-8 (hbk)
ISBN: 978-1-032-99848-0 (pbk)
ISBN: 978-1-003-60732-8 (ebk)

DOI: 10.4324/9781003607328

Typeset in Times New Roman
by Apex CoVantage, LLC

To Mary

Contents

Introduction to the classic edition

I'm honored that the publishers have deemed this book a "classic." This might, though, suggest that the book and the subjects it takes up somehow remain static. One of the leitmotifs of this book is how theory and practice are changed as they pass through generations: Freud to Ferenczi, Ferenczi to Klein, Klein to Winnicott, Freud to Anna Freud, the Ego Psychologists to the Relationalists, and so on. This process has continued in the decade or so since the book was written.

The first sentence of this book promises an integration of infant development findings with psychoanalysis and psychodynamic therapies. I hoped, also, to offer a kind of intellectual history of the developmental perspective in analysis, organized in part around analytic theories' shifting image of the infant. As I featured infancy and worked to contextualize it and childhood more broadly, I also offered an account of the developmental psychoanalytic perspective *in itself*.

In retrospect, though, it seems to me that I didn't quite feature that perspective as an explicit, concentrated theme as much as I might have, although I did provide a history and an orienting summary (Chapters 3–5). In proposing a "relational-developmental perspective," I meant to build on the earlier developmental psychoanalytic interest in how childhood experience endures and is reproduced in adulthood. I took for granted that readers would be more or less familiar with this body of work.

Lately, though, I've come to feel that this core developmental-psychoanalytic perspective has receded from its more central place in the analytic canon. While images of infants and parents are—quite helpfully—commonplace, those drawn from toddlers, older children, and adolescents may be less so. But exposure to actual children and a feeling for them can be an indispensable part of all psychoanalytic therapy, providing rich, insightful templates to organize the complex and often bewildering array of ways that patients repeat their pasts in the present—images, themes and structures, such as separation/autonomy/relatedness; dependence/independence; trust/mistrust; holding on/letting go; initiative-agency/receptivity; and many more.[1] I hope my debt to Erikson is apparent. I often imagine my patients in some small-size version of their adult bodies, in their families of origin, with some of those childhood feelings and dilemmas that have led them to therapy.

The impacts of childhood adversity—especially trauma—can hardly be grasped without some sense of how they vary across different childhood and adult ages and developmental stages. A developmental phase-oriented, life cycle perspective adds a vivid, specific dimension to our listening in the moment and our understanding over time: It makes things more real. In most approaches, much of what analysts and patients experience shares many qualities with parent-child dynamics. This is well-acknowledged, but without some knowledge of those dynamics, it will be hard to really get hold of this. For example, many of us agree that good analysis is like play, but this might remain abstract without all that can be learned from spending time with children playing.

The developmental mindset also highlights the ebbs and flows of time and temporality—present, past, future layering, mixing, sliding through and shaping each other. The backward and forward movement of developmental time—regression, fixation, growth, progression—are at work in psychotherapies of whatever sort (whether acknowledged or not); they are inevitably at the center of the therapeutic action of psychoanalytic treatment. Transference-countertransference shows up in a special form that intermingles childhood ways of imagining and relating with the present actualities of the analytic relationship, however construed and however shaped in each person's individual early and current personal and cultural experience. Some of my colleagues and students today, though, describe transferences in the same language as they would describe an adult's attitudes and beliefs. Although this can be helpful—especially in communicating with a patient—something will be lost without grasping that different and developmentally earlier form that is shaping the way things are feeling. One of the special skills of the analyst is to keep this in mind without infantilizing the patient as a complete person. A strong developmental perspective is at the center of psychoanalytic theory and practice.

It enriches my thinking in every clinical hour, and it's very difficult for me to imagine practicing without it.

This orientation seems to me to have remained so implicit or taken for granted by the older generations that we have neglected to emphasize it. A developmental perspective was regarded as indispensable for most of my generation of analytic therapists. In the late 1970's and 1980's United States, Erikson and Winnicott were opening our eyes to what was special and inspiring about childhood, and developmental-analytic research theorists like John Bowlby and Margaret Mahler were proposing new theories about attachment, separation-individuation, and other reformulations of the original Freudian psychosexual stages. These new theories were leading to new approaches to borderline and narcissistic conditions: Otto Kernberg's and Heinz Kohut's integrative books were the most read among mental health professionals. Critical feminists like Nancy Chodorow, Jessica Benjamin, and Irene Fast were extending these insights to challenge the established phallocentrism. Overview volumes were ubiquitous. In Britain, workers at the Hampstead Child Therapy Clinic in London, led by Anna Freud, were elaborating and codifying a developmental approach, and the Middle Group's interest in infancy and childhood was proceeding apace (based at the Tavistock Clinic), with a growing profession of child psychotherapists, many of whom were inspired by Kleinian child analytic approaches.

This enthusiasm has faded in the last decades. Within the analytic world, in the United States at least, both pre-license and formal analytic training generally include less developmental teaching than in the past; it's hard to learn much about the wide range of experiences of children 0-18 in just a quarter or two. This may be due in part to how much new knowledge has emerged in all the mental health fields, just as so much has developed in psychoanalysis.

Theoretical movements within analysis are involved, too. As I outline in Chapters 3, 5, and 6, the hegemony of the Freudian Structural model and North American Ego Psychology in Anglo-American analysis has waned in the Twenty-First Century. Since developmental psychoanalysis was most fully elaborated there, it has receded, too. Several of the currently ascendant psychoanalytic orientations take a more ambivalent stance toward developmental thinking: While both Kleinians and some contemporary French theorists have shown interest in developmental observation and theorizing, they have also circumscribed it as outside of the purely analytic data available only in the consulting room. In a different key, the early Relational movement was influenced by the Interpersonalist skepticism about development. While significant integration has emerged there—including substantial attention to the infant development research—there has been no comprehensive meta-synthesis of the sort that emerged from Ego Psychology. Indeed, this book is my attempt to close that gap.

The excitement over that infancy research may also have had the paradoxical side effect of pulling interest away from the engagement with the later phases of childhood and adolescence. Complex as they are, parent-infant interactions are most often *relatively* contained, involving just two (or three) people, most often in a single place (either a home or a laboratory setting). As such they are easier to subject to empirical procedures like rating and coding, which leads to the possibility of correlations with other concurrent developmental phenomena (brain development, attachment classification, etc.) as well as data from later developmental periods (borderline personality, adult attachment classification, etc.). Such clarity is harder to obtain as a growing child becomes more affected by more expanded environments like schools and neighborhoods. Even more important, video imagery of infant-parent interactions are so rich and fascinating as to draw attention from those other life stages. That there is now wide agreement that the first months and years are the most influential offers even more reason to give them priority. Nonetheless, something is lost if clinicians are not familiar with the different child and adolescent stages, and the general developmental orientation, with its ebbs and flows.

There are some broader cultural trends that have contributed to this, too. The widespread depersonalization of psychotherapy treatment is a leading factor: Thoughtful linkage of patients' childhoods and adulthoods takes getting to know them over some time, a process which is being increasingly devalued, as ostensibly reproducible, objectifiable modalities have advanced—reaching a kind of apotheosis in the push toward automation in AI-based treatment by text. This has gone along with the aggressive cost-cutting management of mental health services by insurers and often governments. Market forces have transferred human resources (like other wealth) up the class ladder, and cultural forces like social media have devalued the inner life.

Happily, the long-brewing turn toward a more cultural-historical orientation in psychoanalysis has accelerated in the last few years. The developmental psychoanalytic lens can be a key dimension of this move, offering a window into how child-rearing practices are primary sites for socialization and illuminating internalization process in general. Some advocates of a more social psychoanalysis, however, are apprehensive about the prospect of universalizing overgeneralizations drawn from developmental observation in particular cultures, especially developed, Western societies. For example, certain characteristics which may be adaptive or otherwise appropriate for a particular cultural or ethnic group are pathologized while others are overvalued, as when infant attachment to a very few caregivers is regarded as a preferred norm. These are fair criticisms, though, in my view, they sometimes obscure what can be learned from social-developmental studies.

There may be a question about method, too. There does seem to me to be some overreliance on theory at the moment. This takes different forms: Sometimes, one theory or another is idealized and overutilized, or theory itself leads to detachment from the immediacy of what is happening in the "hurly-burly" of the psychotherapeutic encounter. This caution about hypertheory may seem odd coming from me, as this book is quite theoretical, and I have been quite involved with both psychoanalytic and critical social theories for much of my life. In addition to all that I've already mentioned, I think that I have stayed interested in actual children as a counterweight against this tendency to over-abstraction: The immediacy of direct engagement with children is an irreplaceable source of vitality and vivid, experience-near language to describe patients' inner lives and psychoanalytic process.

The infant development theory and research has generated a number of bracing linkages and concepts—intersubjectivity, recognition, nonlinear dynamic systems, vitality, mentalization—many of which are featured this book. These ideas are essential breakthroughs for our fields. Hopefully, our curricular limitations and need to select what we attend to will not force a choice between these and direct consideration of the worlds of childhood. The crucial mission of the developmental orientation is to stay with the children themselves.

January 2025

Acknowledgments

This book would not have been written without Adrienne Harris, the co-editor of the Relational Perspectives Book Series. Along with convincing me that this was worth it and reading several drafts, she lent me her extraordinary frame of reference and keen understanding of all the nuanced complexities involved in synthesizing psychoanalysis with adjacent fields. I'm grateful for her steady encouragement and ongoing insight.

Muriel Dimen made a comment as we crossed the street one evening about her interest in an orientation to the emergence of developmental psychoanalysis that got me writing what is now the first half of the book. It might have seemed a bit casual at the time, but I suspect that she had something up her supportive sleeve. Muriel's spontaneous interest has sparked more projects than anyone probably realizes. I wish she were still here.

Many mentors and supporters encouraged and facilitated my finding a voice, such as I could: Robert Wallerstein, Owen Renik, Jonathan Slavin, Joseph Afterman, Calvin Settlage, and others whom I may be, regretfully, omitting. Dialogues with Daniel Stern, Mary Main and Erik Hesse, and especially with Louis Sander helped me believe that new ways of looking really could work. The regular meetings of several professional organizations have provided ongoing contact with colleagues and ideas as well as an opportunity to present earlier versions of some of these chapters: the Division of Psychoanalysis (39) of the American Psychological Association, the World Association of Infant Mental Health (WAIMH), the National Center for Clinical Infant Programs (now called Zero to Three), and later, the International Association of Relational Psychoanalysis and Psychotherapy (IARPP) and the American Psychoanalytic Association.

For three decades, my colleagues at the Infant–Parent Program at the University of California, San Francisco offered nearly daily lessons in how intellectually conscientious and caring work in the most difficult psychosocial circumstances could make a dramatic difference—in both clinical intervention and in social policy. Weekly lunch meetings with Jeree Pawl, Alicia Lieberman, Judith Pekarsky, Graeme Hanson, and Barbara Kalmanson were a remarkable chance to learn with some of the most serious and committed colleagues that I have ever met. I'm grateful and proud to have worked with each of them.

Some of these chapters were written over a number of years, during which many colleagues and friends supported their writing. I was fortunate to collaborate with Alexandra Harrison and Rebecca Shahmoon Shanok on related papers, and they graciously agreed to allow our joint thinking to be included in this book. Over the last decades, the original editors of *Psychoanalytic Dialogues*—Stephen Mitchell, Neil Altman, and Jody Davies—offered a platform and vote of confidence. My own co-editors-in-chief at *PD*—Anthony Bass, Steven Cooper, and Hazel Ipp—have given me the chance to have a collaborative experience that is uncommon in the usual private psychotherapy practice career. I have been very lucky to have them as partners.

More recently, many friends and colleagues commented on the chapters: Randy Badler, Edward Corrigan, Luca DiDonna, Pearl-Ellen Gordon, Michael Kazin, Lisa Koshkarian, Anne Krantz, Katherine Leddick, Mary Margaret McClure, Thomas Rosbrow, David Wallin, Michael Windholz, and the students and colleagues in my seminars in Los Angeles, New York, San Francisco, and the University of California, San Francisco. Orna Guralnik and Thomas Cohen took on my writing as if it were their own, challenging me to figure out what I really wanted to say. Karen Rosica read repeated drafts and spent hours talking with me about them. With typical enthusiasm, she reread evolving versions often enough that I couldn't believe that she wasn't bored to tears. She has been a special colleague and an even better friend. Michael Kazin and William Greenberg helped me sort out the book's structure and listened to my complaints and anxieties along the way, as did Steve Anker and Richard Bloom. The Inverness and Point Reyes Station branches of the Marin County (CA) Public Library offered quiet, pleasant places to write. I'm glad that I rediscovered the peace and clarity that public libraries still preserve.

Jeff Jackson was the editor that I have always wished for: one who loved what language could do, who understood how ideas and writing structure each other, and who could put that together so as to help me find the best way to say what I was trying to say, sometimes before I quite knew it myself. Kristopher Spring's steady hand and mind backed up the completion of this project; I'm not sure that I could have finished without him. Kate Hawes and Charles Bath at Routledge have helped more, I suspect, than they realize. Kate's clear understanding of what sometimes felt to me to be insolubly amorphous puzzles might have seemed to her to be just what she does every day, but she got me around some corners at which I might still be stuck if I hadn't found my way to her.

My wife, Mary Amsler, and our daughter, Molly Leigh Amsler Seligman, have had to put up with a fair amount so all of this could get done, and I haven't thanked them enough. I'm grateful for their patience and flexibility, and most of all, for the light they bring into my life.

Stephen Seligman
San Francisco
May 2017

Permissions

Some of the following content has been adapted and revised for inclusion in this book:

- Chapter 6: Seligman, S. (2001). The new baby settles in: Commentary on paper by Frank M. Lachmann. *Psychoanalytic Dialogues, 11*, 195–211. Reprinted by permission of Taylor & Francis LLC (http://www.tandfonline.com).
- Chapters 6, 7, 8 and 10: Seligman, S. (2003). The developmental perspective in relational psychoanalysis. *Contemporary Psychoanalysis, 39*, 477–508. Reprinted by permission of the William Alanson White Institute of Psychiatry, Psychoanalysis & Psychology and the William Alanson White Psychoanalytic Society (http://www.wawhite.org).
- Chapter 8: Seligman, S., & Harrison, A. M. (2011). Infant research and adult psychotherapy. In G. O. Gabbard, B. E. Litowitz, & P. Williams (Eds.), *American psychiatric association textbook of psychoanalysis* (2nd ed.), pp. (239–252). Washington, DC: American Psychiatric Publishing. Reprinted with permission from the *Textbook of Psychoanalysis, Second Edition* (© 2011). American Psychiatric Association. All rights reserved.
- Chapter 9: Seligman, S. (2012). The baby out of the bathwater: Microseconds, psychic structure, and psychotherapy. *Psychoanalytic Dialogues, 22*, 499–509. Reprinted by permission of Taylor & Francis LLC (http://www.tandfonline.com).
- Chapter 11: Seligman, S. (2009). Anchoring intersubjective models in recent advances in developmental psychology, Cognitive neuroscience and parenting studies: Introduction to papers by Trevarthen, Gallese, and Ammaniti & Trentini. *Psychoanalytic Dialogues, 19*,

503–506. Reprinted by permission of Taylor & Francis LLC (http://www.-tandfonline.com).

- Chapter 12: Seligman, S. (2000). Clinical implications of attachment theory. *Journal of the American Psychoanalytic Association, 48,* 1189–1196. Reprinted by permission of Sage Publishing.
- Chapter 13: Seligman, S. (2017). Recognition and reflection in infancy and psychotherapy process: Convergences of attachment and research with psychoanalysis. *Psychoanalytic Inquiry, 37*(5), 298–308.
- Chapter 14: Seligman, S. (1999). Integrating Kleinian theory and intersubjective infant research: Observing projective identification. *Psychoanalytic Dialogues, 9,* 129–159. Reprinted by permission of Taylor & Francis LLC (http://www.tandfonline.com).
- Chapter 15: Seligman, S. (2016). Disorders of temporality and the subjective experience of time: Unresponsive objects and the vacuity of the future. *Psychoanalytic Dialogues, 26,* 110–128. Reprinted by permission of Taylor & Francis LLC (http://www.tandfonline.com).
- Chapter 16: Seligman, S. (2011). Review of Daniel Stern's *Forms of vitality: Exploring dynamic experience in psychology, the arts, psychotherapy, and development. Journal of the American Psychoanalytic Association, 59,* 859–868. Reprinted by permission of Sage Publishing.
- Chapter 17: Seligman, S. (2014). Paying attention and feeling puzzled: The analytic mindset as an agent of therapeutic change. *Psychoanalytic Dialogues, 24,* 648–662. Reprinted by permission of Taylor & Francis LLC (http://www.tandfonline.com).
- Chapter 18: Seligman, S. (2005). Dynamic systems theories as a meta-framework for psychoanalysis. *Psychoanalytic Dialogues, 15,* 285–319. Reprinted by permission of Taylor & Francis LLC (http://www.tandfonline.com).
- Chapter 19: Seligman, S. (2002). Louis Sander and contemporary psychoanalysis: An introduction. *Psychoanalytic Dialogues, 12,* 1–10. Reprinted by permission of Taylor & Francis LLC (http://www.tandfonline.com).

What to expect from this book

This book integrates developmental findings about infancy and early attachment with psychoanalysis and the psychodynamic therapies. It places this project in the context of both psychoanalytic history and the present intersubjective-relational turn, clarifying the core concepts and clinical implications involved. Introductory sections trace the history of developmental psychoanalysis and the place of infancy and childhood in different analytic approaches: The different "analytic babies" are described and compared. Along the way, I describe the institutions and people involved so as to humanize, contextualize, and enliven the ideas, and I link them to the European and American historical and cultural milieus that influenced them.

I mean to offer a non-reductionistic integration that preserves the classical analytic attention to the irrational, turbulent, and unknowable aspects of the mind and of human interaction, along with verbal meanings, narratives, and fantasies, without sacrificing the long overdue re-orientation of analytic thinking toward the place of relationships and care in development and psychoanalytic therapeutic action. This is rooted in the last decades' new findings in the areas of attachment, infant-parent interaction research, developmental neuroscience, trauma, and the like, integrated with current models of intersubjectivity and nonlinear developmental systems theories. This focus joins with the task of rediscovering what remains vital in the grand psychoanalytic traditions: Freud's original models; child psychoanalysis and psychotherapy; the Kleinian, Bionian, and Independent Group object relations views; and the Anglo–American Ego Psychology, with its developmental psychoanalytic turn.

In doing this, I have tried to both follow and add to the already strong integrations of new knowledge about infancy with analysis[1]:

applying analogies between infant–parent and patient–therapist interaction patterns; bringing the lived experience of the body back into analysis; calling special attention to the importance of the nonverbal, emotional, and interactive realms; elaborating new links between psychodynamics and related disciplines; describing the contemporary emphasis on relationships in the psychoanalytic field; and more. I consider these themes along with special attention to the interrelated subtleties by which early experiences are transformed into later psychological structures and then emerge in the intricacies of the adult analytic situation, with all its puzzling twists and turns.

The book's broad scope reflects my experience in several related, but somewhat disparate fields: everyday analytic practice as a psychoanalyst-psychotherapist with adults and children; infant mental health work in the tradition of the original "Ghosts in the Nursery" model developed by Selma Fraiberg (1980); and ongoing writing and teaching engaged with the integration of infancy and child development research with psychoanalytic theory and practice. I've also tried to maintain an overview of the historical and current analytic scenes, including as co-editor-in-chief of *Psychoanalytic Dialogues: The International Journal of Relational Perspectives*. Bringing developmental findings and analysis together involves both the enthusiasms of interdisciplinary convergence, on the one hand, and the tensions of contradiction and translation, on the other. I've tried to highlight this lively and intriguing edge. Perhaps my having "lived" in all these domains gives me the possibility of conveying the multi-dimensional impact of the worlds of children, their caregivers, and their cultures, along with the fascination and depth of psychoanalytic practice, so as to capture the commonalities and diversity among various analytic and non-analytic ways of thinking.

I try to anchor all this in the immediacy and vitality of direct experience with babies and their parents, and of therapists and patients. The book presents engaging images of infants and their parents throughout, interweaving them with complex theoretical concepts and debates so as to make those sometimes abstract matters seem immediate and experience-near. For example, such frequently discussed, but not so well-understood concepts as "intersubjectivity," "mentalization," and even "projective identification" are revisited and illuminated. As the integration develops, clinical themes are continuously evoked and clinical material is presented throughout, including a series of thoroughly clinical chapters. An online appendix with additional images, videos, and other material can be found at www.routledge.com/9780415880022.

Stephen Seligman

Note

1 See, among the classics, Alvarez (1992, 2012); Beebe and Lachmann (2002); Boston Change Process Study Group (2010); Lichtenberg (1983); Schore (1994, 2003a, 2003b); and D. N. Stern (1985).

Why developmental psychoanalysis?

Psychoanalysis illuminates how childhood affects adult lives: how we find our way in the world, organize our strengths and suffering, and come to understand ourselves. At the same time, the intensity and seclusion of adult analyses tempt analysts to overlook the world beyond the consulting room. This book is an attempt to bridge this gap.

Imagery about childhood has always sparked—and expressed—the psychoanalytic imagination. Analysts evoke childhood—and especially infancy—as a kind of natural state, a realm in which to see the originary psychic principles and causes. Since Freud (1905b) cast the net of infantile sexuality over childhood, analysts have used their ideas about infants and children to construct master narratives that establish coherence between their theories of development, personality, psychopathology, and hence, clinical work, with widely varying blends of observation and imagination.

Each psychoanalytic group has relied on its own "metaphor of the baby" (Mitchell, 1988, p. 127) to buttress its own core assumptions: There are as many "psychoanalytic babies" as there are psychoanalytic orientations. Psychoanalytic views of infancy and childhood sometimes seem like those of the proverbial blind men who take their part of the elephant as the whole. I aim to provide a more panoramic view by moving between the compelling worlds of actual children, on the one hand, and psychoanalytic theory and clinical practice, on the other. I believe that this integration can strengthen the original analytic insights about the deep, unconscious, irrational mind by bringing them into contact with the evocative, immediate, affectively vivid worlds of childhood—especially infancy.

This leads to what I call a "robust developmental psychoanalysis." Developmental psychoanalysis has attended most closely to the actualities of infancy and childhood and their reciprocal extensions with adult

DOI: 10.4324/9781003607328-1

psychopathologies and therapies. With roots in the early twentieth century, it has drawn on direct analytic therapeutic work with infants and children as well as adjacent fields, including psychology, pediatrics, child psychiatry, education, community-based interventions, social and historical awareness, and more recently, developmental neuroscience. (See the chapters in Parts I and II.) This book integrates the remarkable progress of these fields over the last decades with a variety of psychoanalytic perspectives. Babies are now understood as evoking and responding to caregivers and other important people from the very beginning of life, while the traditional analytic theories have focused on the more irrational, solipsistic feelings and motivations. I aim to offer a complex, non-reductionistic mediation between what we have learned from direct exposure to infants and children and the broader analytic field.

Some analytic groups have embraced the developmental perspective, while others have been wary of it, insisting that empirical research and non-clinical observation distract from the purer understanding of psychic realities that is only available in clinical psychoanalysis. While sympathetic to this view, I believe that it is possible to stay attuned to the immediacies of childhood and infancy without sacrificing the deep focus that is so crucial to the analytic project. Bringing apparently divergent perspectives together disorients our given frameworks and strains the imagination, as it works against the reassurance that internally consistent theories and clinical schemes can provide. But it's worth the trouble, for it challenges our boundaries and deepens our understanding of what might otherwise be taken for granted. New ideas and approaches emerge, and established concepts that have outlived their usefulness can be renewed, displaced, or even discarded.

Engaging directly with infants and children offers exceptional access to experiences that psychoanalysts otherwise approach more provisionally and inferentially. As in the best moments in analyses, the compelling physical and emotional immediacy of infancy offers the prospect of analytic models rooted in direct experience of the most compelling sort. Infant-parent interaction has much in common with fine arts like dance, music, and film, where form and motion, varying over time, evoke the most compelling feelings. Learning about infants and older children enriches our understanding of what happens between therapists and patients, as well as all the remarkable intricacies by which childhood experiences transform over time, as they are lived out in the remarkable multiplicities of adult lives.

"The metaphor of the baby": Infancy, child development, and clinical practice

Images of children and parents are omnipresent in everyday psychodynamic psychotherapeutic practice. We learn what we can about patients' childhoods, form pictures and narratives about how those experiences have shaped the present, and imagine ourselves as parents or other crucial figures from that past—real and imaginary. Analysts configure interventions so as to heal childhood wounds and open new possibilities for the future, through a variety of more or less direct pathways. We all assume that there are basic commonalities between the processes by which children and patients change: internalization, affect regulation, containment, enhanced reflectiveness, insight, and more.

Each analytic group's adherents play out their different analytic orientations as they apply their images of patients' childhoods in momentto-moment clinical thinking and interaction, privileging different dimensions in their accounts of psychopathology, analytic practice, and cure. These are all transmitted in our literatures, training programs, supervisions, personal analyses, and institutional cultures (Seligman, 2006). In responding to a hostile transference, for example, a contemporary Kleinian will be more likely to attend to destructiveness emerging from a patient's psychic reality (influenced by the image of an infant struggling with aggressive instincts). In contrast, a Self Psychologist might think about the empathic responses that were missing in the patient's childhood (thinking of empathy as the key to adequate emotional growth). These differences are not absolute, but they make a difference. That their influence is often implicit does not make them any less important.

Thus, each analytic orientation can be understood through how it approaches childhood, child development, and their relationships to adult personality, psychopathology, and psychodynamic therapy. With all of this in mind, this book addresses these and other central clinical and theoretical questions that lie at the heart of psychoanalysis, as well as at its boundaries:

- How is knowledge about infancy and childhood relevant to psychotherapy and psychoanalysis with adults?
- What are the origins of psychopathology and other problems in living?
- What are the core motivations?

- What makes for change in psychotherapy, especially in psychoanalytic therapy?
- What is the relative weight of reality and fantasy, of the internal and external, of social engagement and private, personal experience? What can we learn about adult "psychic structure" by looking at infants and children?
- What can we learn from the nonverbal world of infants and toddlers that we can apply to adulthood? What are the best ways to think about this: phantasy,[1] internal object relations, self-states, attachment categories, character defenses, brain anatomy and physiology?
- How does the past present itself in what is happening now? How much do we balance the present relationship and the reconstruction of the past in clinical work?
- How can we be most effective in really making a difference in the lives of the most people?

Infant development research, the relational baby, and the intersubjective turn

This book emerges from a lively and disruptive phase in psychoanalytic history, during which many of the core assumptions and institutions have been transformed, especially in the United States. A relationship-oriented, "two-person" approach has dislocated many of the core orthodoxies about the centrality of the endogenous primitive instincts and clinical orientations about the analyst's oracular, abstinent position that followed from them: Relationships, rather than drives, are the basic organizers and motivations of psychic life, and the individual and her environments—especially other people—are seen as inextricably intertwined. This "intersubjective" perspective has emerged in the many fields especially concerned with child development—developmental psychology, attachment theory and research, neuroscience, all supporting contemporary developmental psychoanalysis.

My own approach to these questions reflects my exploration of the implications for psychoanalysis of direct observational research into infant–parent interaction and early infant–caregiver relationships that has emerged during the last several decades. These inquiries converged on several core propositions, including that human infants are born prepared to respond to and evoke care from parents and others; that the creation and maintenance of ties to other people are primary and central motivations for infants and, indeed, for humans in general; and that the relationship between infants and caregivers is the fundamental unit within which early development occurs. Neonates, for example, prefer human faces and voices to other sounds, are most visually acute focusing on objects about 27 cm (8") from their eyes—about the distance to the faces of their nursing mothers—and display the same basic emotions as adults, across cultures, so as to directly communicate a great deal about their inner states. (Imagine the different impacts of seeing a two-month-old smiling and cooing in a supermarket—as I did an hour before I wrote this—or another one crying inconsolably during an airplane landing.) Although the "relational baby" is very dependent, his or her mind is already organized and primed for complexity and integration as it meets a responsive caretaking environment. (This is elaborated in the second part of the book, Chapters 6 to 10, along with the more specific accounts of intersubjectivity and attachment theories in Chapters 11 and 12 in the third part.)

As early development proceeds, infants and parents engage in increasingly complex patterns of mutual influence and mutual regulation, signaling and affecting one another's experiences and behaviors. Infants and parents, like adults and older children, evoke changes in one another's brains and bodies that follow along with these more obvious behaviors, often at microsecond intervals more rapid than can be apprehended in conscious reflection. Overall, there has been an explosion of new understanding of, and attention to, the importance of the dyadic caregiver-infant interactions in early development and as crucial determinants of later personality and psychopathology. (See Chapter 9.) Some of these findings are consistent with traditional analytic models, but many are not.

Conversely, some of the strongest observations of those classical approaches seem to lie outside the direct observational methods of the infant development researchers; this is particularly noticeable in regard to much of the compelling, irrational, fantastical material that emerges in analytic clinical work. I have generally tried to explore the possibilities for translating from one sphere to the other, so as to refine the concepts and clinical strategies on either side. But this is not always possible; the inconsistencies and contradictions are not always reconcilable, and theoretical and clinical choices may need to be made. In general, translation is a complex and often awkward business, with different outcomes in the hands of different translators and in its various forms—between languages and from basic science research to clinical application, for example (Davis, 2016; Galassi, 2012).

Relational-developmental psychoanalysis

The infant development research has been most supportive of the Relational and intersubjectivist Self Psychological analytic schools, but all of the Freudian schools have been affected (as have the interpersonalists, to a lesser extent). Core classical psychoanalytic assumptions have been challenged, especially those about the image of the baby as solipsistic and chaotic, the primitive, endogenous libidinal and aggressive instincts, and the analogies between normal infancy and serious psychopathology. In parallel, there has been a movement toward flexibility in clinical technique, toward a view of the analytic situation as an interactive system co-created by the patient and analyst: Much like the baby and parent, each analyst–patient pair creates its own unique, mutually regulated relationship in which understanding and growth can be sustained in a joint enterprise (one which is not always harmonious or even progressive, of course). In line with these commonalities between infant and child development and psychodynamic process, therapeutic action is seen as following multiple lines. These include the reactivation of blocked adaptive potentials, the direct effects of new experience, disconfirmation of previously rigid expectations about relationships, and more. This contrasts with the classical position that insight following interpretation is necessary for true therapeutic action: Interpretation remains a powerful tactic, but not the only one.

There have been other influential perspectives emerging within and around the contemporary psychoanalytic scene: feminism and queer theory, the influx of women into the analytic profession, critical theory, cultural studies, neuroscience, psychopharmacology, and an array of historical and political-economic factors. (The historical evolution of psychoanalytic theories of development and their images of infants and children is described in the first part of this book, in Chapters 1 to 5.) As in psychological development, different dimensions and situations are in dynamic transaction in the movement of the analytic field itself. Throughout this book, I am rooted in the proposition that the mutual and intertwined effects of the various domains that shape our experiences must be considered in all their complex interactions. Historical, social, familial, biological factors, as well as individual–psychological, all transform one another as they change over time.

All of this comes together in the term, "Relational-Developmental Psychoanalysis."[2] This phrase marks the shift to the view that relationships are the fundamental motivators and organizers of human behavior and experience, both influencing and being influenced by social and bodily experiences in their many dimensions; these range from economies, cultures, and neighborhoods, through sexualities, families, and intimacies of all sorts, to organismic factors, including cellular and genetic. The interrelations of all these evolve over time over each lifespan and culture, in various transformations and integrations, more or less coordinated and strained, both within each person and between persons and their varied environments. The ongoing interplay of the past, present, and future is featured, with all the different progressive and regressive possibilities and combinations imaginable. With this in mind, I've been drawn to the nonlinear dynamic systems models that have emerged in the last decades and have more recently been applied in psychology and psychoanalysis. (These models are elaborated in the last part of this book, Chapters 17 to 19.)

About the author: The personal backstory

A brief account of the evolution of my own interest in developmental psychoanalysis offers another perspective on the themes animating this book. I finished graduate school in 1981, completing an innovative doctoral training program that included a strong introduction to life sciences, neurophysiology, and neuroanatomy, along with psychoanalysis and other psychologies and child development, followed by three years of hospital-based clinical training. I was impressed with the immediacy of the physically present body, and the methods and findings of the medical and natural sciences, even as I was aware of their limitations. At the same time, I remained engaged with political and philosophical themes and communities that had enlivened my own late adolescent and post-college years. I was a 1960s New Leftist in college, and afterwards a labor organizer and community mental health clinician, working for what I still regard as very just purposes, along with sorting out personal-developmental concerns. I had an intellectual interest in both social–political theories and psychoanalysis, along with wanting to include something of a social service or social action agenda in my everyday work.

There seemed to be a gap between analysis and the social theories that were influencing me: Marxism, the Frankfurt School (e.g., W. Benjamin, 1968; Marcuse, 1955), structural–functional sociology (Parsons, 1964), and emerging critical social theories like Foucault's (1978). By and large, these theories concerned themselves with power inequities, but they did not propose a strong psychological theory. However, psychoanalysis privileged asocial, individual motivations and personality structures at the expense of the social world, even as it offered a method suitable to the radical project of unearthing the hidden dynamics by which people collaborate with forces that frustrate, deprive, and even oppress them. But if the primitive instincts were driving the system, then how could one remain optimistic about the prospect for the basic changes that seemed so needed? And, as so many of my comrades in the New Left movements were returning to the more mundane challenges of personal and professional life as the movements waned, how could we think about these more private domains in a way that carried some of our earlier zeal for social justice (Harris, 2012; Seligman, 2012a)?

During my clinical training, I spent a fair amount of time working with children. There seemed to me more opportunities to intervene into the social environments that were ordinarily neglected in most of the adult treatment settings, and I liked playing with kids. This practical bent was reinforced by my interest in conceptual questions about the comparative effects and influences between environmental and constitutional influences. As these were the same years during which the direct observation of infant–parent interaction was coming of age, I was becoming aware of the new generation of bold and sensitive researchers who were providing the new understanding of the baby as active, social, and psychologically alive from birth and sowing the seeds of the new paradigm that was to transform the broader analytic landscape (e.g., Bowlby, 1969; Brazelton et al., 1974; Emde, 1988a; Greenspan & Pollock, 1989; Sander, 2002; Stern, 1985).

The "Relational revolution" was taking hold within psychoanalysis during these same years. Even as I began formal psychoanalytic training at a more established psychoanalytic institute affiliated with the American Psychoanalytic Association, I found the Relational turn best adapted to provide the overarching framework for an integrative and flexible analytic synthesis.[3] Its broad and inclusive approach drew on the more socially-oriented tradition of interpersonal analysis, as well as insurgent feminism, critical social theory, and the new developmental research; it was critical of the Freudian psychoanalytic roots without rejecting them. The iconoclastic and flexible Relational approach to clinical work suited me well, both temperamentally and intellectually, offering a considered and serious alternative to the more traditional analytic clinical method in which I had been trained. Although many of my Ego Psychologically oriented teachers were impressively dedicated, intelligent, and thoughtful, and some could be quite flexible (especially in practice), there still was a more or less uncritical acceptance of the established theoretical and technical conventions about drives, neutrality, and the like. Similarly, there was a surprising lack of cosmopolitan interchange with the various currents in the analytic world of which I was becoming aware, including Self Psychology, Lacanian and other French innovations, and of course, the British Object Relations groups (by which I had been most impressed for some time). The hegemonic North American Ego Psychoanalysis seemed to err on the side of asserting and exporting itself, without much self-critique or dialogue with other perspectives, within and outside of the analytic field.

My own enthusiasm for a broader view was further fueled by continuing work with children and especially by my special interest in work with infants and their parents. Earnest contact with babies washes away blocks to spontaneity and authenticity: Infants can communicate and respond directly and efficiently without the subtleties of language and are usually receptive to even small changes in the emotional and physical environment. I have generally maintained an ongoing child psychotherapy practice along with seeing adults, but I have also worked throughout my career in the development of the infant-parent psychotherapy model proposed by Selma Fraiberg et al. (1975, 1980), adapting its psychoanalytic attention to the "Ghosts in the Nursery" to work at the homes of the psychosocially and economically compromised, largely African–American and Latina families (Seligman, 1994, 2014b). There, straightforward and immediate responsiveness seemed as compelling with babies and their parents as it always has with children in psychotherapy. Many of these cases involved episodes of child abuse and neglect, recent immigration, and addiction amidst poverty and other sociocultural difficulties. As I was encountering this in the homes of such troubled families and in the midst of varied social service, governmental, and medical systems, I found that the core analytic ideas could be compelling in these unconventional and challenging circumstances, if conceived and offered in a clear, available, and experience-near way. (See Chapters 7 and 8; see also Seligman, 1994.)

In my clinical work, I find value in all the analytic orientations with which I am most familiar, as they are called forth by each emerging analytic situation, usually without much awareness of my particular sources at any particular moment. These include the classical Freudian, the structural model with its emphasis on defenses and psychic conflict, the Kleinian emphasis on phantasy and deep internal object relations, the deeply imaginative and developmentally oriented Middle Group, Self Psychology, and the contemporary Relational view, with its affirmative approach to the analyst's engagement and participation. The anthropologist Clifford Geertz (1973) has proposed simultaneous "thick description" as a method of looking at phenomena from multiple perspectives at once so as to present a textured description of an array of details and processes and from varied perspectives that can convey and capture some of the depth of what is going on. In many respects, psychoanalysis relies on such methods in its everyday practice. (See also Chodorow, 1999.)

Psychoanalysis has always seemed to point toward this kind of intensity, but is too often distanced from these potentials by its own organizational, procedural, and epistemological hierarchies and rigidities, as well as its insistence on the primacy of the verbal. Beyond this, though, the Freudian illumination of ambiguity, conflict, fantasy, and the irrational, elusive nature of what can be said and known about oneself is indispensable—not just for our field but for the culture as a whole, especially as it seems bent on abandoning interiority for the worlds of commodities and pre-packaged communication. But these core virtues are not fulfilled by the mystifications and orthodoxies that have stood in the way of a pragmatic, contemporary approach that could encompass what is most evocative *and* accurate and, I would dare to say, points us toward the truest experience.

Building bridges: Strengthening traditional insights with new knowledge

With all of this in mind, I take a synthesizing approach that discards outmoded ideas when necessary while retaining the most worthwhile insights available from whatever source. I believe that the vitality of psychoanalysis will emerge most deeply from the polyphonic transactions between adult analysis, developmental research, child psychoanalysis, and clinical infant work that are presented here. This integrative project calls for a balance of reconciliation and confrontation between differing conceptions of the analytic project, some of which may be contradictory. Although there are many ideas and attitudes that should be discarded, some contradictions should be entertained rather than resolved. Inconsistency is at the heart of psychoanalysis.

This evokes intellectual, cultural, and institutional tensions of all sorts. Critics of the applications of infancy research have regarded it as overemphasizing what can be directly observed so as to dilute the core psychoanalytic method of learning about the dynamic unconscious through interpretation and other aspects of the psychoanalytic situation. I do not agree: Embracing contemporary developmental perspectives does not mean that those core analytic conceptions need to be abandoned. Instead, they can be fortified as they are rendered more flexibly, made clearer and more accessible to colleagues in other disciplines and to our patients. At the same time, contemporary analytic communities who have been perceptively critical of the established traditions, such as the Relationalists and other intersubjectivists, can take advantage of the Freudian vision when it is updated with new findings and understandings in mind. (See Cooper, 2014; Corbett, 2014; Seligman, 2014a, for example.) My own view is that the applications of early development research to psychoanalysis have deepened it, exposed flaws in established orthodoxies, called attention to the observable details and patterns of dyadic interaction in psychotherapeutic process, and all in all, brought lived experience—especially of emotions and the actual body—into the analytic field. They offer support for the basic analytic strategy of making thoughtful, reflective contact with people in their distress, and open up space for us to think about the range of emotional and interpersonal stresses that we face every day.

Effective practical applications emerge, too: Programs to encourage parents to read to babies can be anchored in brain science; theories of internal representation and defense analysis support treatment of abused children and their parents; juvenile courts can be linked to relationship-based therapy programs, which are in turn illuminated by understandings about primitive countertransference and the associated fantasies; fMRI- (functional magnetic resonance imaging) supported research about very rapid implicit emotional communication can help analysts in the grip of intense emotion with their analysands.

Psychoanalysis is a profound and generative enterprise, but we have been overconfident for too long. Twenty-first-century theory, like other twenty-first-century efforts, calls for a hybrid sensibility. Analysts have sometimes been too eager to tell others what we know, rather than letting ourselves be influenced by what they understand. If we can do a better job of importing, we can think more clearly and work more effectively.

How this book is organized

The book moves from a more general historical–conceptual overview (Part I), through a more detailed elaboration of the current observation-ally based image of the baby with its extended parallels in a relationship-oriented intersubjective-developmental approach to analytic theory and practice (Part II), to an extended series of more specific explorations of core themes within that field (Parts III to IV). Each part begins with a brief introductory summary. These are intended as general orientations, as well as to guide readers who might find one or another[4] of the chapters to be presenting familiar material. There are also references to links to video recordings of infant–parent interaction and other childhood events in the text, as well as in the online appendix, which is accessible at www.routledge.com/9780415880022.

The first part of the book offers an extended account of the place of child-hood and human development in psychoanalysis, beginning with Freud's "discovery" that childhood experience determined adult personality and his theory of infantile sexuality, through the evolution of child analysis, the core evolutions of analytic theory in Ego Psychology, Kleinian psy-choanalysis, the Middle Group's object relations theory, and the post-World War II flourishing of the analysis in the United States. I trace the movement from Freud's regression-oriented model to include the forward, growth-oriented movement of the developmental perspective, but with reference to complex and sometimes controversial interactions between different analytic orientations, and their views of infancy and childhood, including their larger cultural and historical contexts.

Along the way, I present each analytic group's view of the infant: "Freud's baby," "Klein's baby," "Winnicott's baby," and so on. The dif-ferent discourses and disciplines each see a different aspect of what is there, of what matters for clinical work and theory. When we can take them together, we can understand "the baby" in a new way, an under-standing alternatively manifest as metaphor, as clinical image, as the most evocative, rapidly developing and vulnerable type of person, as embodi-ment of our hopes (and fears), as remarkable force, whether in families or the species' reproduction, and even as sacred presence (and so on).

The second part presents a more extensive profile of "the observed, intersubjective baby," in a summary of the infant observation research that emerged in the late twentieth century. The mutually influencing support between these findings and relational-intersubjective analytic theory and clinical practice are then elaborated in some detail. Finally, specific topics within this area are quickly presented in what I hope might work as something like "executive summaries": attachment theory, continuities from infancy to adulthood, intersubjectivity theory, and contemporary relational-developmental ideas about gender, sexuality, and the Oedipus complex. These first two parts also include a "theory strand," which tracks the evolution of specific *theoretical issues*. Although such theoretical nuances have been foundational in determining key clinical practices and attitudes, I've set these apart, since they are conceptually distinctive in some respects, such that some are less interested in them. The second of these, Chapter 4, is an elaboration of the "Robust Developmental Perspective," which is a pivotal dimension here.

The final three parts present an extended series of more specific explorations, organized around three core themes: recognition, reflection, and mutual regulation; vitality and activity; and nonlinear dynamic systems theory and the creative potentials of uncertainty. Each part presents extended case reports that illustrate and extend the clinical implications of the conceptual material. These groupings reflect something of my way of organizing the multiple dimensions of the infant development-psychoanalysis intersection, although there could be many others.[5]

I hope to engage the reader in the different frameworks, controversies, and syntheses that have surfaced and submerged as analysts have conceptualized the relations between infancy and childhood, on the one hand, and adult personality, psychopathology, and therapy, on the other. With this aspiration in mind, I hope that the underlying themes and connections among the different chapters here will emerge, such that a pragmatic and contemporary integration of deep psychoanalytic thinking with biological, social, and clinical conceptions of development—especially infant development—will come into view. Many of the chapters are directly animated by the transaction between the infant-parent interaction research or attachment theory and clinical psychoanalysis, in the context of the intersubjective-relational perspective. Others focus on theory building; many consider psychoanalytic child psychotherapy, especially infant–parent psychotherapy; most draw on the transactional-dynamic systems model. Methodological, philosophical, and scientific questions also come up. As in the broad developmental field, however, most of these issues are at least implicit in the background throughout, influential even when not elaborated or featured. I've tried to organize this book in a dynamic and "user-friendly" way, with different sections and strands that reflect these complex and intertwining themes, sometimes separating them out and sometimes intertwining them.

Notes

1 There are two different spellings of the term "fantasy/phantasy" in the psychoanalytic literature in English. The first is most commonly used among the Ego Psychologists in both Britain and the United States, and more generally in the United States, while the second is most used in the Kleinian traditions. "Fantasy" connotes the more conventional sense of imagery or ideas that are representations of wishes, needs, fears, memories, etc., as in "I had the fantasy that my entire family reunited for the holidays, including those who have passed away." "Phantasy" points toward the deep structures at the threshold of the bodily based instincts, as they move toward mental life. (See Isaacs, 1948 or Spillius et al., 2011.) Projective identification is one of the central phantasies for the Kleinians—a phantasy built from the even more basic phantasies about evacuation and incorporation that emerge in the primitive oral stage. Throughout this book, and at the risk of inconsistency, I will use whichever spelling seems to best capture the intended meaning.
2 Adrienne Harris (2005) has used a similar term.
3 I sometimes use the term "Relational" to refer to the specific psychoanalytic movement, and at other times, to a more general perspective that stresses the centrality of relationships in development and personality. Although these often overlap, I've tried to capitalize the R for the first connotation, and use the lower case for the second.

Part I

How we got here

A roadmap to psychoanalytic theories of childhood and development

This part of the book offers a "roadmap" of sorts that sets the stage for the rest of it. It traces the evolution from Freud's original formulations to a full-throated developmental psychoanalysis, as it developed amidst several influences—most of the traditional analytic theories, contemporary intersubjectivist and Relational psychoanalysis, psychoanalytic clinical work with adults, developmental research (especially about infants), child analysis, and infant mental health practice. In so doing, I hope to offer a basic orientation to several different core analytic theories through the window of their way of approaching childhood, child development and their relationships to adult personality, psychopathology, and psychoanalytic therapy.

While Freud established childhood as meaningful and influential in the center of his revolutionary psychology, his approach was primarily retrospective: He relied on imaginative reconstructions drawn from the fantasy-inflected memories and traumas that he considered to be the source of his patients' pathologies. He presented childhood as embodying the disorganized primary process and asocial instincts that he saw at the primitive core of human nature. The evolution of the analytic view of childhood was influenced by members of Freud's inner circles and other associates, including a number of women who were especially interested in children, their families, and schools; some of them remained marginal, while others became the leaders of psychoanalysis' next generation. As Freud's own models evolved further, he included social, growth-oriented motivations: Childhood was cast as containing endogenous, progressive, adaptive motivations parallel to the sexual and aggressive instincts. Divisions emerged between different groups of analysts around how central those adaptive currents should be in the core psychoanalytic models in general, and in clinical

DOI: 10.4324/9781003607328-2

work in particular. At first, these centered around the Kleinian, Ego Psychological, and British Middle Groups.

Nonetheless, the central place of child development became established in much of the analytic world, analogous to physical growth, as a matter of the emerging potentials for "forward-moving" engagement with external reality and the social world; this added to a more exclusive reliance on the "backward-looking," reconstructive method of generating hypotheses about childhood. Eventually, a more general turn toward relationships as central motivations has taken hold in the psychoanalytic scene, especially in the United States. Relational psychoanalysis and intersubjectivist Self Psychology have been especially influential, supported by the direct observation of infants and infant–parent interactions, along with other emerging historical and theoretical currents. Interpersonal analysis and innovations from Continental Europe and Latin America are increasingly garnering attention. Overall, a more flexible and multimodal approach to therapeutic technique has followed.

A narrative in context: A historical-developmental approach

Although I generally follow the standard organization of the central Anglo–American psychoanalytic orientations as they flow into the contemporary scene, this account is not meant as a positivist narrative of a field getting ever closer to some truth or scientific validity. I contextualize the changing analytic theories and their views of infancy and childhood with the different analytic cultures and organizations within which they emerged, as well as in relation to the broader historical, cultural, and economic environments, such as is possible in a brief set of chapters. As in individual development, not all the ideas, methods, and languages present at any moment are the most influential, whether implicitly or explicitly. Some are overlooked; some are suppressed or repressed; some transformed, diluted, and even co-opted. Some are marginalized, sometimes to be rediscovered later— again, implicitly as well as explicitly.[1]

All this has been further amplified by the extent to which analytic organizations and discourses have often been personality-driven, if not charismatically organized. These ebbs and flows are inscribed in the history of any discourse, not least psychoanalysis, as it is so located in the field of the elusive.

In a sense, I am taking a developmental perspective about the developmental orientation in psychoanalysis—seeing it as reflecting a number of different influences and environments. Changes in analytic theory do not occur in a vacuum. Just as each element in a child's development affects and is affected by the whole person and the broader surround, the analytic view of the child has emerged in concert with the evolution of the field overall—as a movement, a clinical practice, a set of theories, an institution with its many factions and local and national organizations, and as a discourse with its own core concerns and styles. Historical and cultural contexts have always been involved, too: the place of women in the psychoanalytic establishment; the two World Wars and the rise of fascism and anti-Semitism in Europe; the subsequent emigration of Central European analysts to Britain and the United States; post-World War II prosperity, especially in the United States. I hope that this approach adds something to the many useful accounts that have been more focused on the specifics of the analytic developmental models.[2]

The emergence of the psychoanalytic development viewpoint

The origins of psychoanalysis:

- Freud's "discovery" of childhood, in his conception of infantile sexuality and the primitive instincts, with its retrospective/reconstructive approach;
- The emergence of child psychoanalysis within the early Freudian context, led by women who were not otherwise admitted to Freud's inner circle;
- The evolution of a new interest in early development and, finally, of a more fully developmental approach, emerging through three broad schools:
  1. The structural model and ego psychological approaches that developed in both Great Britain and the United States (including the postwar expansion and "expanded scope" of psychoanalysis in the United States);

2. The Kleinian object relations theories;
3. The Middle Group and their British object relations theories.

- The diversification and pluralization of psychoanalysis, especially in the United States, including:
  - The flourishing of psychoanalysis after World War II, especially in the United States;
  - The breakup of the post-Freudian hegemony and the emergence of Relationally oriented, "two-person" psychoanalyses;
  - The current infant observational-intersubjective turn in the last decades of the twentieth century, with its greater interest in social interactions and direct observation of infants and their caregivers.

The psychoanalytic orientations: A timeline

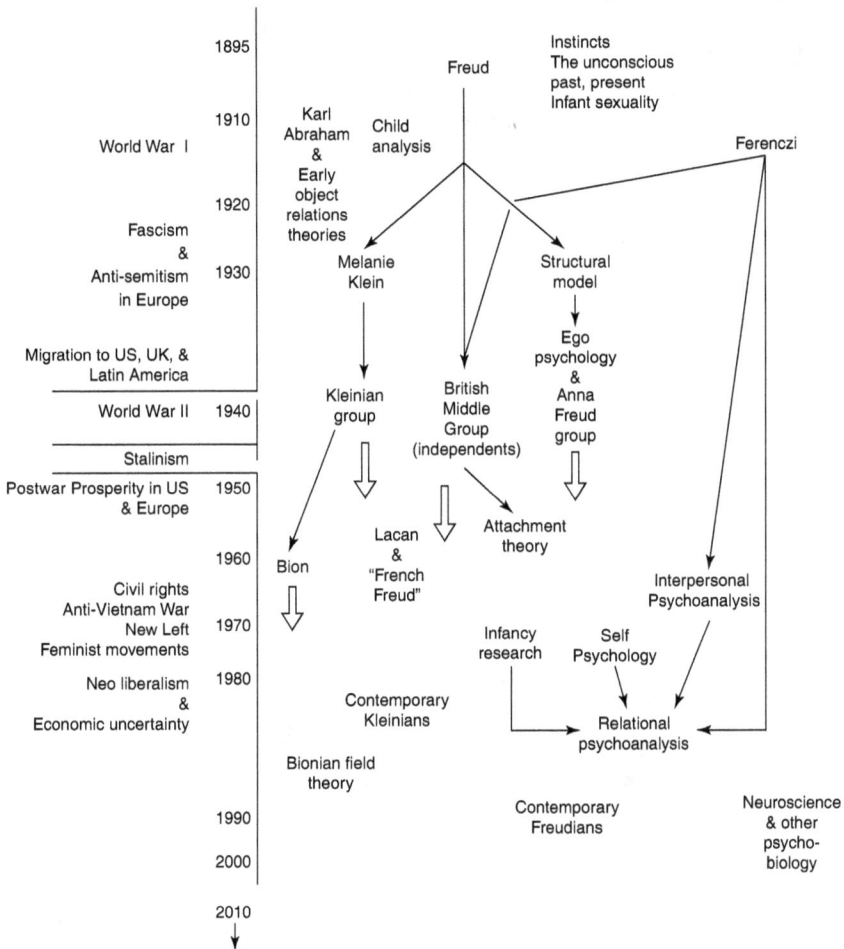

Figure 1.1

Notes

1 This standard Anglo–American narrative has sometimes underestimated the value of the French and other Continental psychoanalytic schools. While sympathetic to this criticism, I don't include these schools much here, as they don't feature childhood and instead rely on retrospective approaches drawn from Freud's earliest models. Perhaps I'm guilty of the same omission as those whom I have criticized.

2 See, for example, the useful recent books by Fonagy (2001), Gilmore and Meersand (2014), Mayes et al. (2007), Palombo et al. (2009), and Renn (2012), as well as classics by Blanck and Blanck (1994), Lidz (1968/1983), and Tyson and Tyson (1990). For a general overview of psychoanalytic theories, see Mitchell and Black (1995).

Chapter 1

Childhood has meaning of its own

Freud and the invention of psychoanalysis

Psychoanalysis launched one of the great cultural revolutions of the twentieth century: Childhood was now vested with meaning on its own terms and seen as the key source of adult emotional suffering and mental health. Freud's "revelation of childhood" was one of the essential elements of this remarkable transformation: His core formulation of the childhood libidinal stages established the more general conceptualization of developmental phases. This intertwined with a model of an irrational unconscious life that was oriented to instinctual gratification. Regression and fixation to childhood traumas was at the core of his theory of psychopathology and analytic therapeutic action. Freud brought the emotional and physical experience of being a child into view in a way that changed both popular and clinical thinking.

Freud's early models are the source of the rest of the history of analysis. Most, if not all, of the current innovations and controversies are anticipated in Freud's work, so basic and integrated that they are easily overlooked. He saw analytic clinical practice as both a medical treatment and a research method from which he could build a comprehensive system, one that explains the widest range of human experience—dreams, sexuality, psychological suffering, family life, culture, religion, and history.[1]

Freud established the groundwork for developmental psychoanalysis and, in a sense, for the whole of developmental theory. Freud's breakthroughs, though, did not comprise a fully developmental model. Freud was reliant on the retrospective method, which led him to look backward in time and "downward" in the psyche, at the expense of the more adaptive, socially oriented, and forward-moving aspects of childhood. He did not place growth and progressive change as central aspects of childhood or psychoanalytic therapeutic action. Instead, these remained secondary to the problem of taming the instincts.[2]

DOI: 10.4324/9781003607328-3

The early psychoanalytic movement led to child psychotherapy and child analysis, which emerged primarily from significant, direct engagement with children in their natural settings, mostly by women. However, many of the early child observations were not actively integrated into the analytic "mainstream" for many decades, although child analysis eventually became quite influential.

Freud's legacy for developmental psychoanalysis: Childhood at the origins

Instincts, childhood, and the unconscious: How does a mind emerge?

Freud's linkage of childhood, memory, unconsciousness, and trauma to human joy, suffering, and fulfillment remains one of the most generative ideas in our present discourse. He saw childhood as definitive in determining individual development, offering the clearest access to the basic forms and forces of personality and culture. Freud was especially interested in childhood trauma and infantile sexuality, especially during the earliest phases of his work (1895–1915). This was intertwined with his core theories of infantile sexuality and the instinctual drives, and the unconscious and repression, which emerged along with his accounts of childhood and its enduring effects. Although many readers may be quite familiar with all of this, I will offer a quick review.

Childhood, infantile sexuality, and the retrospective method: The genetic model

Freud sought to reconstruct the past from the present, especially in the patient's symptoms, depending on the *reconstructive* method to search for the origins ("genesis") of the patient's difficulties.[3] He called his retrospective-historical perspective the "*genetic* model." Childhood was the key determinant of adult personality, especially childhood trauma.

In developing this method, Freud built a theory of "infantile sexuality": childhood motivation and experience were dominated by the instinctual drives,[4] organized through a series of endogenous, predetermined series of psychosexual (libidinal) stages, associated with bodily zones—oral, anal, "phallic"—to be interrupted by the quiescence of latency, followed by the surges of adolescence. The baby was the most "primitive," psychically merged with the external environment and other people and internally disorganized, in a state of "primary narcissism."

Bodily based instincts at the center of motivation and human nature: The dynamic-economic perspective

For Freud, the instincts are the basic source and motivation for mental life. They emerge from the body, as energic tension, pressing for discharge through whatever pathways are available—people, things, images, and so on. They thus followed the "pleasure/unpleasure principle." Even interpersonal relationships are secondary to drive satisfaction, rather than originally significant in themselves. (Essential as it is, this idea is often overlooked by contemporary readers.) In this *dynamic-economic* perspective, Freud built a motivational theory along the lines of the prevailing physicalistic scientific models of his time, in which energy was seen as a matter of fluid-like forces in play: Freud saw himself as a scientist–physician and was avidly interested in scientific legitimacy. Although Freud's view of the instincts changed over the course of his decades of writing and practice along with much of the rest of his model, these core principles remained in place, generating many of the evolving innovations and controversies.[5]

The unconscious as repressed and distinctively (un)structured: The topographic model

Freud, of course, placed *the unconscious* at the center of psychoanalysis. Most mental activity is actively repressed by the inner conscience. Further, the unconscious mental processes are chaotic and fluid, governed by the pleasure principle and thus distant from reality. Such as they are structured, unconscious "ideas" are in the relatively "primitive" forms of fantasies, dreams, raw emotions, anxieties, bodily symptoms and tensions, and the like. In most of the Freudian canon, then, "the unconscious" differs from ordinary awareness in both content and forms, such as "condensation" and "displacement." (Some of the new models of the unconscious that have emerged recently will be discussed in Chapters 7 and 8.)

Freud (1911) proposed the term "primary process" to describe this chaotic and turbulent substrate. In his early models, he saw the primary process and the unconscious as co-located, much like the terrain (primary process) depicted in a particular place (the unconscious) on a map (hence, the *topographic* model). The *primariness* of the primary process refers both to its fundamental and temporal position, in that it is the base of mental life *and* came first in time.[6]

Overall, the intrapsychic, unconscious, instinctual factors are the most important and powerful determinants of behavior and subjective experience, especially (but not only) in childhood. In this way, Freud's early models are not fully "developmental" in the sense in which I use the term in this book. (See Chapter 4.) The adaptive, growth-oriented processes by which the social world and the body are integrated over time are regarded as secondary.

Freud and infancy

Freud's depiction of infancy as the most dependent, disorganized, body-based, and boundaryless stage led to analogies between it and the most severe pathologies. The more profound the pathology, the earlier in development to which the drives were fixated; both the psychotic and infantile minds are dominated by primary process.[7] Although his imagery was vivid and has been exceptionally generative, Freud reported few observations of children.[8] Psychoanalytic interest in direct observation and research about infants and older children grew substantially as psychoanalysis evolved (a central theme of this book, whose emergence I trace in these first chapters). Some analysts still maintain that the retrospective method is the exclusive pathway to the deepest knowledge of the mind, through the regressive processes of clinical psychoanalyses (Green, 2000).

Development as civilizing socialization: The oedipus complex and its vicissitudes

The instincts were asocial, if not antisocial, given to gratification, greed, and destruction (especially once Freud added the aggressive drive to his model); they "pulled" the personality downward and backward as they pushed it forward through the inexorable press for discharge. Human biological nature and culture are thus opposed, with conflict between instincts, on the one hand, and collective morality and conscience, on the other, as the organizing source of mental life. The key moment for drive-taming socialization is the resolution of the Oedipus Complex: the child internal-izes the authority of his parent(s) to suppress the primitive and infantile sexual and aggressive forces, so as to enter into civilized social life.[9]

Freud later extended his model to highlight adaptive motives and pro-cesses by which cooperation and civilization were internalized, including language, identification with parents and other adults, and mourning and loss. But the Oedipus Complex remained at the center of his conception of socialization. Indeed, the various analytic approaches to development specifically reflect these different emphases, including the balance of social, reality-oriented motives and structures as opposed to asocial, irra-tional motives, the nature of human relationships as primary motivators rather than objects for drive discharge, and others—all debates over what is "primary." These shape the rest of this historical section and, indeed, run through the entire book. (Chapter 10 will return to the Oedipal model from a contemporary perspective.)

Clinical implications: Trauma, fixation, regression, and the recovery of the repressed

Freud, then, built his clinical theoretical apparatus around the idea that adult personality was shaped in childhood. Neurotic symptoms emerged from the displacement of drive energy from early childhood trauma, through pathways that bound that energy while keeping those experiences out of awareness. At first, Freud (1917b, 1917c, 1917d) stressed the memories of trauma, and later shifted to the drives and fantasies that accompanied those experiences. The therapeutic action of psychoanalysis involved unpacking these symptom-fixation complexes (*analyzing*, as when a chemical com-pound is analyzed into its elemental parts), such that problematic fantasies and memories could then become available for remembering and rework-ing, and the bound-up drive energy could now be available for more flex-ible and adaptive purposes, more oriented toward external realities. The symptoms were thus relieved through retrospective interpretation. Freud first advocated direct and rapid interpretation of the trauma, but eventually was to engage the defenses against it, especially its compelled repetition in the transference (Freud, 1914a, 1914b).

In light of all of this, the original psychoanalytic method was oriented toward the pathways that could make the individual patient's unconscious primary process more available to awareness, as in the regressions of dreams, fantasies, slips of the tongue, and the psychoanalytic situation itself. Along these lines, the invitation that the patient associate freely on the couch is not only a way to get through the repressive barriers, but also to approach the more unbound nature of childhood language. Similarly, the orthodox prescription for the analyst's emotional detachment aims at maximizing the frustration of the patient's drives, so as to lead back to the intrapsychic bedrock and the conflicts surrounding it. All in all, this supports the recognition of early fixations; undoing these through insight can lead to increased freedom and symptom reduction. The focus is on the analysand's mind, with the analytic work set up so as to bring about the patient's engagement with what is "inside" of him or herself. Although Freud's actual ways of working with patients did not always match this, his overall approach was certainly a "one-person psychoanalysis."

Real women and children: The emergence of child analysis

The emergence of child psychoanalysis in the 1910s and beyond offered new pathways to a more rounded and robust developmental approach. These early child workers were usually women, in "feminine" roles, as mothers, teachers, and the like. They spent time in immediate contact with children, both in their consulting rooms and in real-life situations like schools, clinics, and families, including their own.

Such direct contact led to new directions for direct observation and interaction with children and new methods of inquiry and clinical mind-sets, featuring direct observation and engagement. As teachers, social workers, mothers, as well as therapists, the child analysts engaged with those "infantile" mental (and physical) states that carried so much weight in analytic theorizing. But rather than relying on reconstructions and hypotheses about patients' memories and fantasies, they connected with children's physical presence, languages, and imaginations. Child therapists join their young patients in worlds in which the ordinary distinctions between the "objective" and the imaginary are blurred—play, fantasy, transitional space, symbolic equivalence, preverbal affect, immediate action, and the like. Making contact with children means suspending the usual adult modes, making oneself available to forms of experience and communication that might otherwise not be acknowledged or understood. With this access, they could see the physical and emotional immediacies of childhood, together with the compelling and yet routine "primary process" of fantasies, displacements, and condensations that is more conspicuous in childhood.

Anna Freud (1936, p. 38) summarized this:

> In the play technique advocated by the English school for the analysis of little children (Melanie Klein, 1932), the lack of free association is made good in the most direct way. These analysts hold that a child's play is equivalent to the associations of adults and they make use of his games for purposes of interpretation in just the same way.

Children's use of such modes thus allows for a more direct experience of a terrain that often takes some time to reveal itself in adult analytic work. Here are two episodes from my own cases that illustrate how the condensed displacements of primary process thinking can be readily available in play therapy, leading to special opportunities for often rapid therapeutic progress.

Seven-year-old Jack expressed his images and fears about his parents' bitter divorce in a vivid, emotion-laden way, while hardly referring to it explicitly. I was able to understand his experience of this very trying event so as to help him reflect on it in the special play-therapeutic format. Jack's parents had been fighting in front of him for much of his seven years and spent most of their private parent consultations with me denouncing each other. He spent every session setting up battles between two warring factions of Lego figures. We pretended to be journalists covering the conflict, writing stories and taking photos every week, to which we then returned the following week. We rarely mentioned the divorce, but it was clear that in orchestrating these battles, he was telling the story of his parents' constant attacks on one another. I talked about how difficult it felt to be powerless and alone, watching a fight to the death, without being able to help anyone, seeing myself as providing a steady, available space to work through his overwhelming feelings.

Another one of my patients, a two-year-old, misses his mother since she has returned to her job, but hits her when she returns from work. This toddler is engaged in a defensive and apparently paradoxical reaction to the array of feelings emerging around his longing for and transient separation from his mother, relying on a form of intense contact that both reveals and conceals his frustration, powerlessness, and anxiety, along with wishes to make intense contact and have a strong impact. A child therapist informed by both psychoanalysis and attachment theory might help the mom become more aware of her son's distress, suggesting a response like: "Oh, sweetheart . . . I know how much you missed me. I missed you, too. But you mustn't hit me. That hurts!"

The first of these rather ordinary episodes illustrates how young children can use symbolic but nonverbal play as communication, while the second shows the use of the affect and the body, with its muscularity and movement through space. There is something especially immediate and evocative about children's use of their bodies: Language is not the key mediator of meaning and communication in either situation. Infants are especially effective at using their sensory and motor abilities to organize and express their needs, longings, pleasures, upsets, and other inner states with great clarity and evocative power for those who pay attention to them: Imagine a baby cooing, or alternatively, crying or even going limp with exhaustion after crying for several minutes without response. (See Chapter 6.) Older children rely on a wide repertoire of nonverbal modes: A four-year-old girl runs away from me in my office when she feels frightened of some unbearable feeling that has come up; a three-year-old hangs onto the doorknob and pounds on the door as his mother leaves him at pre-school, only to turn to his friends and gleefully join their play within a minute after she is out of sight.

Overall, child analysts are especially involved with children's novel and inventive interplays of reality and fantasy, and are directly exposed to the varied forms of nonverbal meaning that are most conspicuous in childhood but persist throughout adulthood. Those working with children cannot help but be aware of the importance of direct physical care and the different social environments in which children find themselves. Child analysts have highlighted the apparent paradox that children are quite vulnerable and dependent, yet uniquely creative and capable of remarkable growth. They are similarly aware of how these dynamics evolve over time, both in general and in each child's life, and how their potentials can be enhanced or impeded by different social, economic, and cultural environments, as well as in psychotherapy with both children and adults. All of this opened toward what would become the developmental psychoanalytic perspective, as will be elaborated in Chapters 3 and 4. (Erik Erikson's, 1950/1963, explorations of the relations between "childhood and society," and his (1958, 1969) subsequent innovations in psychoanalytic psychobiographies of Luther and Gandhi remain extraordinary examples of the extension of this beyond the consulting room.)

Child analysis and adjacent fields: Practical and scientific

In its direct access to the worlds of childhood, child analysis has shared a common domain with fields like education, social work, and even developmental psychology. As they were mostly women, many of the child analysts began their careers in such fields. Anna Freud was a teacher; Hermine Hug-Hellmuth (1921) and Melanie Klein (1932), the "founding mothers" of child analysis, often carefully observed their own children. Karl Abraham (Geissman & Geissman, 1998) did the same. (This was quite an original approach, although Charles Darwin (Darwin et al., 1872/1998), among a few others, had drawn on such observations in his path-breaking work on emotions.) Later, many of the most influential child therapists were social workers or directly trained in child therapy, as was possible in Great Britain, where child psychotherapy is an autonomous profession. This group includes, among so many, Anne Alvarez, Selma Fraiberg, and Adam Phillips (Seligman, 1997). The child analytic tradition has been especially influential for me, as it has combined the deep analytic vision with a pragmatic and vital sensitivity to the real concerns of children and families.

Outward-looking as they are, analytic child workers are predisposed to collaborate with practitioners and researchers in related fields: Child development reflects transactions between many domains—familial, individual, educational, affective, cognitive, and so on; there are often synergies from simultaneous interventions into several such areas. The career of the remarkably creative Sabina Spielrein reflects such interdisciplinary potentials. Spielrein made substantial contributions about the development of language based on observations of her own children, introducing important ideas about transformation and integration over time into the analytic literature (Harris, 2015). Jean Piaget, who was in analysis with Spielrein, may well have been influenced by her, as he rooted his own majestic studies in the systematic observation of his children. Spielrein had contact with and probably also influenced the influential Russian developmentalist, Lev Vygotsky (1962), who was himself interested in psychoanalysis in his early years. Vygotsky's idea of "the zone of proximal development" remains influential, close to a century after he first proposed it.

Child analysis became the central source for what has become the broader field of developmental psychoanalysis. (See Chapter 4.) Interdisciplinary crosscurrents have been elaborated, in transaction with developmental psychology and child psychiatry, and sometimes, adjacent fields such as anthropology, sociology, neuroscience, linguistics, and philosophy. At its best, all of this was cast in the temporal frame of childhood, with its complex transactions between the external and the internal, the environment and the individual, with their great transformative potential. In suggesting that direct observation and interaction with children would be fruitful for analysis, the child analysts have rendered much of the original analytic imagery on the unconscious fantasies and bodily processes with new vitality and vividness. While their observations of children's fantasies and play supported many of the Freudian ideas, they also dislocated the retrospective, psychosexually-oriented view of childhood.

Progress and resistance to the child analytic project: Gender and authority in psychoanalytic method and politics

Substantial as they were, the early child analysts worked at the margins of original analytic theories and institutions, centered in Vienna. Most members of Freud's inner circle were male physicians, more medically oriented than the women who worked with children, often outside the usual consulting rooms and without advanced degrees. The relationship between parents or teachers and children was less formal and authoritarian than the oracular, physicianly mindset within which the early analysts built their theory and practice. Working in the classical interpretive method, the analyst or doctor looked inside the patient, figured out what was wrong, and told him or her, so that she or he could be cured. Freud was engaged with the traditional imperial, paternally structured conventions and definitions of authority and virtue of his Viennese-Central European surround, even as his revolutionary work strained against and, ultimately, broke through their constraints.

Notes

1 Harold Bloom (1997) describes Shakespeare's "invention of the human": He views Shakespeare as proposing images and terms that shaped the subsequent consideration of what it means to be a person. Freud did the same for childhood.
2 Freud (1917c) was not unaware of the complexities inherent in a developmental phase model. In one of the lectures mentioned, he also wrote: [I]t is bound to be the case that not every preparatory phase will be passed through with equal success and completely superseded: portions of the function will be permanently

held back at these early stages, and the entire picture of development will be qualified by some amount of developmental inhibition . . . I regard it as possible that in the case of every sexual trend that some portions of it have stayed behind at earlier stage of its development, even though other portions have reached their final goal . . . we are picturing every such trend as a current which has been continuous since the beginning of life, but which we have divided up, to some extent artificially, into separate successive advances. (pp. 339–340)

3   Freud's later (1905a, 1914b) coming to regard transference as the richest representation of the past was a crucial development.

4   At first, Freud stressed the sexual instinct, but later added a destructive drive.

5   Late in his career, Freud (1927, 1930, among others) wrote a series of social-theoretical monographs in which he depicted the instinctual roots of various social phenomena about which he was troubled (e.g., mobs, religions, tyrants). Many have seen these in the context of his own anxieties about the rise of fascism around him, but he rarely makes these connections explicit. (See Chapter 2 for more on this.)

6   The term primary appears in various core phrases in the psychoanalytic canon, where it carries similar significance. Examples include "primary narcissism," "primary identification," and Winnicott's "primary maternal preoccupation." These are all linked with infancy.

7   Edward Said (1978) regards Freud's "othering" of the "primitive" instincts as a form of what he called "Orientalism," in which Western ideology assigned a kind of underdeveloped, childlike and/or wild quality to non-Western cultures. In this case, infancy is "orientalized" in much of Freudian analysis. (See Chapters 6 and 8.)

8   Two noteworthy exceptions are frequently cited: the famous fort-da vignette in *Beyond the Pleasure Principle* (Freud, 1920) and the case of Little Hans (Freud, 1909). This frequency, however, illustrates how few other examples of direct observation of children of any age can be found in Freud's extensive writings. Further, Freud never actually saw Little Hans, as he treated him through his father.

9   In contrast, current relationship-oriented developmentalists view cooperation and mutual regulation as basic motives from birth onward.

Chapter 2

Theory I

Foreshadowings: Core themes and controversies in the early Freudian theories

The grand themes of the most creative and original philosophical and scientific systems are articulated in their core controversies as much as in their direct elaboration. The limitations, omissions, and sensitive points mark their most generative dimensions. Newton's classical physics, for example, proved unable to accommodate many of the problems and data that subsequently emerged, bringing forth the questions that spawned Einstein's relativity theories, which have themselves been subject to new paradigm shifts. Such processes are at the core of scientific change (Kuhn, 1970): New ideas generate a set of new questions which the earlier models may not have anticipated, often in such a way as to affirm their essential value.

As I have said, the place of childhood in psychoanalysis is a key area where such processes have played out in regard to the core questions of the larger field. In this chapter, I delineate some of these key questions as they emerged in the early Freudian contexts, with an eye toward how they unfolded in the emergence of a more fully developmental-psychoanalytic perspective: the tensions between instinctual and social motivations; the relative influence of fantasy and actual experiences, including the shift away from the "seduction theory" of trauma; the place of the body in analysis; and gender, sexuality, and the Oedipus Complex.

Object relations and the interpersonal world

While many take the term "object relations" to refer to relationships with other people, Freud used it intentionally to connote the instincts' disposition to use whatever is at hand for discharge, including, as I said, inanimate objects, ideas, and other mental imagery, parts, or contents of the body, as

DOI: 10.4324/9781003607328-4

well as persons. The core theory of infantile sexuality is built around the bodily orifices, oriented through their particular contents (mouth–food; anus–feces)—not people as such: Freud's oral stage *is not a metaphor* for the infant's global dependency on his mother. Even as the Oedipal phase marks a shift in the social direction, genital satisfaction and anxieties mark its basic dynamics. These complexities became a central dimension of the various controversies and developments which ensued in the century following Freud's original proposals.

It is in this context that "Object Relations Theories" are named as such, since they do formulate such relations in a way which is closer to the person-to-person interchanges. Even those theories that cast those relations as substantially built on fantasies, such as the Melanie Klein's, point toward the kinds of needs and threats that are typically part of interpersonal relations—comfort, hunger, abandonment, annihilation, and the like, even when these are hardly acknowledged in the main currents of the theories. In their masterful and influential exegesis of *Object Relations in Clinical Psychoanalysis*, Jay Greenberg and Stephen Mitchell (1983, p. 4) wrote:

> *Accounting for the enormous clinical significance of object relations has been the central conceptual problem within the history of psychoanalytic ideas. Every major psychoanalytic author has had to address himself to this issue, and his manner of resolving it determines the basic approach and sets the foundation for subsequent theorizing.*
>
> (italics in original)

The Ego Psychologists tried to resolve the dilemma by giving increasing weight to the role of actual realities and relationships while also keeping the instincts and primary processes in their model (spurred, in fact, by Freud's mid-career revisions of his early models). The British Middle Group and the American Self Psychologists argued that social motives and actual caregiving relationships were more important than the life and death drives, which extended into their interest in the direct effects of the analyst–patient relationships. Interpersonal and Relational analysts have made similar arguments, taking them even further to encompass the mutually influential interchange between the analyst's personal subjectivity and that of the patient, as part of the analytic therapeutic action. It is these various ways of resolving these tensions through different clinical-theoretical transactions that are at the core of this book. When pressed to answer the awkward question about my own "psychoanalytic orientation," I've described myself as "an intersubjectivist-object relations Freudian." Even as these different perspectives are not always explicit in my clinical work or theorizing, they are usually close at hand.

Ferenczi: Actual relationships matter in childhood and in the consulting room

Both the original analysts and the child analytic pioneers were engaged with such controversies. Sándor Ferenczi, a key member of Freud's original circle, was the most explicit.[1] Ferenczi emphasized the impact of real events and the confusions that followed when the social world, especially families, failed to acknowledge the damage that they were inflicting on the child. He was especially attentive to the actualities of the analyst–analysand relationship, including asymmetries of need and power. He advocated reassurance, reciprocity, and self-disclosure, generally affirming the analyst's activity as part of the therapeutic process, rather than something to be avoided. He considered the analyst's attention to his own experience as a key element of providing help for the patient, and experimented with a more participatory version of the analyst's role (Aron & Harris, 1993; Bass, 2015; Dupont, 1995).

Ferenczi's vision opened toward a more frankly developmental perspective, as analysis was seen as capable of remobilizing developmental progress that had been arrested, anticipating and even influencing the Middle Group, Self Psychology, and Relational analysis. Although Ferenczi had been one of the most trusted of Freud's key lieutenants in the very small official inner circle, he was eventually marginalized. Freud (1933a) never lost his admiration for him, however, as can be seen in his quite moving obituary. Ferenczi is widely considered the first "two-person" psychoanalyst.

The body and (human) objects in instinct theory

Freudian psychoanalysis takes a complicated stance toward both the body and the experience of other people. At the same time that instinct theory places the physical at its center, it does not feature the direct lived experience of having or inhabiting a body or being in contact with another's. The variety of bodily experience is subsumed into the sexual zonal imagery.

Although he worked hard to span the physiological and the mental, Freud, finally, maintained a mind–body dualism that keeps classical psychoanalysis at some distance from the more direct manifestations of the body.[2]

Infancy research plays a special role in my approach to the body in psychoanalysis, both clinically and theoretically. It illuminates how we feel ourselves in the world: Observing how babies can be so compelling without words offers a direct window into how bodily positions, emotions, gestures, vocalizations, touch, gazes, and the like, all organize and communicate mental states. We are thus pointed toward understanding the mental and the physical as deeply intertwined (as Winnicott understood so well in coining the term "psychesoma"). Such diverse disciplines as brain research, somatic studies, physical and occupational therapy, trauma studies, and phenomenological philosophy have also been influential in highlighting the immediacy of emotion, movement, and sensation. All of this has had an effect on psychoanalytic clinical practice, especially among the Relational and Self Psychological circles (e.g., Knoblauch, 2000; Ringstrom, 2001; Sletvold, 2014). It has been particularly highlighted lately among trauma-oriented therapists, some of whom have been quite critical of psychoanalysis (e.g., Perry, 2007; Van Der Kolk, 2014).

Fantasy, reality, and trauma: The place of actual events in development and therapy

In his earliest theories, Freud stressed the direct pathogenic effects of actual traumatic events, in the "seduction theory." Memories and other feelings would be dissociated with symptoms both expressing and concealing the trauma. Early theories of therapeutic action turned on the undoing of these blockages. In the case of Frau Emmy von N., for example, the patient recovers from an array of somatic symptoms as hypnosis helps her recall an array of disturbing experiences and feelings (Breuer & Freud, 1895).

During the first decade of the 1900s, however, Freud shifted the focus to the instincts and fantasies, rather than actual events. Although the symptoms might be stimulated by external events, the pathogenic effects would ultimately depend on the internal dynamics, especially the fantasies about them. Psychopathology in Freud's second model was a matter of primary process and instinctual energy, rather than of memory itself. Feminists, historians, psychoanalysts, and others have criticized Freud's abandonment of the seduction theory as concealing actual sexual abuse and other real trauma. For example, in Freud's (1905a) analysis of his patient, Dora, a young woman whose father was having an affair with a married woman who was a family friend, he interpreted her erotic transference to him without talking with her about the fact that her father had arranged for Dora to spend time with the woman's husband while he was with the wife (Bernheimer & Kahane, 1990; Erikson, 1964; among others).

These critiques point toward a broader critique of analysis: that the emphasis on the intrapsychic unduly turns attention from compelling social realities, just as it devalues real trauma. This tension between realities and fantasies is a central concern within analysis, which has been configured in different ways. Generally, there has been a movement toward an increasing attention to actual events and environmental conditions in analytic theory and clinical work. This movement is traced in the next chapters: A robust developmental perspective pushes the field toward greater attention to the actual events of childhood, stretching to encompass both the internal and external worlds.

Beyond the intrapsychic: The social and political worlds

Some in Freud's early circles broadened the initial psychoanalytic focus by linking it to various political and cultural matters, which were very much alive during the years that psychoanalysis was emerging in middle Europe. These included gender, class, and political power. Wilhelm Reich (1927/1933), for example, was a member of Freud's original circle as well as an activist and member of the German Communist Party. In that role, he organized free clinics in working-class communities, something which has been often repeated in venues ranging, for example, from the national health services in European social democracies to liberation-oriented community mental health clinics in the 1970s in Italy, the United States, Great Britain, and elsewhere.

Reich also theorized how matters of class and culture were inscribed in the mind and in the body, along with sexuality. Reich proposed the central concept of "character" to describe deep, ongoing structures that were more general than symptoms alone, but are instead basic ways of living that might, nonetheless, be organized around conflicts and tensions around instincts.[3] Reich further extended his concept to encompass the deep, structural role of culture in organizing the instinctual energies,

through the varied array of regulatory pathways and prohibitions for gratification and self-expression. He thus anticipated many of the subsequent
integrations of psychoanalysis and sociological theory, ranging from Levi-
Strauss' (1949/1971) and Parsons' (1964) interest in the social functions
of the incest taboo to Althusser's (1971) Marxist–Lacanian notion of how
political and ideological power are "interpellated" into the individual personality, among many others (see also Aron & Starr, 2013).

Freud's views of gender and sexuality and the Oedipal narrative

Freud broke through the Victorian sensibility of his day with his frank talk
about sexuality and desire. Still, his view of girls and women conformed
to the gender-ideological view of his day that women were inferior to men.
Even as he argued that the variety of sexual preferences and orientations
are part of the innate human endowment, he built his theory around the
normative Oedipal narrative of the boy renouncing his sexual desire for his
mother in response to the fantasized threat of revenge from father, eventually leading to a more "mature" heterosexual object choice.

Paternal authority marks and resolves the conflict between individual
impulses and social order; it is thus granted special legitimacy. Since the
core anxiety here was castration, the male's moral and self-regulatory
capacities were based in an imminent threat, while the female's was compromised by the fact that the damage had already occurred; hence, the
theory that girls and women lived with "penis envy." Since Freud viewed
morality as a matter of restraint rather than empathy or mutuality, he
thought that men developed stronger consciences than women, and het-
erosexuality was treated as the normative outcome of the resolution of the
Oedipus Complex, as the "polymorphous perversity" of the earlier phases
was thus subdued.

The Oedipal theory also reflects Freud's inattention to the influence of
infancy and very early childhood. This can be viewed as a kind of patriarchal
blindness to the "women's work" of caring for children. In addition to this
(at least implicit) devaluation of what women do as mothers, the Freudian
formulation of the instinctual baby links mothers to the least civilized and
most instinct-driven aspects of human nature. The downgrading of maternal
care diminished the field's access to all of what women, especially mothers,
knew about children, love, and human development in general.

Creative and groundbreaking and generative as it has been, then, the Oedipally centered approach has been criticized since early in the history of analysis (e.g., Horney, 1935) and has been largely discredited today; indeed, it is a source of much antipathy toward analysis on the contemporary scene. A variety of new viewpoints and models have emerged, especially influenced by feminist, gender, and queer theories, as well as child analysis, infancy research, and other socially oriented currents. (These are discussed in more detail later in this book, especially in the review of the contemporary perspective in Chapter 10.)

The Oedipal emphasis and the Oedipal/pre-Oedipal distinction in clinical theory and practice

This also has had clinical resonances. The "Oedipal/pre-Oedipal" distinction has been canonical for many analytic schools, with "Oedipal" pathology referring to those conflict-organized neuroses that were "analyzable" and "pre-Oedipal" referring to what might now be called narcissistic, borderline, and psychotic personality organizations. These were not organized around psychic conflict, not treatable through interpretation, and thus "unsuitable" for analysis. These more severe diagnostic categories have often been conceptualized developmentally; they are regarded as analogous with and having their origins in infancy and toddlerhood abandonment, neglect, abuse, and other kinds of childhood trauma, especially chronic traumatic caregiving.

As I will describe in Chapters 3 to 6, all of this eventually changed, as a wide array of new concepts and treatment strategies emerged in a shifting analytic landscape. Ego Psychologists became more interested in developmental "deficits" along with fixations and regressions. Kleinian and Middle School analysts elaborated deep, imaginative images of the infant's mind and the effects of early caregiving, both "good enough" and otherwise. Relationalists, interpersonalists, and Self Psychologists looked at how relationships, rather than instincts, could be sources of conflict and explored direct parallels between the interaction between infants and parents and analysts and patients, buttressed by the late twentieth century explosion of infancy research. Generally, there has been a broad shift to considering the basic character organization of all patients, rather than just the specific neurotic conflicts, although the "pre-Oedipal/Oedipal" has not disappeared from the psychoanalytic canon. All of these developments have been intertwined with tensions and shifts in the entire psychoanalytic field—theoretical, clinical, and organizational.

Psychoanalysis' inattention to its own historical situation: Freud in the midst of turbulence and violence in central Europe

Another way of putting all this is that Freud looked away from political, economic, cultural, and ideological conditions, even as he made the most profound advance in considering. Similarly, he did not consider the influence of his own historical situation on his theoretical development, although he did comment from time to time on current events, as in his famous correspondence with Einstein on the origins of war (Freud, 1933b). It may well be that, despite many notable exceptions, analysis has overlooked its own social situation—in its theories, accounts of itself, and in the consulting room.

Freud introduced a personal-historical perspective to the emerging fields of psychiatry and psychology when he saw adults' mental health problems as a matter of the repetition of the past traumas. However, he built his model around individual, childhood trauma, rarely extending his accounts of psychopathology beyond the family or into adulthood. Freud's irrationalist instinct theory may be read as a reaction to the turbulent, violent and deeply insecure early decades of twentieth century Central and Eastern Europe, including World War I, the fall of the Austro–Hungarian Empire, and the rise of fascism, Stalinism, and similar state terrorisms, and toward the end of his life, the advent of the Holocaust. Vienna was at the very center of these storms,[4] but Freud rarely alludes to them, writing a series of social theoretical works in the interwar years that analyzed the risks of social chaos emerging from the instincts in which he made few references to the terrifying events surrounding him. Similarly, Freud rarely comments on his own Judaism, although anti-Semitism was a central force in his life, including hearing his own father's story of humiliation at the hands of a group of village thugs who threw his new hat into the mud, leaving him to retrieve it, to the role of his Jewish identity in his difficulties being appointed to a Professorship at the Medical School in Vienna (Gay, 1988).[5]

In the following chapters, I hope to keep in view some sense of the historical and cultural surrounds within which the field has developed especially as it has influenced and is reflected in the image of the child and developmental psychoanalysis. Just as with the movements from childhood to adulthood, our own theory and practice will be enriched when we can think historically.

Notes

1 Jung recast many of Freud's key concepts, including the instincts and fantasies, but has not been influential among non-Jungian analysts, having founded his own psychoanalytic movement separate from the Freudians.
2 This is a version of the current critique of "one-person" psychology as Cartesian. Descartes considered the mind as superordinate to and separate from the body, rather than as embedded in it. Phenomenologists such as Husserl, and especially Merleau-Ponty, have started from the direct experience of the body to build psychological theories.
3 There are many parallels here to other analytic concepts, including the widespread current use of character, which originates with Reich, as well as Sullivan's (1953) "self-systems" and the Ego Psychological idea of "psychic structure," which I will elaborate on later.
4 Timothy Snyder's *Bloodlands* (2010) presents a grisly picture of the lands between Germany and Russia, between 1933 and 1945, as the most murderous regions in all recorded history. Joseph Roth's (1924/1987, 1932/2011) books cover the fall of the Austro–Hungarian empire, including in Vienna, and the chaos that followed World War I. Various writers have proposed links between more ordinary aspects of Freud's social surround and his emerging theory. (See, for example and recently, Makari, 2008.) Peter Gay (1988), for example, offers a complex argument about Freud's negative, if ambivalent, critique of the Victorian sexual moralism of his day. Fred Weinstein and Gerald Platt (1969) see the Oedipal theory as a reaction to the new family situations produced by the shift from rural economies in which the entire nuclear family worked together, to urban industrial economies, in which fathers were often away at work and thus more likely to be viewed as remote, authoritarian figures. Carl Schorske (1961/1981), a noted historian of pre-war German culture, notes parallels between Freud's theories and specific power struggles in the fin-de-siècle Viennese government which, he argues, would have been of great interest to Freud.
5 Similarly, Freud's contemporary, the composer Gustav Mahler, converted to Catholicism to obtain the appointment as conductor of the Vienna Philharmonic Orchestra.

Chapter 3

The baby at the crossroads

The structural model, Ego Psychology, and object relations theories

In the 1920s, Freud proposed a new "structural model," organized around the three-part mental structure of id, ego, and superego, and the resulting psychic conflicts. The emerging "Ego Psychology" included a more adaptive side to mental functioning, leading to increased attention to growth-promoting potentials in child development.

After Freud's death, new controversies emerged, in which competing interpretations of infancy and childhood were central. Melanie Klein and her followers stayed closer to the earlier fantasy- and instinct-oriented views of the early Freud, portraying a baby in the grip of the most primitive instincts, while the "Anna Freudians" presented a baby with a mixture of drives, needs, and adaptive orientations to care.[1]

Klein placed the destructive, instinct-driven world of internal object relations and phantasies, configured in mother–infant relations, at the center of her models. She and her followers were strongly influenced by their analytic work with very young children. They called for direct, blunt interpretation of psychosexual and aggressive material, rather than working through resistances.

Many in the British Society stayed unaffiliated with the independent "Middle Group" putting forward several related theories of infancy that combined elements of both approaches. The Middle Group, however, were more radical in their general agreement that actual human relationships were central and original motivations. In this way, they anticipated much of the current movement toward a social-intersubjectivist model.

DOI: 10.4324/9781003607328-5

Ego psychology—psychic structure, adaptation, and external realities

Freud's innovative "teens" and the consolidation of the structural model

In the decades immediately preceding and following World War I, Freud reworked his established models. He developed new theories of object relations, narcissism, depression, masochism, chronic guilt, the persistence and unconscious quality of defense, resistance and transference, and more. Finally, in the 1920s, he settled on the new "structural model." This featured the tripartite mental structure of the primitive instinctual id, the ego, and the superego, the internal site of the moral, regulatory proscriptions of culture. The instinctual drives and irrational primary process remained essential, located in the id. But there was a new stress on innate adaptive motivations, located in the ego, which faced both "backward" toward the drives and outward to the demands of reality, and, of course, the superego. Both the ego and the superego evolved through identification with important people and social structures, and so development included an ongoing process of interacting with and incorporating the social world.

Ego psychology: Further movement toward an adaptive-developmental perspective

The original structural model was extended in the new "Ego Psychology," especially in the United States. The Ego Psychologists theorized and investigated the ego as having its own independent and adaptive dynamics and functions—integration, cognition, adaptation, reality testing, delaying gratification and tolerating frustration, language, object relations, impulse control, judgment and, importantly, defenses. The ego was now the "strong rider" of the drives. The leading Ego Psychologists, including Erik Erikson (1950/1963) and Hartmann (1958) and his colleagues, emphasized innate adaptive motives and structures, such as "apparatuses of primary autonomy" and "ego nuclei."[2] New models of development, psychopathogenesis, and analytic therapeutic action emerged from this refocusing.

   Coordination and conflict between the different psychic agencies, especially between the drives and the ego, was now featured. Defense became especially important in the emerging clinical orientation, as the earlier conceptualization of repression was expanded to include an array of different mental operations that restrained or altered the expression of id-impulses, including organizing perceptions of the world to protect against anxiety about those impulses, such as rationalization, denial, projection, reaction formation, dissociation, and others. Defenses could become structured over time, especially if they developed in response to traumatic situations. Driving patterns of experience and behavior, these could contribute to the formation of relatively stable "psychic structures." Neurosis was increasingly seen as a matter of character as well as of discrete symptoms (Reich, 1927/1933).

Anxiety played a special role here as the (often unconscious) trigger of defense, reconfigured by Freud (1926) as the psychic signal of danger, whether from an internal or external source (rather than as the residue of instinctual frustration). Freud offered what amounted to a chronological sequence of distinct anxieties that set the stage for a new developmental model—annihilation (a global, fragmented, terrifying non-being) associated with infancy; separation and loss; loss of love of the object; castration (damage to the body and to the self, fear of punishment); and, finally, superego anxiety (guilt).[3] This "anxiety series" was especially influential in the emerging object relations theories as well as in Ego Psychology. Much of Klein's and Winnicott's work may be read as an extended account of annihilation anxiety; Bowlby begins his monumental study of attachment and loss with reference to Freud's separation anxiety. Overall, Freud's revisions and additions of the 1920s opened toward a more elaborate developmental approach, most directly following the Structural Model, but throughout most of the analytic orientations.

Clinical technique

The emphasis on defenses, anxiety, and psychic structures contributed to a subtle but significant shift in technique. Rather than interpreting the instinctual impulses or repressed fantasies or memories directly, as Freud did in his early work and Klein continued to do, the analyst was to work through the patient's defenses and character structures, including the anxieties propelling them. Defenses would give way to new contents, but also to new defenses and anxieties: Such sequences might recur for extended periods. Transference remained central, but now, also, understood as something that might be resisted, as well as a source of resistance, since it might cover up other dynamics, including other transferences. (See Greenson, 1967, and Sandler et al., 1991, for authoritative reviews of this orientation.)

If the defense mechanisms were not adequate, psychic breakdown might ensue. Freud clarified what was to become a central distinction between neurosis and more severe characterological psychopathology. The more pervasive pathologies came to be regarded as reflecting deficits in pre-Oedipal development, while the neuroses reflected a more satisfactory, if flawed, Oedipal resolution. In *The Ego and the Id*, his definitive statement of the structural model, Freud (1923) wrote that "[I]t is advisable . . . especially where neurotics are concerned, to assume the existence of the complete Oedipus complex" (p. 33). Neurosis was organized around the more "advanced" anxieties, such as castration and guilt, while "pre-Oedipal" pathologies involved the more basic, "primitive" fears of annihilation, separation, and unlovability.

A two-tiered approach to analytic technique and therapeutic action became standard: The interpretation of defenses and psychic conflicts was to be offered to neurotic, "Oedipal-level" patients, with a developmentally oriented approach offered to characterological, pre-Oedipal patients. The new clinical theory gives strong weight to the impact of incomplete or blocked development, with terms such as "developmental lag," "deficit," and "fixation" becoming quite common (A. Freud, 1965; Group for the Advancement of Psychiatry, 1966). This suggests that the therapeutic relationship and its growth-promoting, nurturant effects could bring about real change in psychic structure, whether in tandem with or in lieu of interpretation of psychic conflict: Forces for psychological growth could thus be nurtured and hence, reactivated. This approach remained controversial, as some analysts have continued to contend that deep, "structural change" could only be achieved through interpretation of transferences, resistances, defenses, and other conflicts.

Toward a more full-throated developmental psychoanalysis: Progressive development, clinical work, and analytic therapeutic action

A more complex developmental approach emerged from the adaptive, social/reality-oriented dimension of the structural-ego psychological model. The basic and innate tendencies to engage with and adapt to the external world promote a natural, primary progressive side to childhood and child development that would emerge with adequate environmental support. Development is an active process of increasing competence, mastery, and an overall broadening and movement into the social world, as well as a passive one of tolerating and adjusting to frustration. Forward movement in childhood (and even adulthood) is thus conceptualized and considered fundamental, in addition to the backward pull of the instincts and the unresolved past. Overall, the integration of inner and outer, the social and the personal, work and love, potentials, actualities, and limitations all became subjects for psychoanalytic interest, and relevant to clinical assessment and intervention. This also implied a turning toward environmental intervention, as this could make a difference in personality development—indeed, even reaching into the intrapsychic.

Sigmund's daughter, Anna, played a special role in the new developmental thinking: Attuned to the forward-moving dimensions of development in the maturational progress of the body and the ego, she proposed the "concept of developmental lines" (A. Freud, 1963) that spanned the life cycle, such as the ones leading to autonomy in eating, self-care, interpersonal relationships, and the like. Along with her colleagues at the Hampstead Clinic in London (now the Anna Freud Centre), she developed an array of integrated developmental concepts to be applied to children, adolescents, and adults. In addition to developmental lines, she studied "normality and pathology in childhood" (A. Freud, 1965) and sponsored a detailed scheme for profiling patient's anxieties, fixations and regressions, defensive structures, deficits, and more. She was the leader of the Freudian group in the "controversial discussions" with Mrs. Klein's group that split the British psychoanalytic community in the 1940s, remaining at the political helm of the Anglo–American Ego Psychology movement until her death in 1982. The child analytic annual, *The Psychoanalytic Study of the Child* (directed by Miss Freud and her associates), was highly influential throughout the post-World War II decades. In addition, even as she was an advocate of developmental practice and theory, Anna Freud (1936) also wrote the definitive study of "The Ego and the Mechanisms of Defense," which remains the core statement on the matter.

Ego Psychology, developmental psychoanalysis, and interdisciplinary orientations

The interest in actual environments and interactions supported both direct observation in naturalistic settings and empirically oriented research as relevant for analysis. This was continuous with the early child psychoanalysts' interest in nonclinical settings and sources, especially as many of the leaders of the Ego Psychological groups were child analysts themselves. This accelerated during World War II and after. Anna Freud (Freud & Burlingham, 1943) observed children separated from their parents during the World War II bombing of British cities (as did John Bowlby). Analysts of different persuasions, especially child analysts, drew on child psychology, psychiatry, and pediatrics, along with expanding work in a variety of child-oriented settings that were becoming more common, such as pediatric units, schools, juvenile courts, and child welfare agencies. Along with this, child analysis gained increasing prestige and influence both within psychoanalysis and in the broader mental health communities. This was to accelerate in the post-World War II prosperity of the United States and Europe.

In the inaugural issue of *Psychological Issues*, a monograph series dedicated to the project of psychoanalysis becoming a *"general* psychology in the broadest sense of the word" (Hartmann, 1958, p. iii), the editors offered what amounts to a core summary of the leading edge of Ego Psychological theory and research:

> [I]n the last twenty-five years psychoanalytic interest has ranged with profit far beyond psychopathology, unconscious fantasy life, and the therapeutic process . . . This means that to develop its theoretical potentialities psychoanalysis must scrutinize data from all fields of psychological and psychiatric inquiry.
>
> The advances in Ego Psychology during the last quarter of a century are good examples of how psychoanalytic theory has broadened in scope and altered its perspective. Issues of structure formation and its change, and of adaptation and reality have become increasingly important to psychoanalysis. Concomitantly, important revisions have evolved in its developmental propositions. In this connection Piaget's work and that of the ethologists have aroused psychoanalytic interest; so have studies of the mechanics of thought, and of perception and learning as tools of adaptation. Further theoretical advance requires not only new types of data gathered by nontherapeutic methods . . . In our opinion, relevant contributions can come from experimental studies as well as from clinical ones, from controlled developmental studies as well as from the genetic explanations of psychoanalytic therapy itself.
>
> (p. xx)

Critiques and limitations of Ego Psychology

The language of structures and functions can seem overly mechanical, losing the person in the enthusiasm for structures and processes. (See Lacan, 1953, for an especially pointed statement of this general critique.) Kleinians, especially, argued that the Ego Psychologists abandoned Freud's greatest discoveries about the instincts, fantasies, and the unconscious. Others have argued that the interest in adaptation has been too "adaptationist," overlooking the range of social and economic conflicts and inequities, as well the strains that arise within individuals as they encounter social constraints. Human relationships were still not viewed as primary motivations; even at those moments when that might be implied, it was the ego structures and the instinctual needs, rather than the basic interpersonal motivation systems, that were featured. The ego remained a fundamentally individual structure, such that Ego Psychology stayed far short of becoming the "two-person" psychology that later relationship-oriented analysts were to advocate.

The movement toward a more fully developmental view opened windows that have led to much that is compelling in the current scene, that was not anticipated in Freud's early theories (nor in Klein's), as I will describe in the next chapters. I've found the structural model and Ego Psychology to offer many very useful ways of clarifying and organizing all the different things that happen in each analysis. For example, my moment-to-moment thinking typically includes observing defenses, resistances, specific anxieties, along with the mix of adaptive and regressive motives and processes. I do think that many of my colleagues—even those that identify with other analytic persuasions—think similarly.

Kleinian psychoanalysis—internal objects, phantasies, and the centrality of the infantile primitive mind

Following Freud's death in 1939, an extended battle between Anna Freud's and Melanie Klein's groups for theoretical and political control of the British Psychoanalytical Society ensued. These were the passionate and creative "controversial discussions," in which members of the opposing camps presented fundamental papers to their colleagues in the British Institute for Psychoanalysis. The disputes were settled when the Institute was divided into the three cooperating groups, including these two and a third, the "Middle Group" (later "the Independent Group"), who remained unaffiliated with either. While the Ego Psychologists were hegemonic in the United States until the 1980s or later, the Kleinians have been influential in Britain, and increasingly in Latin America and the United States, and their perspective has evolved considerably, with such key contributors as Bion, Rosenfeld, Segal, Joseph, and others.

Klein transformed the analytic landscape by relying on infancy as the central metaphor for psychoanalytic psychology. For her, the infant's mental life was organized in phantasies and internal object relations. These were only dimly influenced by the baby's interactions with his caregivers, since these were always mediated through phantasmatic projections, identifications, and introjections. This was in contrast to Freud's view that there was no relationship at all because the infant was too undifferentiated to be able to have such capacities.[4]

The mother thus became a player on the psychoanalytic stage, first in this shadowy form and eventually from a more realistic perspective: The move to a greater interest in infancy inevitably moved toward an interest in the dynamics and effects of maternal care. Klein was the first object relations theorist, and the Kleinian focus on infancy served as an ambivalent point of departure for many of the seminal Middle Group analysts, including Winnicott, Balint, and Bowlby, all of whom were supervised by Klein in their child analytic training.[5] In quite varied ways, the Middle Group analysts drew heavily on the Kleinian interest in infancy, deep psychopathology, and primitive anxieties and phantasies. However, they also proposed the most frankly social and developmental models, emphasizing the primacy of social motivations, actual caregiving relationships, and other environmental influences, and the possibilities of analysis re-activating previously fixated developmental potentials.

The Kleinian baby

For Melanie Klein and her followers, infancy is the central metaphor for deep psychic life throughout the life span. Klein consistently linked her theories to her clinical experience analyzing very young children. Unlike today's infant developmentalists, though, she focused on primary process play and fantasies as a matter of the conflicts between the libidinal and destructive instincts, stressing direct interpretation of deep fantasy material. In her (1961) seminal case of ten-year-old Richard, for example, she quickly told him that the toy train with which he was playing symbolized his penis and feces. This approach was extended to analytic work with adults. This placed her at odds with Anna Freud and the rest of the structurally oriented analysts.

Klein insisted on the centrality and continuity of the instinctual, primary side of mental life into adulthood, especially the destructive "death instinct." Freud (1923) had introduced this idea as a complement to the libidinal drives, but Klein rendered it more central and featured it more definitively as presenting itself in psychic life as a destructive force. Phantasy and *internal* objects were at the bedrock of personality throughout life. The social adaptive motivations and the recognition of the actual environment emerge over time, rather than being influential in earliest infancy.

The experience of actual caregivers is mediated by these phantasmatic internal object relations. The Kleinian *ph* connotes the depth of those instinctual structures that were prior to the encounter with reality—bedrock psychic processes that give form to the conjunction of the instincts with the bodily sensations (including sense-perceptions) at the most basic levels. (See Isaacs, 1948, for a remarkable outline of this concept.) This contrasts with typical use of the term "fantasy" to refer to the somewhat more ordinary, daydream-like use of imagery of different kinds as a holding place for the drive energies, wishes, memory traces, and other motives and meanings. Phantasies are primary in the sense that they are prior to the experience of external reality; they are the first format for mental life in the Kleinian model.

The Kleinian infant is never far from a state of psychic emergency. Organized around the opposing instincts and relying on projection and introjections, she splits herself and her objects between idealized and destructive; the bad internal objects are incompatible with and too threatening for the good internal objects, so they are expelled or projected, following the format of the oral phase. But this leads to further psychic threat, since the projected hateful objects now turn persecutory, imperiling the very survival which their projection was primed to protect. The "Kleinian baby" is thus caught in a vicious cycle, in the "paranoid-schizoid position."[6] These basic anxieties persist into adulthood: None of us are very far from a kind of psychotic-like shattering of the sense of self and objects.

Klein and the origins of object relations theories

Klein transformed the psychoanalytic landscape by describing earliest infancy as one of relationships, albeit internal and fantastical: She thus brought object relations into the center of psychoanalysis. In her elegant late-career summary of "Some Theoretical Conclusions Regarding the Emotional Life of the Infant," Klein (1952, p. 209) noted that she had

> described some aspects of mental l ife during the first three or four months. (It must be kept in mind, though, that only a rough estimate can be given of the duration of stages of development, as there are great individual variations.) In the picture of this stage, as I presented it, certain features stand out as characteristic. The paranoid-schizoid position is dominant. The interaction between the processes of introjections and projection—re-introjection and re-projection—determines ego development . . . Destructive impulses and persecutory anxiety are at their height. The desire for unlimited gratification, as well as persecutory anxiety, contribute to the infant's feeling that both an ideal breast and a dangerous devouring breast exist, which are largely kept apart in the infant's mind.

Klein (1935, 1940) eventually described a more "mature" developmental position—the "depressive" position, in which mourning, loss, and the possibility of reparation were possible. She saw the paranoid-schizoid and depressive positions as alternative modes in every personality organization, rather than simple genetic hierarchies. Rather than focusing on the instincts alone, her thinking became more oriented toward emotional states characteristic of different kinds of relationships (such as longing, "pining," disintegrating). She became more interested in integration and other developmental processes. She refined and applied her conceptualization of projective identification, so as to influence most every subsequent psychoanalytic approach. Overall, her writing became clearer and more direct in both tone and content: Her late masterpiece, *Envy and Gratitude* (1957), is a tender and compassionate ode to longing and grief.

Subsequent elaborations and the contemporary Kleinian view of development: Bion and the development of "thinking"

There have, of course, been countless other elaborations, refinements, and innovations from within the British Kleinian Group, leading to a remarkably rich body of clinical and theoretical work. (See, for example, Isaacs, 1948; Rosenfeld, 1971; and Segal, 1957.[7]) Importantly, the Kleinian-oriented Tavistock group has ensured that infant observation is a required part of training in both adult psychoanalysis and child psychotherapy in Great Britain, an approach that has gained wide acceptance and influence throughout the analytic world.[8]

W. R. Bion (1962) has been the most influential of the Kleinians after Klein herself. He described the mother transforming the baby's projections of intolerable, destructive phantasmatic feelings by "containing" and re-presenting them to her. This ushered the baby into a more advanced level of managing that primitive internal world, which he called "thinking," and which was open to external reality. He thus specified a process by which the infant might be extricated from the terrors of the original, instinctual psychic reality. Bion extended this model to therapeutic action, offering the term "container/contained" to capture a similar process of analytic transformation of psychic realities, including the analyst's attention and ability to reflect on what is at hand. Along these lines, the careful attention to countertransference and the analyst's handling of the patient's projective identifications is now considered central to analytic process among the contemporary Kleinians (Heimann, 1950, for example): The analyst uses the emotions that the patient has evoked in him or her, first by containing them and, often, eventually translating these feelings into interpretations. (See Chapter 13 for a discussion of this in light of contemporary developments in attachment and mentalization theories.)

Bion eventually went beyond the established Kleinian models to develop a more radical view of psychical transformations. He left the London analytic scene to live in Los Angeles, only returning to London in the last years of his life. The later Bionian ideas have been crucial sources for a number of writers on the current scene, especially among analysts in Latin-language speaking countries, including Bionian Field theorists (e.g., Baranger & Baranger, 2008; Bleger, 1967; Civitarese, 2005; Ferro, 2002; Ogden, 2007).

Critiques and integrations of the Kleinian model

Compared to the Ego Psychological and Middle Group orientations, the baby's relationship orientation and innate potential for growth is hardly credited: The direct experience of the creative, physical, and psychological vigor of infant care, later childhood, and even adolescence are sacrificed for the radical insistence on the intrapsychic and the primitive. Even as they are implicit in the background, vulnerability and dependence are hidden behind the overemphasis on destructiveness. Compelling as it is, the Kleinian image of the infant doesn't correspond with the everyday experience of infants with their caregivers or the infant developmental researchers.

Contemporary intersubjective critics note that the Kleinian model does not attend to the mother's own personality or the actualities of the caregiving relationship. This parallels the Kleinians' focus on the patient as the source of countertransference, in contrast to the analyst's personal and specific contribution to the transference-countertransference. Both "the Kleinian mother" and the Kleinian analyst are recipients of the phantasmatic processes of the baby/patient, rather than collaborators in the potentially generative, reciprocal process of mutual interaction that is featured in Relational analysis and, to some extent, in the Middle Group's developmental orientation. Even in Bion's work, the emphasis is on the management of the (very) "bad" experiences emerging from the destructive side of the instinctual cauldron, rather than anything intrinsically progressive in the infant or even in the mother–infant relationship. I think of Bion's model of the containing mother/analyst as an example of "one-and-one-half-person" psychoanalysis.

Despite these constraints, I find the radical focus on the intrapsychic and their specific accounts of the torturous and deeply disorganized side of inner experiencing to be indispensable in my own clinical work: The Kleinian focus preserves and asserts something that we might otherwise be tempted to neglect. A variety of disturbing psychotic-like and post-traumatic states become more comprehensible and tolerable with both the original and subsequent Kleinian ideas in mind, including all the chaotic and sometimes bizarre relationships (internal and external), projections, transferences and countertransferences dilemmas, and more. Without all of this, I could not practice as I do.

In some respects, the Kleinians' core assumption that the most basic mental processes are organized in relationships (albeit internal) opens the door to the more reality-oriented recognition of relationships with other people. Moreover, the centrality of projection and projective identification points toward the intertwining of selves and objects, even as the Kleinian approach insists on the primacy of the intrapsychic. The effort to synthesize the intersubjectivist, object relations and structural approaches animates this book and is an effort to explicate the ideas that organize my everyday thinking. (See, for example, Chapter 14.) My approach to the apparent contradictions between the Kleinians' dedicated intrapsychic focus and the more socially oriented paradigms is to view them as paradoxes which define and animate the psychoanalytic field, to be juxtaposed so as to enliven and deepen one another rather than be resolved.

The Middle Group—toward a relationship based theory of psychic realities and environments

The Middle Group analysts took the object relations theories to the next step, with the then radical view that human relationships were the key psychological and physiological organizers. Growth and development were at the center of their project, yet they largely retained the Freudian focus on the often hidden and deeply idiosyncratic dimensions of the imaginative emotional internal worlds. In keeping with the Middle Group's independent spirit and ambivalence about analytic politics, there was considerable variation among their individual approaches, making it harder to provide a general summary than with the other groups. (They were later renamed "the Independent Group.") Openness and irresolution have always been part of the Middle Group style, continuing through recent writers like R. D. Laing, Christopher Bollas, Adam Phillips, Juliet Mitchell, Neville Symington, and others. There is often something literary and "outside the box" in the "Independent Tradition."

The Middle Group babies: Winnicott and Bowlby

The range and imagination of the Middle Group is well illustrated by juxtaposing the very influential work of D. W. Winnicott and John Bowlby. Both featured the actual infant–parent relationship, with very different imagery and emphases. Yet their models are largely compatible and supplementary.

Winnicott's psychoanalysis of the development of intersubjectivity: Imagination and paradox in relationships and the psychesoma

The depth, imagination, and novelty of Winnicott's theories are often underestimated, despite how widely disseminated and influential they have become. Winnicott rereads and supplements Freud's models in several ways: He starts with the baby's actual body, rather than the instincts. In the same move, he locates that embodied baby as inextricably engaged with its caregiving surround, at the most basic level; this is the significance of the oft-quoted, "there is no infant . . ." (without the mother) (1960b). Winnicott sees a natural, adaptive dynamic in the meeting of children's physical and psychological growth with a supportive environment. In doing this, he invents a remarkable set of new concepts that start from what can be observed at the same time that they point toward the unconscious depths that have always been so central in the Freudian project.

An object relations theorist at the most basic level, he sees the shapes and qualities of our experience as they emerge from how the world of both internal and external object relations are constructed in the earliest relationships. With a combination of direct description and poetic interpretation unparalleled in the analytic literature, Winnicott delineates three stages in the development of object relations in the first few years of life, which corresponded to three basic modes of psychological organization that persisted throughout life.

At first, the baby is immersed in the maternal caregiving environment, with mind and body undifferentiated, rather than with a mother seen as a separate person or even a separate internal object. The baby has a relationship with the mother, but as a medium for existence ("going-on-being"). This contrasted with Klein's more differentiated internal object world (and also with the later infant observation researchers). The baby is thus protected from the potential for acute helplessness that might emerge from premature awareness of his absolute dependence. The mother's devotion to the baby, which Winnicott captures in the term "primary maternal preoccupation," allowed her to accommodate this most basic of the infant's psychic needs just as she and her support systems ensured his physical survival.

For Winnicott, the infant's "omnipotence" was not a distortion or a fantasy, but an imaginative "illusion" that protected the baby from awareness of the tremendous vulnerability of his absolute dependency. He used this rather ordinary word to capture a basic imaginative capacity that linked the individual to the world. Winnicott referred to this as the phase of the "subjective object." If the mothering was "good enough," the baby would come to trust "going-on-being" in the infant–parent environment. The tension states that were inevitable for Freud and Klein would not have much relevance for Winnicott's baby if she were well cared for.[9] However, if the caregiving environment failed in its protective provision, a "basic fault" (Balint, 1968, p. 149) might well emerge, marked by emotional catastrophes such as "falling through space," and "disintegration of personality." Winnicott calls these "primitive agonies,"[10] which could persist through childhood and into adulthood.

As the baby and mother developed, "transitional" object relations emerged. In relation to "the first not-me possession," key psychological boundaries, such as self/other and internal/external, became more relevant, but they were still vaguely defined (Winnicott, 1951). "Illusion" and omnipotence, are now transformed, re-rendered in projection, play, and the like, which make use of the transitional capacity to override the independence of external objects at the same time they are handled as if they had a separate existence. The beloved blanket, teddy bear, family member, or playmate can all be taken up in this way. Meanwhile, the caregivers provide an unobtrusive background while the infant–toddler imaginatively expands her physical and psychic horizons; in play, for example, sensitive adults don't remind the child of the facts that the play is overriding. Winnicott expansively applies this to such diverse situations in which imagination is as prominent as "reality," such as religion, romantic love, the arts, and more. Importantly, Winnicott sees the "as if" quality of transitional space as crucial to the capacity for transference, and he sees the capacity to play as a key part of psychic vitality and analytic cure.[11] Winnicott's affirmative conception of "illusion" captures the role of imagination as a basic psychic principle. (For further elaboration, see Phillips (1988) and my (2018) review.)

In the third phase, this move toward separateness in the context of relatedness becomes clearer. This emerges as the child repeatedly "destroys the object" in her imagination, which nonetheless survives. In this process, "objective reality" is both discovered *and*, as Winnicott stresses, *created*, as it is the child's active encounter with others through his ability to reach out and change things that places things and people in this new realm of independent existence (Winnicott, 1965b, 1970; for more on his complementary work on the constructive place of concern, see his (Winnicott, 1965b) paper and my review (2021)).[12]

Winnicott is clear enough that all of this is fundamentally a psychic process for the child, even as he treats it as if it were actually happening. This *apparent* contradiction is at the core of the Winnicottian method: He remains loyal to the Freudian project of following how whatever is going on is *experienced at the level of the psychic reality*, taking the imaginative psychic processes as of the greatest interest. But, unlike Freud, Klein, and the earlier Bion, Winnicott does not see these deep psychic processes as having to be constrained in order to support the development of an adaptive, collaborative, and reality-oriented mindset; instead, they are their source. In the same vein, Winnicott, who spent his mornings practicing pediatrics, also stays closer to the evocative and moving power of actual, observable bodies, needs, and emotions: He is attuned to how much of what goes on in infancy and childhood goes on in relationships and in physical encounters with the worlds of bodies and things.

There is a paradox here: The observed and the physical are always there and yet usually appear through what the baby makes of it in his own psychosomatic imagination. Winnicott is fundamentally concerned with how the ordinary distinctions with which we live are actually quite elusive and fluid—those between "reality" and "fantasy," internal and external, subject and object, self and other, and even parent and infant or analyst and patient. (See, for example, Winnicott, 1967.) From his own perspective, Winnicott is thus loyal to core Freudian project. Energized by paradox, then, Winnicott builds an account of how these *apparent* opposites are integrated as they held in tension, in different ways in different situations and different developmental stages. This makes his work alternatively enigmatic, enthralling, resonant, and, at times, mind-opening and illuminating. I regard Winnicott as the deepest source for the intersubjectivist Freudian orientation that I am working toward here.

Bowlby: The child's tie to the mother as primary motivation and source of psychic structure

John Bowlby, the inspiring inventor of attachment theory, worked from a more empirical orientation, with a complex relationship to the psychoanalytic traditions. He was influenced by analytic concepts of danger and safety, defense, loss, and mourning, and especially separation and other anxieties, but he relied on a wide array of developmental research, including ethological studies of primates and other species' parent–child relationships, and observations of infants and children, including his own experience with babies who had been separated from or lost their parents in World War II. Directly critical of the established analytic theories of instinctual motivations, Bowlby (1969, p. 179) began his definitive *Attachment and Loss* trilogy by declaring that the "child's tie to its mother is . . . as important as sex and hunger."

Bowlby conceived of early parent–infant attachment as a basic motivational system, rooted in species-specific evolutionary processes. Attachment took specific forms—the organized categories of secure and insecure attachment—which are influential over the lifespan. Extensive research here has been conducted by both developmental psychologists and psychoanalysts. Chapter 12 elaborates on this, including clinical implications. Chapter 9 presents findings about continuities from infancy and childhood and adulthood. Other chapters examine and apply emerging conceptualizations, such as reflective functioning and mentalization. They offer detailed clinical illustrations illustrating developmental processes that lead to increased attachment security in adults and other progressive outcomes of psychoanalytic psychotherapy (Chapter 13).

Bowlby's work was harshly criticized by both the Anna Freud and Kleinian groups, who objected to his radical departure from the sexual and destructive instincts and the irrational primary process. After Bowlby's death, the British Psychoanalytical Society offered a formal apology, which was accepted by John's son, Sir Richard Bowlby.

Development, psychopathology, and clinical style in the Middle Group: Child analysis and other influences

Like Winnicott and Bowlby, many of the other Middle Group analysts were quite involved outside their consulting rooms, with diverse scholarly and clinical influences: Most were child analysts and interested in the worlds of children.[13] Michael Balint directed a child clinic and, with Enid Balint, developed an influential approach to the emotional responses of medical practitioners to their patients; Balint and his first wife, Alice, had been closely influenced by Ferenczi before their emigration from Hungary. Marion Milner was a painter as well as an analyst, authoring books with titles like *On Not Being Able to Paint* and *The Hands of the Living God*. W. R. D. Fairbairn developed his very influential models while largely working independently in Edinburgh.

It is not surprising that the Middle Group heavily weighted environmental failure and its consequences in internal object relations. Michael Balint (1968) described how inadequate early maternal care led to a "basic fault," while W. R. D. Fairbairn (1952) featured splits in the internal object world and painful attachments to "bad objects," as Winnicott (1960b) evoked the "false self," dissociation, and other defensive processes that help with psychic pain. For example, prolonged separations from caregivers, early maltreatment, and other difficulties in early parent–infant communication are increasingly shown to be associated with borderline personality disorder (See Dozier, Stovall-McClough & Albus, 2008, for a review; Hesse & Main, 2000, offer further links to psychoanalysis.).

Overall, this perspective flowed toward a more inventive and flexible technique: The Middle Group analysts affirmed the possibilities for the psychoanalytic relationship to evoke the natural motivations and remobilize previously frozen developmental potentials, as they remained respectful of the power of conflict and interpretation in appropriate cases. Although there was not a one-to-one correspondence, this meant that analytic treatment had much in common with the complexities of parental care of actual children by actual parents, including its compelling emotional intensity and the special vulnerability, dependency and need for care that is especially obvious in infancy but central throughout childhood. Winnicott called for the remobilization of developmental progress that might occur from a "regression to dependency" in a sensitive analytic setting and saw analysis as mobilizing developmentally processes that were previously fixated or interrupted. Michael Balint (1968) illustrated how analysis offered a "new beginning" with a clinical vignette in which a patient danced without the inhibitions that long restrained her, as a turning point in the treatment.[14] In his famous paper on "Hate in the Countertransference," Winnicott (1947) described how he put an adolescent patient who had come to live with him outside the front door in a moment of impulsive near rage. Elsewhere, he (1970) proposed that analytic change in adulthood often depended on the capacity of the patient and analyst to play together, especially in the transference. Whether explicit or otherwise, the links to Ferenczi may be more important than are even realized today.

The Middle Group and contemporary psychoanalysis

Although the Middle Group analysts were influenced by both Ego Psychology and the Kleinians, their clinical approach was thus more innovative, if not radical. Theoretically, too, the Middle Group analysts questioned the established instinct theories more decisively than any of the other Freudian groups, especially the idea of destructiveness as a primary motive. The Middle Group's interest in the actualities of infancy and the push for development foreshadowed and influenced today's developmental psychoanalysis, including much in the infant developmental research.

Some contemporary Relational analysts have noted the Middle Group's in attention to the influence of the analyst's countertransference in the analytic process. As they have called on analysts to take their own personalities into account, they have voiced a parallel concern that the Middle Group's image of the mother excludes the mother's own personality and subjectivity, overemphasizing her place as the object of the baby's needs. In doing so, they have found support in current views of infant–parent relationships as involving bidirectional transaction between the caregivers and the baby. (See Chapter 14.) Some Relational writers have worked to fill this gap (J. Benjamin, 1988; Seligman, 2003; Slochower, 1996; among others).

That said, the Middle Group points toward the rich possibilities for expanding the Freudian attention to what lies beyond the surface of ordinary language and interaction, by engaging the vivid presence of bodies, feelings, and the location of individuals in their sociocultural environments. In an array of distinctive voices and without pathologizing, the Middle Group traditions capture the imaginative ways that people can shape their sense of what is real and compelling, whether in bodily experience, emotion, real human interaction, fantasies, illusion, internal objects, and the like. All of this is deeply influenced by a strong contact with the multi-dimensional worlds of infancy and childhood.

Eric Rayner (1990, p. 9) captured this in his book, *The Independent Mind in British Psychoanalysis*:

Independents come together because they are all committed psychoanalysts in the first place, and then, not because they espouse any particular theory within it, but simply because they have an attitude in common. This is to evaluate and respect ideas for their use and truth value, no matter from whence they come. Here the positive use and enjoyment of doubt is essential. Ideological certainty and factionalism are alien to their spirit. Where differences occur, the Independents prefer to settle them by discussion and compromise. This attitude is sometimes seen by other analysts as a sloppy eclecticism. It can certainly deteriorate into this, but essentially it requires careful scholarship and intense intellectual discipline. The demands upon an Independent mind are very high.

Notes

1 Jacques Lacan and many subsequent French analysts advocated a radical "return to (the early) Freud" in a wide array of evolving and brilliant texts. I have not included the Lacanian and other French groups here: Typically, their models are far from developmental in the sense in which I intend it here, and while I have been interested in and engaged with some of their ideas, their influence on my own developmentalist thinking has not been great.

2 Many of the key architects of this project were analysts from Eastern Europe who found a safe haven in the United States, including Erik Erikson, Heinz Hartmann and his collaborators, Ernst Kris and Rudolph Loewenstein, and David Rapaport. Some have argued that the Ego Psychological emphasis on adaptation reflected the postwar American ideology of optimistic (if superficial) assimilation, with émigré (and often Jewish) analysts turning away from their traumatic experiences with Nazism and fearing the McCarthyist persecution of (ex-) Communists and other left wing intellectuals (Jacoby, 1975).

3 Contemporary analytic theories of affect regulation owe an explicit debt to Freud's account of anxiety as a central regulatory affect (see, for example, Bowlby, 1969; Emde et al., 1991), and the current interest in trauma as a response to unmanageable threat also bears striking correspondences to Freud's ideas. (See, for example, Hesse & Main's, 2000, account of disorganized attachment as "fear without solution," or Porges', 2011, "polyvagal theory" of the different ways that the nervous system apprehends threats, whether external or internal.)

4 I am indebted to Thomas Cohen for his clarification here.

5 Winnicott's (1962) essay, "A Personal View of the Kleinian Contribution," is a very valuable document, both in the specifics of his assessment and the perspective it provides on the influence of Mrs. Klein on his work, with regard to conceptions that he took on and modified, and those that he used as he rejected and went on to rework. It is a masterpiece of Winnicottian subtlety, in which he presents his substantial debt to Klein along with strong critiques that seem gentle at first glance, but disclose themselves as more decisive with a bit more attention.

6 *Paranoid* as in persecutory; *schizoid* as in splitting.

7 The "Kleinian Development," as Donald Meltzer (1978) called it, has been very extensive and of course, highly influential. Here are just a few examples: Isaacs' (1948) "The Nature and Function of Phantasy," remains the most generative essay on the subject; Segal (1957) elaborated Klein's original work on the development of symbolism; Rosenfeld (1971) proposed more complex and subtle modes of psychopathological structures, such as pathological organizations that would invest the persecutory internal objects with survival value, such that they were tenacious forces in the way of psychological change; Betty Joseph (1988) transformed the current view of transference by understanding its expression in "the total situation." In addition, the view of the infant has been rendered more versatile, with concepts such as "the second skin" (Bick, 1968) and the place of autistic states in normal development (Tustin, 1981).

8 The Tavistock infant observation approach differs from the intersubjective infancy researchers. Those infant developmentalists generally rely on empirical methods (both naturalistic and quantitative), while the Tavistock approach involves analytic-like observation of infants at home or similar settings, including elaboration of fantasies and feelings that are noticed or inferred.

9 Erik Erikson's (1950/1963) conceptualization of "basic trust" as the core achievement of infancy seems to have much in common with this.

10 Winnicott was here standing Freud's "annihilation anxiety" on its head: Something that has been annihilated has stopped existing, but "good enough" care guarantees the baby's confidence in her existence, in both the physical and psychological realms.

11 I would surely not have reminded the seven-year-old boy that I described, with whom I was playing war while his parents were getting divorced, that the blocks that were building the "forts" were just blocks. This would have violated the basic "rules" of illusion and omnipotence that delineated the play space. (See also Erikson, 1950/1963, on "toys and reasons," in *Childhood and Society*.)

12 Contra Klein, it is only as the baby emerges toward a sense of her own independent existence in the presence of another that destructiveness becomes a major factor in development: It is not innate. In "A Personal View of the Kleinian Contribution," Winnicott (1962, p. 177) wrote "I simply cannot find value in *the* idea of a Death Instinct." Erikson (1950/1963), again, takes a similar stance when he writes that "Freud's original commitment to a mythology of primeval instincts *has* blurred the clinical study of a force which will be seen to pervade much of our material without finding essential clarification; I refer to rage" (p. 68, italics mine).

13 Many of the Middle Group analysts were supervised by Klein in their child analytic training, including Balint, Bowlby, and Winnicott. All describe mixtures of appreciation and negativity. In my reading, this tension was a very generative part of the Middle Group's creative invention. Bowlby (1969), like Winnicott, acknowledges Klein's influence, even as he was outspoken in saying that the Kleinians were misguided in overlooking actual events and influences. In an 80th birthday celebration for him, he told the story of his child analytic supervision with Melanie Klein: As he heard his young patient let him know about his mother's psychological deterioration and saw the same as he sat in the waiting room, Bowlby tried to convince Mrs. Klein to agree that he should speak directly with the mother. Insisting on the primacy of the intrapsychic, Klein refused. Shortly after, the mother had a psychotic breakdown and the child no longer came to analysis.

14 See Stephen Mitchell's (1988) critique of Balint's understanding of the therapeutic action of this interchange from a Relational perspective. Mitchell saw Balint as overlooking the evolution of his own experience of the patient, and the effect of that experience on the patient.

Chapter 4

Theory II

What is a "robust developmental perspective"?

When I refer to a "robust developmental perspective," I mean to capture the inclusive and integrative approach that applies a wide variety of sources and theories to core problems in psychoanalysis: the relations between past and present, change and continuity, repetition and novelty, the social and the individual, separateness and relatedness, the physiological and the psychological, and more. Developmental *psychoanalysis* is, as Erik Erikson (1950/1963, p. 359) wrote, "a way of looking at things" that includes an array of concepts, metaphors, and master narratives, and has drawn on a variety of discourses and disciplines, including clinical psychoanalyses and analytic theory, developmental research, direct experience with children and adolescents in their natural settings, cognitive and affective neuroscience, child and adult psychiatry, and infancy interventions. Current developmental psychoanalysis engages with a wide variety of phenomena—childhood events, unconscious phantasies, relationships past and present, families, historical movements of all sorts, institutions, emotions, brain configurations, cultures, and so on. How analytic groups and individual analysts orient to these matters has a substantial effect on theories of therapeutic action and clinical practice, both in each moment and more generalized thinking.

Like each psychoanalysis and development itself, developmental psychoanalysis calls us toward integrations that accept that there will always be questions that remain unresolved. While it would be difficult to settle on a precise definition of my developmental-analytic perspective, there are several key elements: an interest in natural growth and adaptation; direct engagement with children; stage theories, with their emphasis on the transformative interplay of change and continuity over time; therefore, a complex view of temporality, and the relations between past, present, and

DOI: 10.4324/9781003607328-6

future; an inclusive stance toward findings from nonanalytic disciplines and settings (like families, schools, and pediatric offices); and an orientation toward complexity and integration.

Looking at actual children

Direct contact with children is central to the developmental perspective, beginning with the earliest child analysts. Observing children, especially infants and young children, evokes strong feelings, both positive and negative. This is, of course, quite vivid in the natural enthusiasm most of us feel seeing a baby when things are going well, or in how bad we feel when we see a child who is being mistreated or neglected. (Imagine how you might feel while seeing a mother soothing her crying baby by slowly talking to him and stroking his back in a comforting, synchronous rhythm. In contrast, imagine watching a two-and-a-half-year-old girl and her mother screaming at one another while you walk the aisles of the supermarket after a long day's work.) Children are vitally engaged in their feelings, bodies, and with the people and things around them. (See Chapter 14 for a much more detailed account of two such evocative situations.)

Bodily experience, affect, and biology are thus directly engaged in developmental theory, in tandem with the interest in physiological growth. The place of the body in psychoanalytic thinking has thus been expanded. Even as they brought bodily functions into psychology, the early Freudian innovations dissociated the actual experience of the body into a hyper-theoretical and imaginary construct of the instincts. The developmentalists' interest in normal physiological growth and the vitalities and agonies of emotional and physical experiencing recontextualizes and reinterprets the original instinct theories. In adding direct observation and engagement with children in their ordinary settings, the developmental approach has broadened and, at times, corrected the original models.

Growth and adaptation as core motivations

Looking at actual children also supports the interest in the dynamic, forward-moving side of childhood in the analytic arena: Everyone knows what it's like to "grow up," to get bigger and stronger, learn to talk, have friends, get interested in love and sex, and so much more. As children get older, they get bigger, more mobile, more competent, more articulate, and their physical and social worlds expand. There is not much about children more conspicuous than how they grow—physically, psychologically, socially. This is one of these things that most everyone knows, but that psychoanalysis has sometimes overlooked.

Freud's revolutionary approach to childhood was primarily retrospective, drawn from fantasy-inflected inferences about the childhood memories and traumas that he viewed as the source of his patients' pathologies. His eventual inclusion of an innate orientation to reality and the external world opened the analytic field toward an orientation that included the forward-moving, progressive motives that are part of the natural world. Growth and adaptation became part of the analytic discourse; the developmental perspective added a forward temporality to the backward look of the classical Freudian perspective. The emergence of the potentials and limitations of these dynamics over each lifespan became subjects for psychoanalytic interest, relevant to clinical assessment and intervention. The idea that psychoanalysis could mobilize developmental flows that had been interrupted or derailed became part of the emerging theories of therapeutic action.

Developmental stage theories, temporal concepts, and integrative transformation

In the course of progressive development, new capabilities emerge. Changes at different parts of the developmental systems typically emerge around the same time, and are integrated together in new and existing socio-psycho-biological arrangements. This involves a basic reshaping of the person's way of living in his world—bodily, psychologically, socially. It is the nature of human systems.

In the shift from infancy to toddlerhood at about one year old, for example, neuromuscular development has progressed to support walking and other motor capacities. Around the same time, the infant–parent attachment relationship becomes more organized, providing an emotional basis for the baby to come and go from its caregiver with new independence. The attachment sustains a protective emotional, interpersonal system that draws the baby back to the parent in the face of threats. Parents often consider increasing their own autonomy around the same time, returning to the job market or spending more time outside the home in other ways.

The coordination of these apparently disparate changes is at the core of developmental process.

Similarly, adolescence involves changes in the teenager's physical and cognitive abilities, sexuality, social privileges (driving or work permits, for example), and more. When things are going well, educational and family systems shift reciprocally, as do cultural customs about privacy, sexual contact, financial freedom, and so on.

Developmental theorists have typically organized such processes in stages (or phases or positions) structured around core themes and clusters of a variety of capacities and developmental markers, whether about motor development, object relations, libidinal zone, cognitive abilities, and much more. Freud's original conceptualization of the "oral stage," for example, has been broadened beyond the emphasis on the mouth as the libidinal zone to include incorporation as the primary mode of object relations, dependency on the need-gratifying object, and many other related qualities of relating and psychic and psychosocial organization. The different qualities are structurally related, such that they can be taken together in a developmental moment that leads to an enduring configuration, both in each life course and in the meta-structure of the different developmental theories. Each stage theory works as a master narrative, as both an account of childhood and a way of organizing clinical material.

Normal development and the progressive movement through stages

The forward movements from one stage to the next are viewed as normal "developmental crises" with the potential for a new sense of self in the world. The co-occurring changes toward the end of the first year of life that I have described, for example, comprise a movement into a new, more independent and competent relationship to space, inanimate objects, and other people. Such shifts also involve some strain and risk of development becoming derailed: Problems in subsequent development are often conceptualized in terms of being "stuck" in one or more of the stages, with unresolved or problematic solutions to the challenges of one stage persisting into and even distorting the next. Psychoanalytic developmental theory offers a number of concepts that capture such backward and forward psychic movement over time: regression, fixation, "the repetition compulsion," developmental deficit and arrest, childhood trauma, and many more.

The themes and structures of each stage, and each person's resolution and reorganization of each stage, persist into subsequent development, even as they are transformed. Each phase builds on the ones before it, much as with the stories of a building under construction: If the lower story is weak or misshapen, then the upper stories will be shaky. But the fixations of each stage can be subsequently revisited and often reworked, if with some resistance. Developmental processes have the potential for backward and forward influence, inasmuch as the past is preserved in the current psychological structures and thus accessible to the present.

Temporal bidirectionality is thus a particular part of the robust developmental orientation: The effects of the past moving into the future are powerful, but the present (which is to say, that future) can alter the effects of that past. This is a basic aspect of a developmental conception of the therapeutic action of psychotherapy. From a developmental perspective, case formulation and intervention involve understanding the dynamic relations between the effects of the past and potentials for new behaviors and experience.

In one case, for example, a four-year-old who had been placed in a series of ten foster homes since he was eighteen months old was extremely impulsive, unable to stay in the therapy room for more than five minutes. His therapist thought this was related to this traumatic history, but he could also see that he was able to form an attachment to his current, more stable foster parent, a great aunt. This led her to also infer that there had been something of a stable relationship with his mother before her drug addiction led her to abandon him, one that laid a foundation for subsequent relationship. In another case, without this early history, the therapeutic prognosis might be significantly more pessimistic.

Stage theories are the typical way that analysts (and most other developmentalists) organize the overarching problem of change and continuity over the lifespan, especially in regard to the rapid movement of child development and its influence on adulthood. The strongest stage theories emphasize transformation of the patterns and structures that are most salient at each stage, rather than conceptualizing the movement from one stage to another as a matter of replacement. To take one from among the numerous possible examples: The Kleinian term *position* displaced *stage* in service of this point, and it is now widely accepted that "there are . . . continual fluctuations between a depressive, inter-subjective mode of functioning and a more primitive, ego-centric para-noid-schizoid one" (Likierman, 2002, p. 116; see Chapter 3 of this book for a more elaborate discussion of the Kleinian developmental model). Klein herself wrote: "[P]osition was chosen because—though the phe-nomena involved occur in the first place during the early stages of development—they are not confined to these stages but represent spe-cific groupings of anxieties and defences which appear and re-appear during the first years of childhood" (Spillius, 1988, p. 69).

Continuity and change: Time and temporality in the developmental perspective

Developmental process is thus a matter of complex and varied relations between change and continuity. Even as we grow and change so dramati-cally in childhood and adolescence, and, at a slower rate, in adulthood, we are also the "same person," live in the "same" bodies, mostly with the same families, in the same places, and so on. Patterns from both the immediate and more distant past are brought forward and reworked into emerging new patterns which encompass the past structures, meanings, and relationships—both internal and external.

Time has always been at the core of analytic thinking. Past, present, and future flow into one another in the developmental psychoanalytic imagina-tion. (See, for example, Loewald, 1980, among many.) In clinical practice, we imagine the past from what we hear, see, and feel in the present, and we think of the futures that our patients might have had, if only there had been opportunities for growth, and much more. Since its inception, analysis has been the most profound of the contemporary psychologies in capturing the temporal dimension. But the original approaches emphasized the pulls of the past on the present. Looking at childhood growth and development directly highlights the dynamic movement into the future that is a key part of most living systems, both for individuals and for species survival and evolution. (See Chapter 15 for an extended discussion of temporality in analysis, including clinical implications.)

Strong developmental thinking places temporality in a complex web of mutually intertwined "forward" and "backward" movements, so that time itself is dislocated. This is in keeping with Freud's original psychoanalytic vision of a primary mental process that does not follow the ordinary conventions of perception and other cognitions that structure everyday "reality." Initially, this took the form of intrapsychic conflict or trauma drawing the psyche backward in time and "downward" in such processes as regression and fixation. This historicization of individual psychology was a radical, indispensable addition to European culture and mental health clinical work.

As the developmental perspective emerged, psychopathology was also understood in terms of impediments and interruptions to the forward and adaptive movement of progressive development process. Conceptions of psychoanalytic therapeutic action are similarly expanded so as to move beyond interpretation of conflict or recovery of repressed memories or fantasies, to encompass the multimodal and complex possibilities of remobilizing progressive development. Growth and development, whether in childhood or psychotherapy, are not simple matters of providing support or "corrective emotional experiences," although some have critique d developmentally oriented treatments in this way. (See Chapters 6, 7, and 8 for more on this.)

Relationships are central

Relationships are central to developmental process. Most developmentally oriented models start from the assumption that relationships are the primary motivations, rather than the drives. Relationships are the primary units within which development takes place, beginning with families, and extending into schools, social groups, workplaces, and so on. More broadly, *development* can be more broadly understood as the organization and reorganization of the relationships within and between neurobiological, psychological, social, economic, and cultural elements, at different levels and dimensions of the life systems. (This is discussed later in the chapter and more extensively in Chapter 18.)

Complexity and integration: Nonlinear dynamic systems theories

Development, then, is a matter of transformation and integration, both over time and of the different capacities and environments that change one another as they emerge at any given moment in development. New modes emerge, such that there is an ongoing dynamic balance between novelty and repetition. All of this occurs as new circumstances, resources, and abilities present themselves from an array of sources. Taken together, these emphases all mark a more fully developmental psychoanalytic mindset, one which locates us in a fluid and multidirectional conception of time.

As I have said, such integrative transformation is a key principle of developmental process. From the open and wide-angled developmental perspective, there are multiple factors involved in every life—genetics, physiology, families, personal history, institutional, cultural and political-economic influences of all sorts, and more. These are so intertwined that it hardly makes sense to refer to them as individual factors, with their interrelationships shifting over time in complex networks. Developmental processes take almost infinite forms engaging countless and widely varied elements, from RNA (ribonucleic acid) changes, to neuroanatomy and neurochemistry, to motor developments such as walking or running, to cognitive or language development, through school attendance, vocational choices, marriages, immigration, ethnicity, political and economic change, and so on. These are all in shifting relationships with one another, and the specific elements and their relationships shift over time, transforming and integrating once again. For example, although there are genes that predispose children to schizophrenia, not all those with the genes will become schizophrenic. The occurrence of the disease depends on many factors, most of which are still not well described or understood. The same is true for most genetic factors.

Contemporary developmental approaches, including developmental psychoanalysis, have increasingly relied on nonlinear dynamic systems theories, which stress the ways that systems organize and reorganize, integrating and transforming their various components and capacities, changing over time in response to their own development and new environmental conditions. The nature and effects of specific factors cannot be separated from each other. Since infants are so interdependent with their caregiving environments, these models have been especially prominent in infant development theory and research. (In Chapter 18, I propose that these systems theories can provide an inclusive and experience-near meta-framework for psychoanalysis.)

Interdisciplinarity

Direct contact with children brings our attention beyond the consulting room to the many places and disciplines relevant to their development.

Developmentally oriented psychoanalysis has built bridges between many of the fields that are most concerned with infants and children: developmental research, education, cognitive and affective neuroscience, child and adult psychiatry, infancy interventions, pediatrics, and so on, along with psychoanalytic child psychotherapies. Developmental psychoanalysis has been a wedge by which nonanalytic knowledge has come into the analytic discourses. Contemporary developmental psychoanalysis lends itself to a hybrid sensibility; in this sense, it may be more accurate to call this perspective "psychodynamic" rather than the more narrow "psychoanalytic." Inasmuch as it strives to bring findings from different domains together, developmental psychoanalysis follows the "translational" method that is increasingly common in linking basic life science research with clinical practice in medicine and other health-related fields.

Developmental thinking and clinical work

This open, inclusive spirit can be applied to everyday clinical work, fulfilling some of what is most inspiring in psychoanalysis as well as in childhood. Although we can't see what happened to adult patients when they were children, we can learn about children and their families and transpose what we learn. Developmental approaches prompt an interest in a wide variety of phenomena—childhood events, unconscious phantasies, relationships past and present, institutions, emotions, brain configurations, childhood events, unconscious phantasies, and more. All of these offer images and narratives that help us in each case, in our clinical discussions, and in theory-building. I often find myself creating a kind of hybrid image of an adult patient as a child or even an infant, one whose body resembles the contemporary adult body, but rather small in size and with some childlike features, in some physical location that may well include parents or other key people from the past or a childhood home, often including some interaction that I've heard about, all as I imagine them. On occasion, I even picture an fMRI graphic that shows one part of a brain intensely colored, representing the blood flow corresponding with affect activity; this is most common for me at moments of emotional intensity with post-traumatic patients. All these interact with my own emotional and bodily experience, sometimes contextualized by abstract concepts such as repression, repetition, internal object relations, and more.

Despite its great value, all of this involves a kind of approximation, an imaginative selection from an array of available imagery. And their very variety points to the ambiguity and incompleteness of our descriptions, formulations, and interventions. We have so many possible images and methods at hand, and they sometimes contradict or override one another, even as they seem useful and even convincing, simultaneously. As developmental psychoanalysis locates itself in this necessary ambiguity, it points toward a vision of psychoanalysis with multiple perspectives and languages in dynamic transaction. This is both a matter of content and method, as human development involves shifting and complex processes, that are both in motion and very solid at the same time. For me, this is at the core of any true analytic perspective, as it is manifested, for example, in the always elusive search for the presence of the past in the present (looking retrospectively backward), and for that matter, of the future in the present (looking prospectively). At its best, the developmental perspective leads to an embrace of complexity, of uncertainty, of controversy in service of breadth and depth, of an effort at integration with an understanding that there will always be questions that remain unresolved.

Psychoanalytic multiplicity, developmental psychoanalysis, and this book

All of this has led me toward a broad and inclusive clinical perspective, resistant to dogma and interested in a multimodal view of therapeutic technique and mutative action. While I consider the intersubjective-relational theoretical orientation to be the most comprehensive, I believe that it is not only possible, but critical, to explore the traditional analytic interest in the radically intrapsychic, as it has emerged from Freud's early works and beyond. The risks of insularity in psychoanalysis seem to me to be greater than those of diffusion: Analysts are too confident about what we have to export and too cautious about what we need to import. I believe that it can be very fruitful to (re)consider a wide variety of analytic models and clinical approaches from a multidisciplinary perspective, with an eye toward clarification (including of mystifying concepts) and integration of strong ideas and correction of wrong-headed ones.

The robust developmental perspective opens analysis to encompass the centrality of family relationships and the broader social world to a more complex view of temporality and memory as something more than a simple forward flow of time, to relevant disciplines from which analysts can check our thinking and find stimulating new ideas, and more. The more we can know about real children and how they become adults in the world, the more then we can know about all the different dimensions that go into building deep analytic models and helping our patients as best as we can. I believe that it is not only possible, but necessary, to think in several registers at once.

Chapter 5

The postwar diversification and pluralization of psychoanalysis in the United States

Interdisciplinary expansion, the widening clinical scope, and the new developmentalism

In the years after World War II, Ego Psychology came to dominate much of the Anglo–American psychoanalytic world, although the Kleinian and Middle Groups continued to work quite creatively. Postwar economic growth and the expansion of the welfare state supported the expansion of both research and mental health services to wider populations, calling for more varied and flexible psychodynamic techniques, especially in the United States. In addition, new currents began to surface in Continental Europe and Latin America, which were to eventually garner more attention.

Psychoanalysis was the leading orientation throughout the mental health professions through the 1960s in the Anglo–American world. Eventually, a variety of influences challenged the analytic hegemony, including advances in psychopharmacology and other nonanalytic therapeutic interventions, economic constraints, regulation of mental health care by insurers, and feminist and other social-political critiques. In this climate, new perspectives within the analytic arena garnered increased attention, including the emerging intersubjectivist/Relational movement.

Toward a more fully developmental psychoanalysis: "Expanding the scope" in the postwar United States and Europe

Postwar prosperity and the growth of psychoanalytic therapies

Psychoanalysis had taken hold in the United States between the World Wars, especially as Central European analysts emigrated there, and flourished after World War II. During and after the War, traumatized soldiers required rapid and pragmatic help, and over time, enhanced incomes and

DOI: 10.4324/9781003607328-7

medical insurance supported treatment for many more clients. As postwar prosperity gathered momentum, mental health services were offered to a wider population, with a broader range of diagnoses. Training in the mental health professions, both for practice and research, grew rapidly, with ample government support. In general, psychoanalytic approaches were the treatments of choice both in inpatient and outpatient settings. Overall, the links between psychoanalysis and academic institutions grew, including both research and training in academic centers, medical schools, and social work departments. Broadly, psychoanalysis was established in the public culture as a helpful (if mysterious) practice and mindset, *de rigueur* among intellectuals and many artists through the 1950s and 1960s.

In this climate, new populations were to be treated and new intervention methods emerged, all of which supported the "widening scope" (Stone, 1954) of analytic treatment and the new technical flexibility. This correlated with the new developmental emphases, as the traditional austere, interpretive analytic techniques were not so useful with patients whose needs were more acute and whose pathologies were more severe or requiring more immediate attention. In addition, four or five times weekly sessions, for extended periods, were not feasible for many, especially as there was a shortage of skilled mental health professionals. Increasingly, the mental health services market grew, often around psychoanalytic institutions and traditions, but with a variety of treatment approaches; "proper" psychoanalysis, while in demand, was typically offered to more affluent, educated groups. The mental health professions were organized along parallel lines, with psychoanalysts forming an elite, self-selecting, restricted class, with other therapists offering modified forms of (usually) psychoanalytic psychotherapies.

Later, other populations—children, the underserved, the chronically mentally ill—were included (following, for example, the Community Mental Health Act of 1973 (Seligman & Bader, 1991)). "Supportive" treatments might now be offered to patients who had been deemed "unanalyzable," including those with severe psychopathology. Most of the initial orientation was cautious, toward shoring up or enhancing defenses, rather than on interpretations that could lead to psychic structural change. Direct interventions, such as emotional warmth and advice, could be part of the supportive approach, and the spontaneity and directness of child analysis and child psychotherapy were of increasing interest to adult psychotherapists. The American "can-do" optimism and liberal social welfare policy were also influential.

Clinical theory along two tracks

Conceptually, clinical theory was also proceeding along two tracks, similar to but not entirely parallel with the hierarchy between analysts and nonanalysts. One track reflected the traditional emphasis on intrapsychic conflict and interpretation for neurotic, Oedipal-level patients, and the other, a more developmental approach to ego deficits for the "pre-Oedipal," "subneurotic" patients. In both theory and practice, there could be much overlap: Although interpretation was not abandoned in the more developmentally oriented situations, it might not always be at the center; conversely, in practice, many experienced analysts become quite engaged and offer much noninterpretive help to a range of patients. Still, the "Oedipal/pre-Oedipal" hierarchy was maintained in most quarters in the United States, with many arguing that interpretation, ideally within the transference, was the definitive element of pure "psychoanalysis." Within the dominant American Psychoanalytic Association institutes, the treatment of neurotic patients remains most prestigious.[1]

Further expansion of the interdisciplinary projects in the postwar United States

The general postwar expansion of research in the affluent, scientifically oriented United States applied to psychoanalysis, especially as it was the dominant orientation in academic psychiatry and psychology departments. By the 1950s, there were attempts to correlate psychoanalysis with the behaviorist psychologies that were so popular in the academic psychology departments (Dollard & Miller, 1950) and, later, with Piagetian theory (Greenspan, 1979). Anthropologists and sociologists saw psychoanalysis as a critical source for their efforts to build integrative models of personality and social structure, often including complex applications of the Oedipal theory (e.g., Parsons, 1964, among many). For example, Talcott Parsons of Harvard and Neil Smelser of the University of California, Berkeley, leaders of the very prominent "structural-functional" sociological movement, undertook formal psychoanalytic training of their own.

This also included increasingly influential direct observation of infants, older children, and adolescents, both by analysts and academic developmentalists. Rene Spitz (1965) studied hospitalized infants who failed to thrive and even died when deprived of emotional care, even when their

physical needs were provided for, demonstrating the importance of relationships. Margaret Mahler and her colleagues (Mahler et al., 1975) conducted extensive observations of toddlers separating from their mothers
to describe processes by which they became more autonomous through
internalization of their parental relationships, achieving "separation-
individuation" through the development of "libidinal object constancy";
this included mourning as a part of psychological growth. Pine (1985)
extended this project in his (1985) influential book *Developmental Theory
and Clinical Process*.

Theoretical and clinical bridges

A number of adult-oriented analysts began to incorporate developmental
thinking in new integrations that were both innovative and inclusive of a
variety of the analytic perspectives. Otto Kernberg, for example, drew on
Kleinian and other object relations ideas in theorizing borderline character pathology and psychic structure in general; Heinz Kohut and his Self
Psychological colleagues brought in ideas about empathy and other forms
of direct responsiveness. (Kernberg's and Kohut's books were the most
widely read among psychiatrists in the late 1970s and early 1980s.) Hans
Loewald (1960, 1979, 1980) also took a more frankly developmental perspective, stressing the adaptive motivations for growth and development
while maintaining a strong interest in unconscious forces and fantasies.
Affirming the direct effects of the analyst's constructive, imaginative
interest in the patient, he offered a remarkable account of the progressive effects of the analyst's vision of the patient's better future, a rework-
ing of the place of temporality in analysis, and an expanded and more
fully developmental view of the Oedipus Complex, as did Kohut (1977).
Middle Group writers (notably Bowlby, Winnicott, and to a lesser extent,
Fairbairn and Balint) began to draw attention in the United States.

Erik Erikson: Toward a social psychoanalysis

In my view, Erik Erikson's psychoanalytic integrations of child development with anthropology, sociology, and history are the most ambitious,
wide-ranging, and generative of the Ego Psychology syntheses. Erikson
drew on anthropology and history to see personality development as an
integration of bodily experiences and dispositions with social, economic,

and historical structures, forming in the context of families, ideologies, and other institutions and cultural forms: He reworked Freudian instinct theory toward the natural vitality of childhood and the energetic engagement of children, adolescents, and their parents, organized and reorganized within the social and historical environments within each person develops. He took the intertwining of the individual and the social world as the basis for a re-reading of Freud's project, broadening the psychoanalytic conception of the self and the ego and stressing "mutual regulation" between different levels of biological, individual, familial, and historical influences. In this way, he anticipated the systems approaches to development that subsequently became so important, as well as an intersubjective approach. (See Seligman & Shanok, 1996 along with Chapters 11 and 18 of this book.)

Erikson extended analytic developmental theory over the entire life cycle, proposing an eight-stage model. Especially interested in adolescence, he developed the concepts of *identity* and *identity crisis* to capture the increasingly complex syntheses required to adapt to all the variations and demands of becoming an adult in contemporary society. Further pursuing his psychoanalysis of the reciprocal effects of historical change on individuals, he founded "psychohistory," including biographical studies (e.g., Erikson, 1958, 1969 on Luther and Gandhi) and a number of Ego Psychology-influenced studies of development over the life cycle by him and others (Erikson, 1968).

Erikson's influence on the emerging generation of infant researchers (see Chapter 6) was substantial. For example, the seminal developmentalist analyst Louis Sander (personal communication; see Chapter 19) said that his own groundbreaking research was inspired by his wish to apply the Eriksonian approach in a fine-grained model of infant development. Overall, the mutual interaction between different levels and dimensions of persons and social structure was of the greatest interest to Erikson, in what I regard as the boldest application of the Ego Psychological project.

Erikson became a leading public intellectual, winning a Pulitzer Prize and National Book Award and appearing on the cover of *Time*. However, he was marginalized within the established psychoanalytic organizations, in favor of the more ponderous Ego Psychological theories of Hartmann, Kris, and Loewenstein. (See David Rapaport's, 1959, summary of Ego Psychology for an authoritative review of the differences between these perspectives, from the viewpoint of a very thoughtful leader of the movement.)

The decline of the Ego Psychological hegemony in the United States in the late twentieth century

During the 1970s and later, the Ego Psychological hegemony began to face a variety of challenges in the United States. The "two-track" division between "supportive" and "expressive-interpretive" techniques was now coming into question. By the late 1980s, Kohut's Self Psychology had become broadly popular, both within the standard analytic organizations and the broader psychodynamic arenas. New findings about early development also challenged the basic psychoanalytic assumptions about the drives, infants' solipsism, and the like (as I will describe in detail in the next section).

At the same time, feminist and, eventually, queer theory critiques of analysis gained increasing traction. Psychopharmacological advances accelerated, challenging the analytic focus on talking and meanings by pointing toward the possibility that direct interventions into brain processes could work around the more intensive (and expensive) psychoanalytically oriented approaches. As basic neuroscience began to develop, the "scientific" validity of psychoanalysis came into further question. Empirically oriented psychotherapy research, especially about treatment outcome, became more common; as the complexity and length of psychodynamic treatments eluded the requirements for precise measures, further qualms were raised. Consumers and, especially, third-party payors such as health insurers and government came to regard psychoanalytically oriented therapies as cost ineffective. (This remains controversial today.)

Organizational decline and dissent

In addition, psychoanalysis was beginning to lose its hold over the broader mental health education and service delivery systems. Uneven economic conditions led to more concern about cost among governments, insurers, hospitals, and consumers. Nonanalytic therapies, with their patina of simplicity and market-minded measurability, gained popularity. These trends were to accelerate in ensuing decades, especially as insurers grew more dominant in the health care markets and continued economic strains combined with growing suspicion of government, including taxes. The market-minded, individualist neoliberal ideology, taking hold during the Reagan years and beyond, accelerated a turning away from the inner life, accentuated by the intensification of media consciousness and other broad sociocultural effects. In addition, feminists and community activists were continuing to critique analysis for incorporating ideological, cultural, and economical biases from the larger culture into its canons. Academic psychiatry departments increasingly sought nonanalytic leadership (Wallerstein, 1980), and clinical psychology and social work marginalized analysis, as scientifically and clinically unreliable and even elitist.

As all of this diminished the overall dominance and confidence of the hegemonic analytic Ego Psychology—both intellectually and organizationally—it created openings that were to lead to significant changes in North American psychoanalysis. In the 1980s, a group of nonmedical analysts were successful in reversing the hegemonic American Psychoanalytic Association's exclusionary stance toward nonmedical practitioners, through an antitrust lawsuit. (See Wallerstein, 1998, for a detailed insider account.) During the same years, new psychoanalytic institutes open to all qualified disciplines and usually, to all psychoanalytic orientations, were founded in many major North American cities, independent of "the American." The psychoanalytic division of the American Psychological Association (Division 39) gained prestige and membership, becoming a forum for new ideas and a center for the formation of new networks of like-minded, freer-thinking analytic workers. Many of this new generation (including me, as I wrote earlier) were veterans of the civil rights, anti-war, feminist, environmental, and other progressive movements, and carried their activism forward into their professional organizations (Seligman, 2012a). In some respects, North American psychoanalysis became more open, especially as many of the new members were women, and after some time, gay men and lesbians. Regrettably, there are still relatively few African-American or Latino members of most psychoanalytic organizations. (See the exceptional video *Black Psychoanalysts Speak* (Winograd, 2014) for a series of first-hand accounts from African-American analysts.)

Interpersonal psychoanalysis

The Interpersonal psychoanalytic tradition had proceeded at some distance from the various Freudian institutes and cultures. Centered primarily in New York City at the William Alanson White Institute, the Interpersonalists maintained a socially oriented perspective from their beginnings in the 1940s, both in featuring the immediate interaction between patient and analyst in their approach to clinical technique and in a broader interest in political-historical forces. (See, for example, Fromm, 1941/1999.) Kwawer's declaration that interpersonalists have "continue(d) to eschew treatment based on clinical detachment and instead seek to establish the safe, trusting, personal relationships needed by people whose lives are in distress" is prominently displayed on the White Institute website today (retrieved from www.wawhite.org/index.php?page=our-history).

The Interpersonalists have been reluctant to engage with a developmental approach, seeing it as distancing the analyst from direct, here-and-now engagement with the patient, as he or she will be thinking of the patient in childhood terms rather than as a direct partner in an immediate and intimate interaction (Ehrenberg, 1992; Mitchell, 1988) that can lead to psychological transformation. Such as they have been offered, interpersonalist accounts of development tend to be more sociological. (See, for example, Sullivan, 1953, including his debt to G. H. Mead's theory of social roles.)

Despite this, I believe that there is substantial potential for common ground between the Interpersonalist position and a robust contemporary developmentalism. (See Schachtel (1959) for an early interpersonalist effort in this direction). At the core of the interpersonalist credo is the view that social interaction can carry meaning and feeling as deeply as the internal, unconscious Freudian fantasmatic world. The basic conceptualization of a world of internalized social relations driving each person's sense of present reality, whether called "roles," "self-systems," "self-states," "internal objects," or "self-objects," spans both perspectives. Like a fully analytic developmental view, the Interpersonalist method turns on the recognition of the potentials of a reciprocal and often-shifting dynamic relationship between the influence of the past and the present on psychic life: New experiences today can change the effect of the past on the emerging future. (See Chapter 15.) This idea is a necessary one for any theory of analytic therapeutic action that includes the effects of new experience of whatever kind, and is, in a sense, at the core of what distinguishes a fully developmental view from one which is closer to being purely "genetic." Bridging this *apparent* gap is another one of my goals in this book. Watching babies exquisitely demonstrates the passionate interweaving of the internal world with the interactional field. (See Chapters 6 to 12.)

Current Relational psychoanalysis is especially indebted to the interpersonalist tradition in its extensive explorations of the effects of analytic interactions and affirmation of spontaneity and immediate contact as sources of mutative action, especially in working out therapeutic impasses in service of their transformative possibilities. At the same time, the Relationalists have been more ready to take advantage (albeit critically) of the established analytic schools, including the Freudian, Kleinian, and Middle/Independent Groups, to build sophisticated models of internal worlds that are in dialectical transaction with actual realities, especially other people. This gives the Relational approach a breadth and versatility, both in theoretical and clinical domains, and points toward the generative, rich relational-developmental psychoanalytic perspective that I propose in this book. As I have said, my project in this book is to pursue this synthesis.

The Relational turn

Relational psychoanalysis emerged in the 1980s and beyond. In some respects, it responded to the vacuum left by the limitations of the ego orientation, providing new directions for some of the clinical, theoretical, and ideological problems that were being raised. Led at first by Stephen Mitchell before his untimely death in 2000, the Relational movement worked to integrate the Interpersonalist affirmation of analytic interaction and the social nature of the analytic work with the depth of some of the established Freudian perspectives. Inclusively oriented, it took on a broader cultural mindedness and incorporated new ideas from critical philosophy, such as phenomenology, constructivism, and hermeneutics, as well as feminist and, eventually, queer theories. It also embraced the emerging infant observation research that was transforming the developmental perspective in analysis and elsewhere. Overall, a new "two-person" approach to analysis emerged, stressing the mutual influence between patient and analyst, the importance of the analyst's own subjectivity, the specificity of each therapeutic relationship as co-constructed by the analyst-patient interaction, an affirmative approach to interaction and spontaneity in clinical technique, a new emphasis on trauma, and an array of new concepts, some of which reach back to early, marginalized figures in the history of analysis, especially Ferenczi. (Aron, 1996, offers a detailed account of the origins of Relational analysis, including its organizations.) Some comparable developments have emerged in intersubjectivist Self Psychology, which has taken Kohut's work as a point of departure to build a significantly more varied and elaborate analytic orientation. (See, for example, Shane & Coburn, 2002; Shane et al., 1997; Stolorow et al., 1994.)

As I've said, the Relational movement has provided the clinical–theoretical context within which I have tried to work out some of the clinical and theoretical issues that I have tracked throughout this present series of chapters. For me, the broad intersubjectivist orientation offers a conceptual, philosophical, and clinical freedom that supports creativity and the possibility of new integrations of a variety of ideas, both traditional and innovative—the "big tent," of which Bass (2014) has written. Much of the rest of the book will revolve around my efforts to read developmental psychoanalysis and developmental research from the intersubjective point of view, using this project as the platform to rework some of the more classical approaches so as to render them less rigid and more experience-near and compatible with direct observations of children, especially infants.

Note

1 Some institutes of the American Psychoanalytic Association continue to require that students' training cases involve "neurotic" patients, with Oedipal-level pathology, treated with interpretation of the transference.

Part II

The relational baby

Intersubjectivity and infant development

Relationships, development, and "two-person psychoanalysis"

Relational analysis came along at the right time. Its innovations took the emerging dislocation of the classical assumptions to its logical and pragmatic conclusion—that a new paradigm should supplant the instinct theory. Relationships were seen as the primary motivators and organizers of psychic life; the dynamic transaction between people, rather than within individual minds, was the primary context for theory building and clinical technique; reality was at least on a par with the intrapsychic; and present and past were in a dynamic interplay rather than either being reducible to the other.

Relational analysis provides the context for a strong synthesis of analytic theory and technique with contemporary developmental psychoanalysis and developmental psychology overall. But while Relational psychoanalysis draws heavily on the infant research image of the adaptive, social infant, it does not subsume its own developmental model to it. It has synthesized that point of view with a number of other crucial emphases: gender theory, social theory, trauma studies, nonlinear dynamic systems theories, and view of analytic knowledge and the analytic relationship as co-constructed between therapist and patient. In addition, "the developmental tilt" (Mitchell, 1988) has been counterbalanced by the influence of Interpersonal psychoanalysis on the relational turn. The Interpersonalists' enthusiasm for the immediacy of direct interactions in the present provides a counterweight to the temptation to cast the analytic situation in the form of the child–parent relationship, at the expense of its other dynamisms.

DOI: 10.4324/9781003607328-8

Amidst these multiple developments, direct observational research of infants by developmentally oriented analysts and academic researchers found a warm reception. I'll first review the infant research breakthroughs, and then use them as a point of departure to delineate key dimensions of the intersubjectivist-relational clinical perspective. This approach is an application of how I use developmental knowledge as a pathway to think through different analytic approaches. I'll then review key implications of this synthesis for a contemporary approach to the theoretical questions that I've been tracking, about motivation, psychic structure, and the place of development in the psychoanalytic theory. Two brief chapters will offer orientations to several specific domains within this broad picture: continuities from infant–parent relationships into adulthood and current conceptions of the Oedipus Complex, gender, and sexuality. The following section begins with similar orientations to intersubjectivity and attachment theory and research.

Chapter 6

Infancy research

Toward a relational-developmental psychoanalysis

The social infant

Beginning in the late 1960s, a generation of creative, innovative infant interaction researchers looked directly at babies. Generally, they saw babies as more cognitively and affectively organized and influential on their worlds than previously believed. This research was innovative methodologically *and* conceptually: Meltzoff and Moore (1977), for example, accelerated Piaget's timetable for the development of internal object representations ("object permanence"), showing that infants in the first days of life sucked at different rates when offered nipples, either textured or smooth, depending on whether they had seen them, although they had not sucked on them. They had some stable memory of the original nipple.

The analytically oriented researchers were particularly interested in the power of the early infant–caregiver relationships. They described the articulate choreography of physical states, emotions, gestures, and the like that builds the infant–parent relationship from the beginning. This original group included Louis Sander, Daniel Stern, Colwyn Trevarthen, Robert Emde, Berry Brazelton, Stanley Greenspan, and others. Most of these researchers were developmental psychologists, pediatricians, or psychiatrist-analysts influenced by the Ego Psychology interest in developmental research. Although they were attentive to Bowlby's work, their approaches were more microanalytic than the attachment researchers': The attachment researchers tracked more global relational patterns (such as attachment patterns and their internal representations) that had become stable over developmental time, while the infant interaction researchers observed processes occurring in rather short time intervals (often a few seconds). These perspectives are generally complementary, as responsive

DOI: 10.4324/9781003607328-9

caregiving supports secure attachment. Both macroanalytic and microanalytic research have supported this view (Ainsworth, 1978; Jaffe et al.,
2001).

Daniel Stern (1971), for example, compared side-by-side, frame-by-frame
analyses of twins' interaction with their mothers to show the specific,
meaningful variations in these dynamics, depending in part on the mother's
perceptions of the babies. Tronick (2007), in his well-known "still-face"
setup, observed infants' desperate distress and bids for social interaction
following their mothers' immobilizing their faces no matter how hard the
babies tried to elicit a response. This vividly demonstrated infants' compelling expectation for interaction from the very earliest months onward.
(See www.youtube.com/watch?v=apzXGEbZht0.)

The still-face experiment is one of many that show that social motivations are primary and that infants are motivated to evoke and respond to
other people from the beginning of life. Neonates respond preferentially to
human faces and voices, especially their mothers' voices, and their basic
affective repertoire matches that of adults. Following Tomkins (1962,
1963), Ekman and Friesen (1969) demonstrated this by presenting sets of
100 photos of neonate faces to adults in various cultures, who sorted them
into similar sets that corresponded to the six basic adult affects: anger,
happiness, surprise, disgust, sadness, and fear. Each affect has its own specific configuration of facial muscle positions and neuroendocrine profiles.
I'll consider further implications of this shortly.

Affect and intersubjectivity

Motor activity and affect play a special role here. When we react emotionally, there are immediate bodily changes that register as part of our
own experience of ourselves and of the world around us, simultaneously.
Affect thus links us to our environments at the most fundamental level:
Affect is at the core of the weave of self-perception, external perception,
and the assessment of what's happening. Our emotion systems are core
human processes by which we come to feel ourselves as in the world, in
our bodies, at the same time, and they are working from birth on.

Affects also provide specific information about the inside and outside
world. The basic affects are registered as positive or negative, with positive
affect directing continued action or involvement in the current situation
and negative affect signaling interruption, flight, or action to change the

environment (as in "fight or flight"). Further, the specific basic affects are key building blocks of more complex meaning systems: They are guides to evaluations about whether something helpful or threatening is going on, whether to get more involved, run, or pay attention with something in between, and much more.

Moreover, we display affects automatically and often unconsciously, and they affect those who observe them almost simultaneously, at split-second speeds. This includes brain, neuromuscular, and neuroendocrine changes, including facial displays in the observer. People who observe another's emotions display their reactions to them rapidly, through movement, posture, body temperature, sucking, biting, and more, in addition to facial displays.

Specific research findings, then, show the power of dyadic interchanges between the minds and bodies of human beings, including babies and caregivers: First, observing *others'* emotions leads to physiological changes in the observer within fractions of seconds; second, making changes in *one's own* facial musculature that correspond to any particular basic emotion induces hormonal and neurophysiological changes in oneself that correspond to the profile associated with that basic emotion. For example, anger is associated with a rapidly rising blood epinephrine level, which will be stimulated by following instructions to make one's muscles tighten in an "angry face" configuration, even if we're not subjectively aware of that angry feeling. Thus, imitating another's face, for example, will lead to an internal experience in the observer corresponding to that of the person who is being imitated. Since babies and their caregivers imitate one another so regularly (and so rapidly), this is especially important in thinking about early development. (See Schore, 2003b, for a review.) Similar processes are observable in all sorts of interactions, including psychotherapies. (See Chapters 6, 7, and 13–14.)

Contemporary findings about "mirror neurons" point to similar processes regarding movement and pain (Gallese, 2009; Rizzolatti & Craighero, 2004). Motor mirror neurons are activated in the same patterns as those that actually activate the movement, but the movement is inhibited. The observer thus feels what the movement feels like, even though she or he isn't the one who is moving. Again, this response is extremely rapid, and usually outside of explicit awareness. Still, the immediacy of this process is quite accessible: Just imagine yourself watching someone jump in the air, and feeling something like their moving up and then down, even as you know that it isn't you that is moving. The mirror neuron researchers call this "embodied simulation." (See my essays on baseball (Seligman, 2010, 2013) for an account of the role of mirror neuron processes in the appeal of spectator sports.)

In short, observing others' emotion displays and movements engages the observer with how those other people feel. Without inference, without explicit cognition, without having to "think about" anything, human brains and bodies know about others' experiences. This is at the core of intersubjectivity. (See the remarkable and very popular video of twins interacting at https://www.youtube.com/watch?v=_JmA2ClUvUY.)

Mutual regulation and mutual influence

Since babies and their caregivers share an affective language from the beginning of life, and observe and imitate one another so naturally and frequently (many times per minute, if not per second), they are influencing each other's internal states immediately and very rapidly in the multiple pathways. All of this generates mutual regulation and understanding, when things go well enough, with these processes proceeding so quickly as to elude ordinary reflective awareness but becoming quite obvious when emerging video technologies slow down the action with slow, time-sequence analyses.

The image of the helpless, boundaryless, instinct-driven baby is thus supplanted by a view of the infant as capable and socially related, with a powerful effect on his environment (Brazelton & Cramer, 1990). The baby is still understood as acutely dependent on his parents and the others around him, but also as having a profound effect on them, as is obvious to most any parent of a new baby. Early development, then, is a mutual influence, mutual regulation process, in each moment and over the course of development. "Self," "others," and "self-with-other" are intertwined and mutually organizing. This is at the core of the intersubjective perspective: Each person becomes a subjective self through relationships with other people. Without such relationships, the senses of personal effectiveness, connection, and vitality cannot flourish. As they shape psychological structure, such intersubjective processes are also part of our internal worlds. These are described in various ways by such relationship-oriented theories as object relations theories, Relational psychoanalysis, and Self Psychology.

There is a further implication. As we think of psychic structure in terms of "self-with other," we can think in terms of different "selves" as different in different environments and relationships, especially the most intimate relationships. This approach is further amplified as we have given more weight to the ongoing influence of reality, especially other people. In this view, we are constantly constructed and reconstructed in our interactions with the people around us. Intersubjective-interaction processes that affect our sense of self can be observed in most social situations: interactions between children and parents, friends, couples, coworkers, and many others, in such varied channels as bodily postures, facial gestures, movements, words, brain activation, and more. This way of thinking is central to the relational-intersubjective view that each psychoanalysis is a unique, dyadic system, rather than one in which the patient's psychology is an invariant that will emerge and be described in the course of the analytic exploration. (See Chapters 7 and 8.) The Relational theory of "multiple self-states," with its broad emphasis on dissociation, is also supported by this approach.

Recognition processes

Such interaction patterns, then, are constitutive of a basic sense of personal identity, meaning and effectiveness (See Seligman & Shanok, 1996, for an intersubjectivist reading of Erikson's identity concept.) When a caregiver gives an infant the feeling of having an effect on her, he or she is learning to feel like a person who makes a difference in the world. This kind of interaction—a sense of interpersonal contact with a responsive other—gives rise to a sense of personal and intersubjective vitality, of being someone who moves and matters in a lively and responsive environment. (See Chapter 15 for a more detailed account of this, with special reference to the sense of having a future.)

Sander (2002) has described how such recognition processes build toward more integrated and competent social and personal functioning. Tronick (1998) has discussed the "dyadic expansion of consciousness" that emerges from such interactions. These conceptions elaborate various psychoanalytic currents, including Erikson's mutual regulation, the Self Psychological emphasis on empathy and "self objects," the Middle Group's overall interest in the essential role of caregiving dyads, and the Bionian conception of "containment." These are emphatically featured in the infancy researchers' observations of the dynamics and details of actual interactions. (See Chapters 11, 13–14 for elaborations.)

The intersubjective perspective

To restate the basic postulate: This inextricability of individuals with their social relationships captures the core sense of *the intersubjective perspective*. Some have used this term to refer more specifically to a state of mutual understanding or reciprocity, but I take it more broadly, to capture a wide variety of forms in which, again, each personal identity is formed in the ongoing transactions between individual person and others—that is, *between subjects*. Development depends on and is organized by the relationships within which it takes place. (Attachment theory, for example, is concerned with dyadic relationships, not isolated individuals: A baby may be securely attached to one parent, and insecurely attached to another.) This orienting theme is central to the rest of this chapter and, indeed, the entire book, especially in the set of chapters in which it is elaborated.

In a remarkable statement of what he calls "the intersubjective psychobiology of human meaning," Colwyn Trevarthen (2009, p. 507) wrote:

> Cultures depend on a ceaseless, highly creative learning process, which is not just an acquiring of information by instructing the young. It is motivated by an innate human talent for companionship in experience, which is mediated by an intersubjective transfer of intentions, interests, and feeling in conversations of rhythmic motor activity. All achievements of technique and art depend upon the affections and shared enthusiasms of interpersonal relationships. Research on how infants communicate with parents has revealed the natural process by which this learning grows and how it may recover from traumatic events. Brain science confirms that the proprio-ceptive regulations of intentions can be shared by sympathetic "altero-ception," so that creative actions and experiences may be cooperative. Both language and rational thought rest upon this dynamic intersubjective coordination of conscious ac tivity. Individual personalities and self-consciousness grow in relationships and come to recognize traditional beliefs and practices of the community.

Micro-analysis and the nonverbal dimensions of communication and psychic structure

In addition to this broad conceptual orientation, the infancy research has a powerful micro-analytic component. The dyadic choreography of early caregiving has been graphically demonstrated, including very slow motion videography to present and analyze interactions in time frames as brief as a few hundredths of one second. The infant researchers have described an array of interaction processes in parent–infant interaction, including (among many) Beebe and Lachmann's (1988) "disruption and repair" (imagine a mother who speaks too loudly to her crying baby, and then pulls the infant close and lowers her voice, such that the baby nuzzles in and calms); Daniel Stern's (1985) affect attunement (see Chapter 7); and "social referencing," when a child checks with a parent or other trusted person to assess the safety or threat in an unfamiliar situation (like a new person). Emde and Sorce (1983) demonstrate this with infants who look for their mothers' guiding cues, such as facial emotional expression, before deciding whether to venture out across a "visual cliff," a transparent plastic platform set a few feet above the floor which they have never seen before. Generally, affect, bodily experience, and other nonverbal forms of communication and self- and other-regulation are featured prominently as basic pathways for such interactional forms.

Transactional, nonlinear dynamic systems in development and psychoanalysis

The transactional systems model (Sameroff & Chandler, 1975) points in a similar direction and has been central in developmental psychology: The effects of any factor depend on the other elements with which it interacts, and the various elements are transformed by their transactions together. Further, the entire system may change, so as to alter the relationships of the different elements, and so on. This has become a general model for development.

Here is an everyday example drawn from clinical infant work: An infant with a mild constitutional tendency to become disorganized and reactive in response to what might otherwise be an ordinary amount of sensory stimulation may become overwhelmed with a hypomanic mother, but flourish with a cautious one, who approaches the baby slowly and deliberately (even if she isn't doing this with any idea about the baby's hypersensitivity). Over time, the baby might become calmer and better organized with the quieter mother. On the other hand, the baby with the more stimulating mother might become more tense, such that the mother would become anxious in turn, and then, perhaps, more stimulating. The baby might then become even more reactive, sensitive in both sensorimotor and affective channels. Here, the "same" temperamental attribute becomes different depending on its context.

Human development is highly complex, context dependent and moves in ordinary forward-moving time as it is influenced by the past; it's rare, if not impossible, to isolate the effects of any particular factor from the many others that surround it. Despite popular journalism to the contrary, it is now quite clear that the answer to the "nature–nurture" conundrum is not an either/or, but a transactional both/and. (See, for example, Polan & Hofer, 2008; Plomin et al., 1985.)

The transactional model opens a window toward the broad, nonlinear dynamic systems theories that have emerged from an array of contemporary sciences, to apply them to both development and psychoanalysis. In those models, it is the overall patterning of the elements and factors that shape each system that are most important in how it functions and evolves, as these evolve in relation to the various environments with which it interacts. This approach is applied to such widely varying phenomena as simple organisms, the weather, economic markets, and natural selection, as well as to human development. In Chapter 18, I propose that such an approach can be a new meta-framework for psychoanalysis. (See also, among many, Boston Change Process Study Group, 2010; Coburn, 2013; Harris, 2005; Sameroff, 1983; Sander, 2002; Stolorow, 1997.) This synergizes with a fully articulated developmental perspective. Each life evolves as a complex transaction among genetic and epigenetic factors, individual biological development, family, culture, and all the different societal, cultural, economic, and historical surrounds (Schweder, 2009).

Attachment theory and research

Here, as throughout this book, when talking about *attachment*, I am referring to the specific models concerned with felt security with a caregiver and the related separation reactions, rather than the more generic sense in which some use the term, to refer to the whole of the infant–parent tie. Although these have garnered much interest in the analytic world, they have mostly been developed by academic developmental psychologists.

Bowlby's Attachment Theory has become very influential. In the 1960s and 1970s, the American developmental psychologist, Mary Ainsworth, Bowlby's close associate, proposed and validated the specific categories of organized secure and insecure attachment. Subsequent researchers, such as Mary Main, Alan Sroufe, and many others, have developed the theory further, including applications to different developmental stages. The Adult Attachment Interview (AAI) (Main et al., 2005) has been particularly powerful in this regard. Main and her colleagues (Main & Solomon, 1990) proposed a new category of "disorganized attachment," associated with trauma and dissociation, predictive of borderline personality disorder in adulthood. (See Chapters 9, 12, 13–14.) Fonagy, Target and their colleagues (2002) have extended this to conceptualize "mentalization," linking the attachment theorists' emphasis on security in relationships and coherent self-reflectiveness with the analytic commitment to personal understanding. (I'll also discuss clinical applications of attachment theory and research in Chapters 9 and 13–14; see also, among others, Fonagy et al., 2008; Renn, 2012; Slade, 2008; and Wallin, 2007.)

Interpersonal neurobiology

A continuously expanding body of research has demonstrated that social environments, especially early caregiving relationships, have fundamental, direct effects on neurological development. Many of the key processes that have been described by the infant observers are simultaneously observable as both interpersonal interactions *and* continuous, dynamic neural patternings. Schore (2012) has proposed that we understand dyadic interaction as a matter of brain-to-brain communication, especially stressing "right brain unconscious affect" (p. 3) as simultaneously intrapersonal and interpersonal. (See also, for example, Panksepp & Biven, 2012, and Porges, 2011.) A number of developmental psychoanalysts, such as Emde (1988a), Sander (1988), and Stern (1985) anticipated these more specific models. Overall, the two-person, intersubjective viewpoint is directly supported by the emerging neuroscience.

These findings have led to a rich and impressive array of integrations between neuroscience research and psychotherapeutic theory and practice. Although some of these efforts have fallen into a premature reductionism of experience into brain physiology or architecture, or simple-minded genetics, many have added a crucial and extensive dimension to the transformation of current thinking about development and psychotherapy. This includes the move from the one-person to the two-person orientation, the shift toward social motivations and a body-brain-mind-interpersonal intersubjective view, and the multimodal understanding of psychotherapeutic change processes, including the new receptivity to progressive effects of inter- action. The extensive implications of the discovery of mirror neurons with regard to the innate roots of intersubjectivity in brain structure, for example, have gained substantial attention in psychoanalytically oriented circles (e.g., Ammaniti & Trentini, 2009; see also Chapter 11). The appli- cations within the developmental psychoanalytic frameworks have been especially rich and had widespread influence (Schore, 1994, 2012; Siegel, 2015; and Tronick, 2007, for example).

It is now clear that brain physiology and anatomy, child/family pro- cess, personal psychology, interpersonal relationships, and sociocultural and economic environments are all intertwined at every stage of the life cycle and over the course of development. (Shonkoff and his colleagues (2009) have captured this in their National Research Council and Institute of Medicine report (2000) on the effects of social environments on child development, "From Neurons to Neighborhoods.") Interactive dimen- sions, such as affect regulation, interactive responsiveness and contin- gency, attachment security, and intersubjective recognition, have enduring effects that often last into adulthood: Such early relationship patterns have been shown to have immediate effects on the developing brain that can be observed in an array of markers, including differential blood flow to emo- tion regulating brain regions, blood levels of stress-related hormones, such as cortisol, and sympathetic and parasympathetic nervous system arousal. (For a general survey, see, among many, Cozolino, 2010 and Tronick, 2007; see also Chapter 9.) There is an increasing evidence, for example, that "developmental and biological disruptions occurring during the early years of life . . . can affect adult health" (Shonkoff et al., 2009, p. 2252). Related research, at a much finer, if related, level of detail, demonstrates that early trauma and other stressors in childhood influence brain anatomy and neurotransmitter and hormone secretion patterns in later life as well as in the shorter term (DiCorcia & Tronick, 2011). A growing body of theory is emerging around such findings, including those linking developmental processes and evolutionary theory (e.g., Ellis et al., 2011; Hofer, 2014). Bowlby (1988) and subsequent attachment theorists have also considered attachment theory within an evolutionary biological perspective.

Allan Schore (1994, 2003a, 2003b, 2012, www.allanschore.com) has been especially engaged with the integration of developmentally oriented psychoanalysis with the emerging neuroscience findings. Along with an array of colleagues, he has stretched the boundaries of both fields in areas such as attachment, intersubjectivity, affect theory and research, unconscious mental life, the body, nonverbal dynamics, trauma, theories of psychotherapeutic action and more. Schore's emphasis on regulatory processes, especially with regard to affect and its localization in the right brain hemisphere, has had wide influence among infant mental health practitioners (see below) as well as adult psychotherapists and analysts. (See, for example, Bromberg, 2011.)

Continuities between infancy and later development

Continuities between infancy and later developmental stages, including adulthood, are being demonstrated. Much research has converged with the longstanding clinical conviction that infant care and emotion regulation give rise to a secure sense of self with others, and that deficits and traumata, especially early abuse and neglect, impair emotional and relationship development, including attachment security and self-reflective abilities. The AAI has been an important tool in retrospective–prospective research, showing that attachment classification at twelve months is likely to predict adult attachment security/insecurity decades later. Intergenerational transmission is also demonstrated: Adult AAI classification also predicted the attachment classification of the twelve-month-old infants of adults who took the AAI prior to childbearing. Furthermore, in a remarkable finding, adult attachment security has been shown to depend on the capacity to coherently reflect on one's experiences to a greater extent than the quality of those experiences themselves. (See Chapter 10, on continuities in development, and Chapters 11–13 for extended discussions integrating mentalization theory with relational and classical psychoanalytic views of transference and countertransference in work with trauma and generally with character difficulties.)

These efforts are part of emerging integrative models of development, psychopathogenesis, and psychotherapeutic process. These models synthesize the infant interactional and attachment theory findings with correlated neuroscientific and developmental psychological data and studies of psychopathology. For example, long-term brain changes associated with affect dysregulation are predicted by early trauma, both of which are correlated with disorganized attachment and borderline personality disorder. More broadly, empirical studies are supporting the more general and long-held clinical intuition that the first few years of life make a powerful difference on adult personality. (In addition to Chapter 10, see also Jurist et al. (2008); Schore (2003b); among others.)

Direct interventions with infants and their families

An extensive array of interventions with infants and young children has developed in the United States and internationally, applying psychodynamically influenced models in a broad array of unconventional situations involving sociocultural, economic, and emotional distress (Brandt et al., 2014). These include developmental disability, parental incarceration and substance abuse, and foster care, among many others. Interdisciplinary at its core, the infant mental health field includes occupational and physical therapists, social workers, pediatric providers, specialists in autistic spectrum and other developmental disorders, neuropsychologists, child and adult psychiatrists, as well as specially trained infant mental health practitioners. Its major organizations—the World Association for Infant Mental Health and, in North America, Zero to Three—attract thousands to their frequent conferences. The closely related field of developmental-behavioral pediatrics has grown substantially, strongly influenced by psychoanalytically influenced pediatric leaders such as Berry Brazelton (Brazelton & Cramer, 1990; Brazelton et al., 1974).

Early interventions have been shown to be the most effective in promoting positive development. The most notable studies have been led by a Nobel Prize-winning labor economist (Heckman, 2008) based at the usually conservative University of Chicago economics department, who actively advocates public and private investment in early intervention as a matter of economic benefit. Governments throughout the developed world, including many states in the United States, support such intervention: In California, for example, there is a tax on tobacco products dedicated to funding services for children aged zero to five. That such efforts have persisted through fiscal restraints in American states that have otherwise been reluctant to advance a social welfare agenda, may well reflect concern for infants as the most vulnerable members of our society.

I was involved in the development of the classic Fraiberg model of infant–parent psychotherapy for several decades, beginning in the 1980s.

(Fraiberg et al., 1975; Seligman, 1994). Selma Fraiberg and her colleagues proposed a flexible intervention approach with infants under three and their families. Psychodynamic interpretation of parents' repetitions of their early trauma with their babies (the "ghosts in the nursery") could be interpreted, along with direct support and developmental guidance so as to remove impediments to developmental progress in the crucial, early stages.

In an exemplary case, Selma Fraiberg and her colleagues (1980) reported the following vignette in which "the ghosts in the nursery" were projected onto the therapist: Annie, the young mother of a five-month-old boy, was beginning to open up to her psychotherapist in infant–parent psychotherapy, which had initially focused on her difficulty touching and holding her baby. In the sixth session, Annie began to describe her experiences of physical abuse at the hands of her father, and in the seventh, even more painful meeting, she began to talk about her mother's abandoning her at the age of five. After this, however, Annie was unavailable for two months of home-based sessions. Sometimes she was not there and sometimes she would not answer the door. The therapist believed that she herself had become a figure in Annie's transference such that, in Annie's mind, she was a potential abandoner. Annie was thus avoiding experiencing her more excruciating, emotionally overwhelming memories of the abuse and abandonment.

Eventually, the therapist wrote to Annie to say that she would have to report her to the local child protective services to make sure that the baby was safe if she would not meet her. Annie then made herself available, and finally was able to see that her indifference and anger at her baby reflected her own early trauma, such that her parenting behavior changed for the better. Fraiberg and the therapist believed that the therapist's ultimatum was taken as a firmly protective gesture on behalf of the baby, who was both Annie's daughter and in memory, Annie herself.

The diagram below reflects some of the complexity of such transactions, although it does not attend to the equally elaborate dynamics involved in the parent–therapist or child–therapist relationships, with their different transference and non-transference aspects (Seligman, 2014b).

For me, infant intervention captures what is most compelling about working with children. Working with families, especially in difficult socioeconomic circumstances and at their homes, has challenged me to be pragmatic, flexible, and integrative in adapting my psychoanalytic thinking and manners to *their* circumstances. The early intervention move-ment, with its interdisciplinary polyphony of intervenors and researchers, embodies the best of the child analytic tradition. (See also Daniel Stern's 1995 book, *The Motherhood Constellation*, for an essential psychody-namic conceptualization of mother–infant dynamics.)

Influences on parenting through parental childhood representations from family of origin

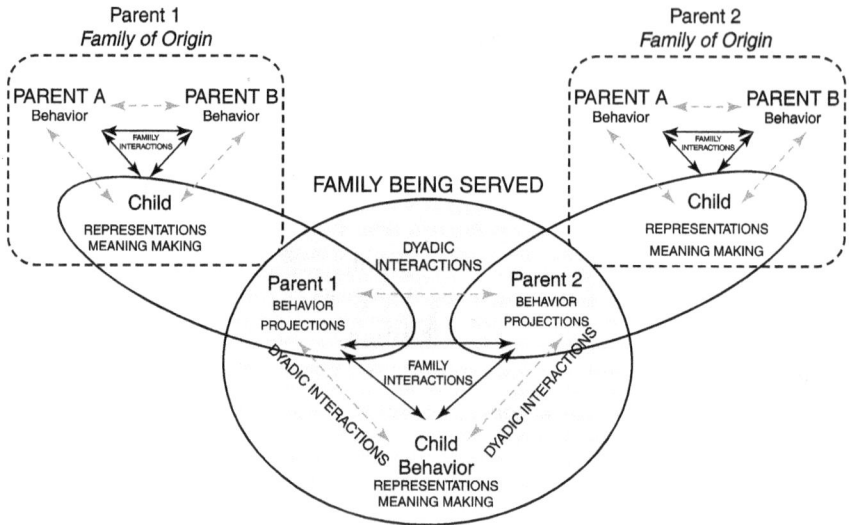

Figure 6.1 Intergenerational transmission and internal representations in infant-parent interaction.

Source: Reprinted with permission from *Infant and Early Childhood Mental Health* (© 2013). American Psychiatric Association. All rights reserved.

Chapter 7

Clinical implications of infancy research

Affect, interaction, and nonverbal meaning

Relational psychoanalysis, developmental research, and the consolidation of two-person psychoanalysis: A core statement

The infant developmentalists' assertion that relationships were primary, dislocated the instinct model's assumptions about infancy and, correspondingly, about the instinctual–primitive core of human psychology, child development, psychic structure, psychopathology, and clinical technique. The classical "metaphor of the baby" (Mitchell, 1988), then, as passive and driven from within, was neither theoretically viable nor sustained as reflecting observed reality.

These approaches to motivation and psychological structure supported innovative relational-intersubjective clinical approaches. Since Relational psychoanalysis was consolidating at the same time as the findings from infant research were emerging, it was in a special position to integrate them from its beginnings, along with the other key influences—feminism, social–critical thinking, the emphasis on reality, dialectical–constructivism, and others.

Action and reflection, inner and outer, and present and past are intertwined in complex models of therapeutic action. Amidst these core developments, a complex set of perspectives has evolved, rather than a single statement or consensus. Although Relational analysis is strongly influenced by developmental imagery and findings, it is not a purely developmental psychoanalysis. Indeed, the Relational turn has included critiques of what it has regarded as excesses of the developmental turn that I described above. (See, for example, Mitchell, 1988, and more recently, Wachtel, in press.)

DOI: 10.4324/9781003607328-10

This led to the consolidation of the fully two-person model. Just as the dyad was the fundamental unit of early development, significant psychic structures are organized in self-with-other, two-person systems that could be manifested internally, externally, or in the intersubjective spaces-in-between. There would also be an individual dimension in both internal and external frames, but these would be in dynamic tension with the relationship matrices within which they formed. The Relational synthesis thus brought forward new dimensions about subjectivity and intersubjectivity and the dynamics of recognition. Overall, the influence of these "two-person" approaches has spread into the other psychoanalytic persuasions in the United States, such that the analyst's subjectivity and participation in the analytic interaction are usually taken as an inevitable part of the analytic process.

The intersubjective two-person orientation

Psychotherapies and caregiving relationships as transactional systems: Co-constructing knowledge and meaning

Engagement is placed at the center of therapeutic action, rather than positivist observation. Like caregiving relationships in childhood, psychotherapeutic dyads are bidirectional and co-constructed, with each partner transforming the other over time. Each analytic process depends on this unique blending, as each analyst will respond in a specific manner to each patient, and vice versa. Transference and countertransference shape one another, in transaction with other factors, rather than in a simple linear manner. Winnicott's (1960a, p. 39) maxim, "There is no such thing as an infant . . .," has been borne out as observable fact and applied to the analytic relationship.

Thus, the analytic situation is cast in terms of engaged participant observation, and the analyst's own psychology and countertransference are implicated in "technique" (Aron, 1996; J. Benjamin, 1995; Hoffman, 1998; among many). As the ongoing interaction changes the situation, each analysis is a dynamic system, changing from moment to moment and over the longer spans of time. The image of the detached and "objective" analyst has thus been dislocated. Analytic knowledge cannot be extricated from the intersubjective field, but rather is created within it. This idea that knowledge and authority are co-constructed in the analyst–patient interaction converges with the mutual influence model of infant–parent interaction and the transactional systems approach.

An open, polyphonic model of therapeutic action and psychoanalytic knowledge has thus emerged, depending on the basic human affinity to be activated and changed in social systems. The original Freudian approach was essentially retrospective, unearthing the psychic facts of the patient's history, with the analyst standing outside of the patient's mind. It was thus a "one-person" theory. The different object relational and ego psychological models included the effects of the therapeutic environment and relationship. But the emphasis was on the analyst's creation of a developmentally progressive environment and provision of various "supplies": need-satisfaction, containment, holding, and the like; this paralleled the developmental models that tracked the mother's role as provider of a more-or-less adequate environment for the child. But the therapist's specific influence on the analytic process and, especially his or her particular personality and subjectivity were not considered, again paralleling the portrayal of the earliest infant–parent dyad as a "need-satisfying relationship" (Edgcumbe & Burgner, 1972, p. 283), rather than a bidirectional one that includes the mother's particular character. I'd call these, then, "one-and-a half-person" theories. In contrast, the relational-intersubjective approach is a fully "two-person" model.

Past and present in transaction

Similarly, both action and reflection and the past and the present have a transactional relationship in the therapeutic process. Just as the past always permeates the present without being reducible to it, analytic interaction inevitably reflects the inner world, but is simultaneously a new creation. The past is carried into the present to be expressed and transformed at the same time. (In his insightful paper on contributions of empirical infant research to adult psychoanalysis, Lachmann, 2001, p. 169, captured this when he wrote that "We have moved from a clinical model that emphasizes a repetition compulsion to a model that sees repetition and transformation in a dialectic.") This bidirectional perspective contrasts with the more "archaeological" classical view, with the analyst doing what he can to enhance the emergence of pre-existing psychic realities. As with the infant and parent, the resonances of the past in the present may be elaborated in interactions, including quite irrational and fantasmatic representations.

With older children and adults, they may be articulated in explicitly reflective thinking.[1]

This correlates with emerging memory research, which shows that memory is a dynamic process in which remembering is understood as new construction based in loosely assembled (and reassembled) neuronal organizations rather than the veridical retrieval of something pre-existing that was fixed when the remembered event occurred in the past. "Recalling" the past also creates opportunities to revise those underlying brain structures and, thus, to reorganize memory. This is particularly likely to happen when affective arousal is strong, but not too strong. Contemporary psychotherapeutic approaches, including psychoanalysis, can be understood in such terms. (See, for example, Carlton & Shane, 2014, among many.)

The multimodal, relationship-oriented view of psychopathology and therapeutic action

The affirmative approach to analytic interaction and the direct observation of actual interaction in development and psychotherapy: Enactments are opportunities

Relational psychoanalysis has featured the opportunities that are presented when patients' problematic internalized relationship patterns are re-enacted in the analytic relationship, often amidst great strain and anxiety (especially when these repeat traumatic situations). From this point of view, there are multiple modes of therapeutic action, such that it is not necessary for self-reflection to subsume action for significant change to emerge. Much Relational clinical writing, in fact, regards enactments as an inevitable and useful part of therapeutic action, and impasses and other interactive crises as offering the greatest opportunities for therapeutic gain (e.g., Bass, 2015; Black, 2003; Mitchell, 1997, 2000). At times, this is presented in very vivid terms: Barbara Pizer (2003) has described the possibilities occurring when "the crunch is a (k)not," and Darlene Ehrenberg (1992) has advocated working at the affectively charged "intimate edge." The Interpersonalist influence is obvious here, with the added Relational interest in the effects of the analyst's own personality and a greater openness to the varieties of more irrational, unconscious, fantasmatic internal experiences portrayed in the more Freudian and object relational theories. (I am especially interested in this synthesis.)

Overall, the relational-intersubjective approach takes an affirmative approach to interaction in the analytic setting, supported by developmental research: Although action may sometimes obviate understanding, recognition, and self-reflection, there is no convincing reason that this is generally true. Interaction is not inconsistent with an interest in interpretation, fantasy, and genetic reconstruction. Indeed, understanding can be established nonverbally and nonreflectively. This is apparent in child–parent interactions, where understanding and recognition, including specific interpretations of psychological states, are conveyed in affectively lively interaction sequences. This is a broader application of development thinking than those approaches that cast the therapist as providing conditions analogous to those that were not provided in the patient's childhood. Despite the misconceptions of its critics, the Relational model is not intended as a prescription for reparenting, or the simple provision of a replacement for missed infantile experience.

Freedom and risk in psychoanalytic practice: New models of therapeutic action

In the midst of such complexity, the analyst's task is not to have the best idea, to make the best interpretation, or to know how to act in advance, but, like a "good enough" parent, to engage in a creative and compassionate manner that is likely to support the therapeutic aims. Contemporary analytic therapists offer multiple modes of intervention to support this array, including helping new awareness and reflective capacities through interpretation, empathy, and other forms of understanding, new forms of affect regulation, re-negotiation of interaction patterns, developmental provisions of different sorts, the analyst's internal work on the countertransference (which might include her own emotional vulnerabilities), and others. The different therapeutic strategies do not exclude one another, although at specific moments there may be choices that tilt in one direction or another.

Once we assume that interaction and interpretation are not intrinsically opposed, the question of how they affect one another can be assessed in each specific clinical situation. For example, self-disclosure is not a prerequisite of Relational technique, although some of its critics have assumed otherwise. I regard it, however, as one option among many, to be used judiciously, in service of whatever dynamic, therapeutic aims might be served. Generally, I believe that many of the models proposed by the different analytic orientations can be applied within the contemporary Relational perspectives. Recasting those theories in terms that stress-relational motives will often strengthen them, making them both more flexible, experience-near, and clinically and scientifically robust.

All of this offers new freedom for the analytic therapist, even as it interferes with our search for guidelines in technical proscriptions, including identifications with analytic cultural norms. Once we acknowledge that our own subjectivities (which are more or less irrational, especially under the intense emotional stresses that occur in most analyses) are inevitably involved in our analytic work, we are challenged to be more self-reflective and aware of even more complexity than in the earlier "one-person" models. The "analytic police" offer a certain kind of security as well as constraint. Often, these norms and identifications help us feel that we know what to do when we are actually imitating or complying with what we think our supervisors (or analysts) would do.

Nonverbal meaning-making and communication in infancy and psychotherapy

Implicit and nonverbal dimensions of clinical practice and therapeutic action: Internal representations, affect, and interaction

The infant researchers have illuminated the meaningful, expressive, and influential nonverbal rhythms and choreographies of infant–parent interactions, vividly confirming the intuitions of parents and anyone else who takes time to look at babies (Beebe et al., 2005; Harrison, 2003, 2005; Harrison & Tronick, 2007). Such details are the building blocks of the more global patterns that form the relational structures, usually implicitly. These accounts can be quite subtle; for example, Daniel Stern (1985) proposed the affect attunement concept to capture a feature of developing intersubjectivity: how one person can show understanding of another's experience while simultaneously showing that she is a different person, seeing this from a different perspective. In both child development and psychotherapy, this can buttress the growing sense of having a subjective self that can be connected with someone separate (whether the patient or the baby). When a baby falls abruptly, for example, experiencing the motor acceleration of the quick motion to the ground, his mother might shout, "ooOps!" thus echoing, but not matching, the pace of the fall. The mother's response takes a different form, in a different sensorimotor modality (vocalization rather than movement), but it still reflects the fall, through its cadence and the accelerating vocal intensity of rising and falling "ooOps!"

Patients and therapists constantly influence one another through minute variations in tones of voice, vocal rhythms, facial displays and bodily postures, physical gestures, pauses and silences, and even the rustlings of clothes or changes of bodily position (Seligman & Harrison, 2011). Although ordinarily invisible to both participants, these all convey fine calibrations of meaning and mutual influence. Just as infants create and experience actual interactions in various nonverbal, implicit pathways, therapeutic interactions affect all the multiple pathways for making sense of oneself and the world (including the plethora of social and cultural forms). (In Chapter 14, I take a similar approach by observing very short time intervals in father–baby interactions to describe different influence patterns that may give rise to different kinds of internal relationship patterns.)

Attention to microprocess, then, shows details less visible in conventional case material. Rupture and repair, and a similar descriptor, "disruption and repair," are offered as important for growth in therapy, as in childhood (Beebe & Lachmann, 1988; Tronick, 2007). (Imagine a therapist switching to a quieter voice and more emphathic mode when her patient starts to raise her voice.) Beebe (Beebe et al., 2005) has used videotape of her own face with a remote, traumatized patient, to evoke safety and potentiate affective recovery. Harrison (2003; Harrison & Tronick, 2007) analyzed videotaped interactions in child cases lasting from split seconds to minutes in order to elucidate the details of transformations in therapeutic process.

Harrison (Seligman & Harrison, 2011) offered the following illustrative vignette from the first session with a child on the autistic spectrum. A four-year-old girl is building a "house for dinosaurs" with blocks. The therapist sits quietly, appreciatively saying "Mmm." When part of the building falls, the therapist asks, "Would you like me to pick up the block that fell down?" The girl says "yes." Another block falls, and the therapist asks again, "Would you like me to pick that one up?" Again, the girl says "yes." They are co-creating a rhythmic predictable regulatory pattern signifying safety in the back-and-forth rather than in the words themselves. The girl places the block on the building, pauses, and then comments—with the same intonation as the therapist had previously used—"Mmm." An instant later (without explicit awareness), the therapist says, "Mmm." Together, they co-created the analyst's original two-part utterance. A sense of safety and mutual recognition is here communicated in vocal and body rhythms and gestures as well as words.

Self-monitoring, countertransference, and nonverbal cues

In keeping with the Relational interest in the analyst's own reactions, therapists are encouraged to follow their own visceral experiences, including minute changes in breathing patterns, vocal cadences, bodily postures, and the like, and musical metaphors are increasingly suggested. (See, for example, Knoblauch, 2000; Sletvold, 2014.)

After sessions with a charming, overly polite, and painfully indecisive young man, a therapist felt vaguely unhappy and irritable, and eventually came to feel clumsy and inadequate. Before noticing this, he had formulated the man's indecision as a perfectionistic reluctance to give up alternate possibilities. But this reasonable, intellectual formulation did not bring him into the patient's experience. In reviewing the hour with a consultant, he noticed that he then shifted to a quieter tone, recalling that he had noticed that he felt annoyed and inferior by something in the patient's tone.

That so much emotion and meaning can be evoked and communicated in these implicit nonverbal pathways intertwines with the emerging ideas about the many modes of therapeutic action other than interpretation, and other modes of explicit reflection. Even when nonverbal communication of psychological states is overlooked, it may still be quite influential, in both positive and negative ways.

Integrative examples

The following examples illustrate how potentials for therapeutic change can be accessed directly through action and emotional interchange, within the co-constructed therapeutic relationship, including attention to nonverbal, implicit influence.

A young man presented with a pattern of "destroying" relationships with women. Over time, he would become "blank" when he began to feel close to his female therapist. He knew that his alcoholic mother had been sexually provocative with him, and speculated that she had been over-stimulating when he was a baby, but without emotional effect. As the therapist carefully pointed out how his posture and breathing constricted in these "blank" states, he gradually linked these moments to fear—first with the therapist and later to the past, recalling his mother's seductiveness. The detached states became less frequent and the patient's relationships improved.

In another situation, the therapist of a woman in her 50s was struggling with his severely depressed patient. Over weeks of the patient's puzzling silence, punctuated by ruminative remarks about the failure of earlier treatments, he felt constricted and frustrated, choosing words fitfully. His apparently empathic remarks were met with more pained silence or corrections. Irritated as he was, however, the therapist held back from pointing out the patient's covert critical attitude. Instead, he concentrated on "getting into her skin" by nonverbal means: Trying unobtrusively to assume the patient's posture and repeat her gestures, he went so far as to time his own respirations to match those of the patient. Unexpectedly becoming immersed in the patient's hopelessness and enormous fragility, he was more able to get past his annoyance. With this expanded visceral awareness, he made occasional comments about his own feelings of sadness and irritability in response to the patient's remarks, acknowledging that his statements could sound "like fingernails on a chalkboard." The patient relaxed, and began talking about her deep depression and wish to die, along with her poignant will to stay alive for the sake of her adolescent daughter.[2]

New conceptions of psychic structure and the unconscious

Psychic structure and the two-person orientation

This attention to dyadic process in psychotherapy is supported by a correlated conceptualization of psychic structure as organized in internal representations of relationships (and relationship systems). The infant development research suggests that both moment-to-moment and long-term interaction patterns become generalized over time and become influential in organizing internal psychic life and interpersonal interactions. Continuities in attachment patterns, brain anatomy and chemistry, and even epigenetic changes have been noted (Polan & Hofer, 2008; see also Chapter 9). In Chapter 14, for example, I approach projective identification as a type of relationship format that can be observed in both infancy and adult relationships, including psychotherapies, building from detailed observations of very brief interaction in which a father brutally handles his three-day-old infant. That the father had been physically abused by his own father suggests that this interaction pattern enacts the internal representation of that abuse, thus demonstrating its intergenerational transmission. (See Chapter 6, on intervention with infants and families.)

Various terms have been offered to conceptualize self-with-other configurations that reflect such continuities, including "self-other-affect units" (Kernberg, 1976), "generalized representations of interactions" (Stern, 1985), "internal working models of attachment" (Bowlby, 1980), interpersonal expectancies and implicit relational knowledge (Lyons-Ruth & the Boston Change Process Study Group, 1998), model scenes (Lichtenberg, 1989), structures of subjectivity (Atwood & Stolorow, 1984), among others (Demos, 1988; Emde, 1983; Fast, 1985). Organized as they are around interpersonal relationships and the intersubjective field, these differ from the classical and ego psychoanalytic models, which are more organized around the traditional drive-defense structures. Those models are not fundamentally "relational," even if they are linked to relationships in their development and expression in current interactions with others; hence they are more "one-person" concepts. Perhaps less conspicuously, they also differ from the classical object relational concepts, especially the Kleinian, in that the internal structures are more directly analogous to effects of actual relationships. These classical theories do organize the intrapsychic in terms of relationships, but even the Middle Group views give greater weight to the more phantasmatic, primary process-like processes featured in most classically influenced analysis.

In practice, these distinctions are usually not so definitive, but I do think there is value to this kind of parsing as a pointer toward greater conceptual and historical clarity. Paradoxically, this differentiation can lead to further integration, just as in developmental process. Relationalists sometimes overlook the potentials for thinking about intrapsychic realities, while some classically oriented analysts neglect the significance and impact of actual interactions, which may be "hidden in plain sight." I believe that there are substantial possibilities for integrative thinking and other sorts of "bridge building" between the intrapsychic and the relational foci. This is a central theme of this book, building around my enthusiasm for the Freudian pursuit of depth and vision in the exploration of the irrational and phantasmatic, taken within an intersubjective orientation rooted in the image of the social, attachment-seeking infant in mutual interchange with her caregivers and the larger environments.

Implicit relational knowledge

The concept of implicit relational knowledge is currently the most widely used conceptualization of relational psychic structure, offering a bridge to new models of mental life outside of awareness. Lyons-Ruth and her colleagues in the Boston Change Process Study Group (1998) coined the term "implicit relational knowing" to capture internalized schemas of self and self-with-other that shape experience and are lived out, often taken for granted and not reflected upon, but neither repressed nor in conscious awareness. Originally, the term *implicit* or *procedural knowledge* was proposed by cognitive psychologists to describe patterns of acting, behaving, or experiencing that don't involve conscious reflection. We follow countless such routines without thinking about them at all; the classic examples include riding a bicycle, turning the key to open a door, or stopping at a red light. Their automaticity may be protective of their efficacy, since such patterns may be disrupted if they are reflected upon (Clyman, 1991; Grigsby & Schneiders, 1991). The concept of implicit knowing now stands beside repression as constituting what analysts mean when we talk about the unconscious, along with dissociation. (See Stolorow & Atwood, 1992, for a thoughtful contemporary conceptualization.)

This "implicit relational knowing" concept describes what might well be called a form of psychic structure, associated with patterns of emotional experience organized in internalized expectations and predispositions to respond with particular ways of interacting with other people. (I've discussed this in terms of "forms of intersubjectivity" that emerge from early infant–parent interaction; see Chapter 14.) Such patternings are also observable in neuroanatomy, chemistry, and physiology, as when the emotion-regulating areas of the brain appear to be underdeveloped in abused or neglected children (including in their adulthood), when examined in functional Magnetic Resonance Imaging (fMRI). Brain development is thus understood as "experience-dependent."

Therapeutic action, interaction, and implicit psychic structure

A new view of the therapeutic action of psychoanalysis and psychotherapies thus emerges. Psychic structures include forms of implicit knowledge, embedded in interaction patterns, senses of self, and biological structures: That these processes go on predominantly out of explicit awareness supports the idea that interaction can be mutative in itself, such that psychoanalytic change processes can reach into what is outside of ordinary reflective awareness without interpretation. Deep meanings and memories are embedded in implicit patterns of action and experiencing which can be affected implicitly. In addition to the growing evidence that psychotherapy can change behavior and relationship patterns, there are also emerging findings that brain structures and functions can be altered by psychotherapy. (See Cozolino, 2010; Schore, 2003a, 2003b; and Wallin, 2007, for example.)

The Boston Change Process Study Group (2010), for example, has applied nonlinear dynamic systems theories to describe several specific dyadic interactional processes that lead to psychotherapeutic change, including "moments of meeting" and "now moments," in which implicit relational structures can be altered. Related processes include the disruption and disconfirmation of affectively charged interpersonal expectations, or the "re-negotiation" of psychic structure (Pizer, 1992). The contention that interactions can change psychic structure parallels the common (and research-based) knowledge that child (and adult) growth and development involves strong change processes which do not depend on conscious reflection. (For other examples, see Beebe & Lachmann, 2002; Sander, 2002; Schore, 2003b; as well as Chapter 15.)

Relationships in development and psychopathology

The emerging findings about the continuities between early development and later psychic structure are illuminating the contemporary view of psychopathology and psychopathogenesis. In this relationship-oriented perspective, there are many pathways to psychopathology, as there are multiple modes of therapeutic action. These pathogenic processes include conflicts between different internal relationships (including their representations and the associated affects and expectations) and conflicts between strong impulses and motives to restrain them, among others, often as a consequence of trauma or other serious developmental strains. Mitchell (1988) proposed a "relational-conflict" model as a conceptual envelope for many of these.

Trauma and the attention to actual experience in both present and past

Relational analysis has emphasized actual trauma in its various accounts of the origins of psychopathology, in accord with a widespread change in both analysis and the broader psychotherapeutic arena. There is now broad interdisciplinary consensus that trauma has direct effects throughout life that can be directly observed. This includes both detailed psychological accounts and a recent array of findings about the direct effects of abuse and neglect on brain development. (For a broader review, see Panksepp & Biven, 2012; Perry et al., 1995; Porges, 2011; Schore, 1994; Van Der Kolk, 2014; Wallin, 2007, for example.)

Traumas of various quality and intensity are often noted, including neglect, sexual and physical abuse, developmental insults and deficits involving poor emotion regulation, early failures of empathy, malignant attribution, anxious and disorganized attachments, and even adverse social and economic conditions. A wide array of interventions have developed, many of which involve making direct contact with repetitions of traumatic situations, including through emotions, bodily states and behavioral re-enactments, as well as the development of new communication and emotion-regulation skills. Frequently, the differentiation of past trauma with present reality is a basic goal, often depending on bolstering the traumatized patient's capacities for affect regulation and reflective thinking. The legacy of Freud's original project can be observed in such apparently distinctive contemporary interventions as the emerging somatically oriented therapies (e.g., Ogden et al., 2006) and dialectic behavioral therapy (Linehan et al., 1999), which has been shown to be effective in treating borderline personality disorder, along with standardized, evidence-based treatments emerging more directly from psychoanalysis (Bateman & Fonagy, 2009; Clarkin et al., 2006; Lieberman et al., 2005). Even analytic therapists who are not specifically focusing on trauma have been influenced by the new attention to trauma and its adverse effects on development. For example, I sometimes suggest to patients that they are viewing intense feelings that are overwhelming in the present as memories, rather than facts (See Britton, 1999, for similar language from a Kleinian perspective, or Winnicott's (1963) related view that patients sometimes experience their trauma as actually happening in the analytic hour.) At other times, I include specific suggestions to support emotion regulation or reflection in the midst of interpretive work.

The relational-developmental emphasis on "what really happened" supports the empathic, respectful, and affirmative attention to the patient's subjective experience of events, including childhood events. This emphasis is supported by the feminist critique of Freud's abandonment of the seduction theory. The contemporary approach takes subjective experience as legitimate in itself, rather than parsing out the veridical events and the contribution of the irrational unconscious. Increasingly, Ferenczi's work is being recovered as a key source.

Trauma and the failure of recognition

This has also renewed attention to an aspect of posttraumatic pathology: that the traumatic situation often precludes awareness of its meanings, in addition to the overwhelming nature of the experience itself. (See, for example, Bromberg, 1998; Davies & Frawley, 1994; Herman, 1992.) The child suffers abuse at the hands of someone on whom she or he depends at the most basic levels, at the same time that she feels compelled to keep the relationship(s) intact. In the classic example, the victim of familial sexual abuse will find it very difficult to apprehend how awful the sexual approaches are when the same man who molests her may be so kind at other times, and is someone on whom she depends. Ferenczi (1949b) was especially attentive to this in his remarkable discussion of "the confusion of tongues."

When others act as if nothing untoward is going on, the difficulties are further amplified. A dissociative stance of not knowing what one knows must be maintained to protect those crucial relationships on which the victim depends, in a mind-crushing bind that blocks reflective thinking: This need to maintain relational ties helps explain the tenacity of painful, maladaptive relational patterns. Such basic modes are often the only ones available to the child in the pathogenic family, who therefore cannot conceive of alternatives at an affectively meaningful level, even as an apparently thoughtful adult. To consider that things could be otherwise is to risk loss, isolation, shame, and the like, potentially at a catastrophic level. This perspective echoes Fairbairn's (1952) interest in the tenacity of "bad objects" and Bowlby's (1988a) recognition of the importance of maintaining the relationships on which one depends, even at great emotional cost. Bowlby (1988, p. 99) captured the therapeutic imperative in such cases in his essay "on knowing what you are not supposed to know and feeling what you are not supposed to feel."

These patterns persist into adulthood, in family relationships and in broader organizational and even political dynamics, as well as in individual personalities. Patients with such traumatic histories may have special difficulties trusting the analyst and the analytic process; these can sometimes be mistaken as primarily paranoid reactions, but they are in fact repetitions of the traumatic situation. Interpretations are sometimes taken as criticism, or even as attempts to convince the patient that his or her perceptions are mistaken, or revealing a distorted or fundamentally flawed mind. (See Chapters 13–14.)

Dissociation, self-states, and the integration of fragmented selves

Dissociation has been central in the Relational arena for some time, intertwined with the emphasis on trauma. The dissociation concept is parallel to and as central as that of repression in classical theory. Freud did attend to dissociation, describing "vertical" splits in awareness and in the ego, in which different parts of the personality were kept separate from one another. Analogizing this to repression's horizontal distinction between conscious and unconscious, he suggested that dissociative defensive organization was most typically associated with more serious psychopathology than the repression-based neuroses. But dissociation was rarely central in his thinking, or that of most subsequent analytic clinical theorizing. Relational analysts, however, tend to see dissociation as central in most cases, presenting with varying rigidity and depth. This can also involve splitting off affects or memories.

Adding dissociation as a basic organizer of the awareness/unconscious dimension of mental life has broadened contemporary models of unconscious mental life. Related conceptualizations are described in terms of experience which is not formulated but is nonetheless quite significant and influential. D. B. Stern (1989) has described "unformulated experience," and Christopher Bollas (1987), a contemporary Middle Group analyst, discussed "the unthought known." Generally, dissociation is currently gaining more traction in many analytic orientations.

Multiple self-states

The Relational conceptualization of "self-states" is closely related to dissociation theories (Bromberg, 1998). These are quasi-distinctive experiences of self-with-other, with different interpersonal expectancies and affective atmospheres. This is to be distinguished from multiple personalities; there is no doubt about the basic identity. Nonetheless, rather than looking at experience in terms of a single "self" or ego, the relational approach starts with a sense of personal experience oriented around tensions between unity and multiplicity. (See Seligman & Shanok, 1995.) Psychological resilience includes the flexible integration of a multiplicity of self-experiences, which may become fragmented and disintegrated in traumatic development. Harris (2005) has captured this conceptualization in using the phrase, "the softly-assembled self." Although with different emphases, there are similarities with the British object relations theories, including Fairbairn's (1952) formulations about different internal objects breaking off from the "central ego," and Klein's view of the integration of different internal objects and developmental positions. These perspectives converge in a view of analysis facilitating the restoration and integration of aspects of self-experience, which have been fragmented or detached; these often make themselves known in interactions whose meaning is not explicit, or even disavowed. Philip Bromberg's (1998) call for analysts to "stand in the spaces" between the dissociated "selves" has been especially influential. Bromberg (2011) has also drawn basic links between self-state theory and the emerging developmental-interpersonal neurobiological research, especially that of Schore (2012).

In a variation on this theme, and drawing on the original Kleinian conceptualizations, Relationalists have linked dissociation theory with a relationship-oriented view of projective identification as involving the analyst's receptivity to the patient's dissociated self-states, bearing them in mind and enduring the anxiety of painful and contradictory experiences coming into the analytic space and (here is the Relational contribution) considering how the analyst's own psychology comes into the mix (Seligman, 1999). In a classic paper, "Whose Bad Objects Are We Anyway?" Davies (2004) described a case in which she found herself absorbing and barely tolerating her patient's projected experience of her as cruel and withholding. Finally, she lost her temper. Shortly afterwards, the patient became more affectionate and reflective, and they were able to talk about their interaction in an affectively saturated way that allowed the patient to integrate and transform these various images of selves and others. Davies considers links to the Bionian conceptualizations of containing projective identification, as I do in Chapters 13 and 14.

A note on regression, dissociation, and the relational critique of developmental psychoanalysis

As Relationalists have emphasized dissociation and self-states, there has been less explicit attention to regression. This caution about regression and fixation links to the Relational movement's general critique of developmental models (Mitchell, 1988), with its Interpersonal psychoanalytic roots. I think that the regression and dissociation models are not incompatible: My own sense is that most of us are thinking in terms of regression much of the time, even when we don't realize it. That said, I mean to avoid a crude developmental approach, where the patient simply moves through previously uncompleted developmental stages due to therapeutic provision, or to insights that free development from fixation to points of trauma or deficit. (See Seligman, 2016.) Something like this might unfold in some cases or at moments in others, but I am more interested in the play of the analytic interaction, and I see that tumult, with all its variations and vicissitudes, as the source of what makes analysis as real and as compelling as it can be.[3] As I've said, a relational-developmental perspective is not the same as a "corrective emotional experience."

Notes

1 In confidently asserting the connections between childhood and adulthood, the psychoanalytic approach to developmental research goes further than the developmental researchers themselves do; the academic developmentalists have been quite cautious about this, oriented as they are by their careful empiricist constraints. The ambitious linkage of present and past is particular to psychoanalysis, with its single-case orientation, its reliance on clinical inference, and, currently, its affirmative use of such hermeneutic validity criteria as narrative efficacy and goodness of fit, at least in some quarters. Psychoanalysis

established itself by linking childhood and adulthood, and remains the most articulate of all the human sciences in regard to such matters.

2 Alexandra Harrison collaborated in the development of the material in this chapter.

3 The concept of regression both asserts and relies on the Freudian interest in the radical fluidity of the intrapsychic and the different levels of psychic functioning, including primary process and the shifts and differences between childhood and adult thinking. In doing so, it marks the vertex of the link between the Freudian commitment to such unusual forms of mental process and a general developmental orientation. Relational analysis has a lot to gain by including more of this orientation, and a lot to lose by overlooking it. (See, for example, Cooper et al., 2014.) Psychoanalysts, of whatever persuasion, are engaged with the mingling of past and present, internal and external objects, phantasy and "objective" reality. Psychoanalyses are especially set up to heighten such unusual blends of modes of experiencing, both individual and shared, in which this kind of softening of ordinary distinctions becomes the dominant form of experience, such that they can emerge and be re-worked in all sorts of ways.

Chapter 8

Theory III

The relational baby: Psychoanalytic theory and technique

We can now revisit those central issues in psychoanalysis that I described in introducing the original Freudian models in Chapters 1 and 2, reviewing those specific controversies from today's robust and inclusive developmental perspective, with infant observation research and the intersubjective-relational models well in mind. The rest of this book builds on this, reflecting my way of working these out, trying to preserve what is most valuable in the traditional analytic models while implementing the energy and freedom of the new analytic approaches.

This summary rests on a number of core contributions, which have approached this from convergent points of view, starting with Joseph Lichtenberg's (1983) *Psychoanalysis and Infant Research* and Daniel Stern's (1985) game-changing *The Interpersonal World of the Infant*. Robert Emde's (1988a, 1988b) Plenary Address to the International Psychoanalytical Association also deserves special mention. (See also Beebe & Lachmann, 2002; Greenspan, 1981.) More recent statements include the remarkable declaration by Colwyn Trevarthen (2009, p. 507) that "culture . . . is motivated by an innate human talent for companionship in experience, which is mediated by an intersubjective transfer of intentions, interests, and feeling in conversations of rhythmic motor activity." Louis Sander's (2008) view of the overarching role of the life-preserving dynamics of living systems, whether in infancy, psychotherapy, or society, has been an essential influence. (See also Chapter 19, on Sander.) Daniel Stern's (2010) final book offers a radical integration of infant research, neuroscience, phenomenology, and the temporal arts of music, dance, and performance to assert that "forms of vitality" are at the core of what brings humanity to life and makes for change in psychotherapy. (See Chapter 16, on Stern.)

DOI: 10.4324/9781003607328-11

Infancy, primitivity, and basic psychopathology

The classical analytic theories assume that early childhood development is an emergence from early primitivity into a more adaptive psychic organization, and thus characterized by a high degree of discontinuity. The infant is to be extricated from the original state of nature, which is chaotic and in tension with the social world; the family is the cultural agency that rescues and civilizes the infant. (See also Mitchell, 1988; Wollheim, 1993.) Basic psychopathology is then understood as a consequence of a distortion or deficit in that process. For example, borderline and psychotic psychopathologies have been traditionally understood as analogous to infancy.

The alternative view that the baby starts out organized and oriented to reality, especially other people, leads to a different perspective. The "infant research baby" is neither basically disorganized, primitive, and solipsistic; nor in dreamlike states and fundamentally motivated to eliminate intolerable affects and tensions; nor undifferentiated from her perceptual, sensory, and human environment. Mental life originates in a relational matrix which is continually co-constructed and transformed by experience: The infant is well adapted to social interaction, oriented to reality, influential on her environment, active as well as passive, depended on as well as dependent, and endowed from the beginning with formidable resources and organizational patterns of all sorts.

Infancy and primitive psychopathology are not analogous

This implies a rejection of the traditional analogy between infancy and primitive mental functioning, including psychosis. Instead, these are separate psychoanalytic categories, the relationships of which we may now begin to explore more clearly and specifically. Instead of assigning the primitive motives to the baby and the more adaptive motives to the social world and its internal correlates in the ego, infant researchers view development at all stages as having adaptive and progressive potentials that inhere in the individual in the same measure in the various stages; indeed, infant clinicians are very attentive to the especially progressive "self-righting" tendencies of early caregiving relationships. (See, for example, Fraiberg, 1980; Seligman, 1994.) This position does not at all overlook how very dependent babies are, nor that early trauma is the most destructive.

Instincts and the lived experience of the body

The Freudian theories (especially in Freud's original form) bring in the body through the instincts, as the pathway by which the physical begins to move into the mental world. This turns attention away from the lived experience of the body, as something known through the senses, in motion, in emotions, in general feelings of wellbeing and malaise, as well as in the ways that one is regarded by others. Relational-intersubjective theorizing features these direct experiences, as a core component of its approach to the relationship between the body and mental life.

The body is thus regarded as organized through relationships, rather than as autonomous and presocial. (See, for example, Aron & Anderson, 1998.) The body and the sense of self-with-others are fundamentally intertwined, evolving in each family and taking on the various constraints and opportunities offered in particular social situations and historical moments. This includes the idea that gender and sexuality are constructed in the transactions between individuals and culture, broadly construed.

A response to instinct theory-oriented criticisms of the relational turn

Some critics of relationship-oriented analytic theory have been concerned that rejecting the classical instinct theories turns attention away from the body, or from passion and sexuality. My own view is that this is "a straw man," misconstruing Relational theory from a position that is rooted in the long-standing analytic tradition that treats the body and sexuality at arm's length through instinct theory and the like. Perhaps Freud felt he had to do that to be seen as something other than a quack or a pornographer in his time and place, but I don't regard that strategy as virtue anymore: Freud, more than any other, opened Euro–American discourse to more talk about the body and sexuality, so the original caution is no longer necessary. In addition, as I have said, much contemporary science supports a relationship-oriented view of development, motivation, and psychopathology. (I say this at the same time that I believe that Freud's instinct theory has been extraordinarily creative and generative; I don't mean to do away with it, but rather, to reposition it as a facet of the psychoanalytic model, rather than at its core.)

Similarly, I don't think that passion is a special problem for Relational psychoanalysis. Strong emotions of all sorts are featured throughout the Relational literature, discussed more frankly and directly than in most other analytic discourses, where it is veiled by references to somewhat ornate abstractions that have to be decoded. Many traditional analysts end up talking about proxies for the body or sexual and other passions, rather than the body itself. Instead, in the Relational arena, there is a more direct discussion of sexual attraction, erotic behaviors, longings, sex itself and sexual practices, as well as other powerful and even peremptory experiences of all sorts, including anger, hatred, fear, and all sorts of other irrational desires, ideas, and emotions. The theoretical basis, as I have formulated it, is in the discussion of affect and the direct experience of the body, as they are shaped in the social field.

The centrality of progressive development

Development is regarded as an innate process that is implicitly integrative and progressively transformative, rather than as an outcome of the conflict between the adaptive and maladaptive forces of the mind and in culture. That progressive development is basic to each human life and to the survival and reproduction of the species supports a more open and affirmative approach to clinical technique and therapeutic action.

The classical view casts the patient as someone whose self-awareness has been impaired (following the paradox of the Oedipus story, in which the boy/king must lose his physical sight as he (re)gains his personal and spiritual vision). Through interpretation and insight, the oracular analyst reduces these blockages to provide the knowledge that will illuminate the patient's lack of awareness. Contemporary analysts see patients' difficulties more broadly, including such factors as developmental failures and traumas and unmet and distorted childhood needs, in addition to limitations of self-knowledge. A developmental psychotherapeutic orientation affirms the restorative potentials for restoring psychological growth processes that have been derailed, both through insight and the various effects of the patient-therapist relationship. The analyst thus oriented is likely to take a more acceptant attitude toward the patient's wishes and accounts of herself, rather than viewing them as defenses or impediments to the analytic process.

Continuity and discontinuity in development

Developmental process here is more continuous than in the classical models. For the infant researchers, the central issues and forms persist over the development course, characterized by transformations within a changing, but continuous, matrix, rather than as one form of organization superseding another, as in the more discontinuous stage theories such as Freud's (1905b) genetic model of infantile sexuality. Growth and development are a matter of intertwining integration and differentiation, as, for example, in how different organs are linked in fetal development as they emerge from the undifferentiated matrix of the original embryonic tissues.

Reality, fantasy, and psychic structure formation in infancy and psychopathology

The classical Freudian model of psychic structure formation gives significant weight to how the experience of what is "actually happening" is mediated through fantasies, defenses, instinctual vicissitudes, and the like, especially in early infancy. But the infant researchers take it for granted that the infant directly experiences actual interactions in a way that leads to basic and enduring transformations of the inner world. Following this, they describe psychic structure as organized into internal representations of these relationships. These are the central concepts used by infant research-oriented developmental psychopathologists to account for how older children and adults encounter "reality" through the templates of their pasts. In this way, they play a parallel function to the classical psychic structure terms like *phantasy* and *defense*.

The challenge is to see how all these different approaches can be used in a flexible and multi-vision perspective that is both synthetic and also retains the specific insights of each perspective. Attending to reality and lived experience does *not* mean neglecting the worlds of primary process.

Findings from adjacent fields and the analytic controversies

At its best, the current analytic field has taken in new knowledge from many other disciplines, and seen itself through their varied lenses. As with our images and accounts of childhood, new views of "the unconscious," trauma, gender and sexuality, socialization, and power dynamics in cultures, families, and psychotherapies have emerged—often in contact with the core concerns that energized Freud's original psychoanalytic project. All of this is exemplified in developmental psychoanalysis's position at the crossroads of the broader analytic field—conceptual, clinical, and even epistemological.

Chapter 9

Continuities from infancy to adulthood

The baby is out of the bathwater[1]

Important methodological issues arise in building models of the infant's mind and theories about how early experience leads to later personality: We are confident that what happens in infancy has substantial effect in determining adult experience, but how? Since so much is different between the first few years and later life, what is it that accounts for the continuity? What is it that "stays the same," what has been transformed, and what is novel, as people move through the life cycle? How does the fundamentally dyadic life situation of the baby find its way into the more individual, "internal" patterns and "structures" of later life? Our responses to these questions have basic implications for clinical practice, since they shape our thinking about the relationship between the patient's history and current situation, and often of the repetitive dimensions of the transference–countertransference. They fundamentally affect what we do and say, almost continuously.

Classically, psychoanalysis has relied on various theories about the development of psychic structure to respond to these questions, with theories of identification and other forms of internalization (see Freud, 1923, and other drive-oriented Ego Psychologists), the development of "thinking" through parental "containment" of infantile projective identification (Bion, 1962, and his followers), and the emergence of innate potentials in the supportive social environment (Erikson, 1950/1963; Hartmann's, 1956, "primary ego apparatuses"; Winnicott, 1960a). Relational psychoanalysis has been less explicit about its developmental models, importing the ambivalence toward them of its Interpersonalist ancestors while nonetheless giving substantial weight to models about developmental fixation and early relational traumas. Infant development research has been welcomed and played a substantial role in the trajectory of the relational development.

DOI: 10.4324/9781003607328-12

Infant development research has proposed links between early development and adult personality and psychopathology. Although clinicians have long taken these for granted, these research approaches raise a number of methodological and clinical issues worth exploring. Analysts have relied on varied formulations of "psychic structure," but these are sometimes elusive and have not lent themselves to the precision, specificity, and validation that some analysts and many developmentalists prefer. New models have emerged over the last decades, including conceptions of internal working models of attachment, implicit relational knowing, and the like. Attachment research has shown strong correlations between infant attachment classification and adult personality. Current microanalytic research focusing on the very fine details of mother–infant interactions has extended the correlations between early relationship patterns, later childhood, adolescence, and adulthood. All of this supports clinicians' interest in attention to the details of analyst–patient interaction, emotion regulation, intersubjective meaning making, and other markers that can be observed in both infancy and adult analysis.

This chapter takes the current findings of Beatrice Beebe, Joseph Jaffe, and their colleagues (Beebe, 2004; Beebe et al., 2010; Beebe et al., 2012a, 2012b; Jaffe et al., 2001) as a point of departure to delve into these issues. In showing how details of mother–infant interactions at four months predict attachment classifications at twelve months, they have empirically confirmed what most infant observers, especially infant clinicians, have taken for granted: that very early interactive patterns are reflected in later patterns of relating and experiencing oneself and others. Although previous research found correlations between general descriptions of maternal sensitivity and attachment security, the current focus on the details of the moment-to-moment interactions adds further precision and dimension.

Further, that four-month mother–infant interaction patterns predict attachment classification strongly suggests that they predict a number of other significant markers. Attachment classification at twelve months predicts the infant's internal working model of attachment in adulthood (as measured on the Adult Attachment Interview [AAI]), as well as the twelve-month attachment classification of the infant's own infant with her, once she becomes a parent (Main, 2000). Thus, we find powerful support for the widespread and popular conviction (held, of course, by many clinicians) that mother–infant interaction at four months predicts the infant's ability to be a responsive and sensitive parent as well as that baby's style of organizing attachment security when she or he becomes an adult. These are remarkable correlations, with few parallels in the developmental psychological literature: There are very few adult psychological characteristics with intergenerational transmissions *of any sort* that can be predicted so strongly, especially from social-emotional factors. In addition, twelve-month disorganized attachment classification has been shown to predict certain differences in adult brain anatomy related to emotion regulation, to predict borderline psychopathology, and to be correlated with infant relational trauma (Gabbard et al., 2008).

Since all these predictions are so closely tethered, subsequent researchers will be able to proceed with broader scope and clinicians to work with more confidence in principles on which they have already relied. Moments such as these are generally quite satisfying for clinicians; infant clinicians have been especially fortunate in having benefitted from (and, indeed, generated) many such findings in the last decades. Overall, we now have substantial empirical support for the view that early parental care has a very substantial influence on subsequent personality organization.

Moving from the developmental-clinical to the developmental-theoretical

I have so far featured relationships between factors that can be observed and at times altered to predict and, also, used to enhance developmental outcome. This effect has been taken as a hypothesis by researchers but relied on by clinicians. The current research, then, moves us from *the developmental-clinical level* to the level of *developmental theory*, working toward a more global model of early development and its longer-term effects that integrates several levels of observation and analysis, from the microanalytic to the psychostructural. Inasmuch as previous research has already shown that more macro-phenomena such as maternal sensitivity in general and attachment classification are both very significant and inter-related, the addition of prediction from microanalytic data now expands the empirical support for the already well-established dynamic, nonlinear complex systems view that integrates different dimensions of development and personality. New data from neurodevelopmental research, including about brain anatomy and physiology and even molecular genetics, are beginning to provide similar support.

In this context, Beebe and her colleagues' work exemplifies the current moment in infant development research. In the breakthrough decades of the 1970s and 1980s, the core strands of attachment theory and microanalytic infant–parent interaction research developed at some distance from one another, albeit with an implicit sense of harmony and a widespread conviction that their obvious synergies might be empirically delineated eventually. Beebe, Jaffe, and their colleagues' work marks a watershed in that project, as they have brought their longstanding microanalytic project in direct predictive correlation with the attachment classifications. As affective and cognitive neuroscience and psychoanalysis—both clinical and theoretical—have also developed along similar lines, there are now multidimensional consiliences between these various fields. In addition to Jaffe, Beebe and their colleagues, Stern (2010), Emde (1988a, 1988b), Schore (1994), Tronick (1998), Fonagy and his colleagues (Fonagy et al., 2002), among others, deserve special mention. In addition, Sander's (2002) and Trevarthen's (2009) path-breaking conceptualizations have now been confirmed as the highly prescient integrations that they seemed to be when they first appeared more than forty years ago, with resonances to Erikson's (1950/1963) seminal, if currently neglected, model. (See also Seligman & Shanok, 1995.)

In general, then, we can now think even more clearly and with empirical support about how infancy affects how adults feel and interact with others and themselves. Our models describe and account for how psychological development is a complex system with continuity and consistency over time and over different situations. Much of this can be translated into clinical work. This is what psychodynamic clinicians have always done, and we can now go forward with some greater clarity and force. For example, there is now extensive empirical support for the imaginative psychoanalytic postulates about understanding the elaboration of past and present in the transference–countertransference field, where the patient is displaying her typical ways of seeking security in the affectively charged therapeutic relationship. To put it another way, working clinicians now have a sense of greater empirical legitimacy behind the clinical imagination,[2] one that both finds and creates workable coherences across a wide range of observations and speculations, whether about someone's expectations of intimate partners, her ongoing sense of personal security, her relationship with her own parents, her interest in offering a communicative account of herself, her way of regulating emotions, the details of how she responds to her baby, characteristic facial expressions, what may well be going on in certain regions of her brain, and so on. In a sense, these become part of an expanded array of observational frames, by which the therapist gets to know the patient, bringing them together to make helpful understandings and models of what is going on. There are many ways that these orientations can work, including generating diagnostic frameworks, orienting behavior, organizing and stabilizing the therapist's own internal experience, and in shaping interventions, among many others.

Mediating concepts

Translating developmental research for clinical value works on different levels. One involves more or less direct transposition of its measures and descriptors to the psychotherapeutic arena. For example, an adult therapist might become more sensitive to her patients' expectations about contingency: Does the patient check often for a response that fits? Is she especially ready to detach in the face of a slightly misplaced emotional gesture? I return to this shortly, but first I want to discuss another dimension: how we think about the links between different conceptual levels and between processes occurring in different time frames. Here I am referring simultaneously to the time frames of each psychotherapy, ranging from the second-to-second and minute-to-minute flow of each hour to the processes that occur across sessions over days, weeks, months, and even years, as well as the decades and eras involved in a development of the individual life.

Beebe and her colleagues are remarkable observers of dyadic interactions occurring in very short time frames, sometimes as brief as tenths of a second. The attachment researchers, psychoanalysts, and other psychological researchers are working with much longer time spans—months, years, decades, and finally lifetimes, as I just said. How do we mediate between these different time frames? What links them? Whether explicit or not, these are core questions for conceptually oriented developmentalists (whether researchers, psychologists, psychiatrists, psychoanalysts, neuroscientists, etc.) and psychotherapists, who use multiple frameworks to understand and communicate with patients. Contemporary developmental psychoanalysts and psychopathologists have elaborated an array of mediating concepts and higher-level hypotheses that link up the different observational frames.

The overall approach looks something like this: The basic phenomena of interest are the mutual regulation and organization of emotion, behavior, and meaning in dyadic interactions, which are intertwined, if not simultaneous. This takes the bidirectionality of such processes into account, with infants and mothers influencing one another's behavior and state of mind almost continuously and at a very rapid pace. These lead to the development of more generalized dispositions, with various references to procedural representations of interpersonal relationships and senses of self, internal working models of attachment, the sense of personal felt security, attachment and attachment classification, and the like. Nonverbal forms of psychic organization are central, especially affect and affectively organized interpersonal expectancies. The enduring effects of trauma, especially early abuse and emotional neglect, are stressed. Increasingly, as I have suggested, these emerging patterns are understood as reflected at various levels of individuals' biopsychosocial organization, from brain to internal representations of self and other to behavior patterns through core patterns of relationship and character. All of this is set within the integrative frame of the nonlinear dyadic systems model.[3] Typically, the current developmental psychoanalysts follow an intersubjective direction, proposing that interpersonal recognition is a key for the development of an adequate sense of self and felt security. Beebe and her colleagues (Beebe et al., 2010, p. 7), for example, have proposed

> that the future D <disorganized> infant represents *not being sensed and known* by the mother, particularly in states of distress. We proposed that emerging internal working model of future D infants includes confusion about their mothers' response to their distress, setting a trajectory in development which may disturb the fundamental integration of the person.

This set of apparent abstractions translates into a picture of ordinary two-person interactions between humans that is experience-near for most people, especially for psychotherapists: People pay attention to those who are interested in, protect, and potentially threaten them; they hope and usually come to expect to be paid attention to in return; emotions and meanings are created in social interaction, which in turn supports the development of individual patterns of regulation, equilibrium, and patterns of experiencing and behaving with other people; the experience of negative emotions such as fear and other forms of distress usually amplifies the search for an attentive other person who can be protective; adequate caregiver responsiveness under such conditions supports individual feelings of coherence, effectiveness, interest, and security; poor responsiveness leads instead to more conflicted, relatively disorganized, and insecure experiences. Those who apply current developmental models to psychotherapy start from the view that such dynamics are also central in everyday psychotherapeutic process.

Along these lines, many adult therapists who are interested in infancy are intrigued by how the baby's world seems to embody the same directness and immediacy that they seek in their clinical practice; it captures the "this is just how it is"-ness of everyday relating. Alongside this, they see a very striking quality of the infant's experience, that it is often reasonably well organized in terms of nonverbal, sensorimotor, emotional patterns, often most distinctive in dyadic interaction, which are meaningful, coherent, recognizable, and communicable. Overall, these conceptualizations are the developmentalists' ways of filling in some of the details and nuances of the psychoanalytic models of the development of psychic structure as an account of personal continuity and coherence over time and space.[4] Since psychodynamic psychotherapists are eager to establish continuities between early development and later life, they will find such models especially appealing, as they call attention to these dimensions that can be observed in infancy and also in adulthood.

Overall, then, the emphasis on nonverbal, nonreflective organizations in these accounts has been of special interest to psychotherapists. Psychodynamic therapies depend on hypotheses about enduring patterns that structure the patient's approach to the world, so as to construct interventions to alter them. Therapists usually communicate with the patient about these, whether in words or other inventive pathways, like direct emotional contact or a focus on the body. Although all these therapies don't invoke developmental findings, it is nonetheless the case that most explanatory hypotheses rely on accounts of the continuity between experience early in life and later in development. Thus, developmental ideas about internal working models, implicit relational knowing, and the like offer very useful conceptual envelopes for the working therapist, providing underpinnings for some of the newer approaches and updating some of the established models, like the psychoanalytic ideas about phantasy and defenses.

Linking the microanalytic with these models: Implications for psychotherapy practice

With this background, some specific implications for clinical assessment and technique come into clearer relief. Current clinical applications of infancy research assert that direct observation and intervention with rapid interactive microprocesses similar to those described in this chapter can be very helpful in psychotherapies. (See, for example, Fosha, 2000; Knoblauch, 2005; Ogden et al., 2006; Seligman & Harrison, 2011; Tortora, 2005.) In one extraordinary case report, Beebe (2004) describes how she observed a patient's dramatic gaze aversion to understand how frightened she was of emotional contact, and subsequently provided video images of her face to her patient when the patient felt emotionally unable to tolerate in-person contact. This eventually led to the recovery and repair of memories of childhood traumatic separations. (This episode recalls Fraiberg's (1982) seminal work on gaze aversion as one of the precursors of defense in infancy.)

In introducing a more mundane example, Harrison and I (Seligman & Harrison, 2011, p. 245) have declared:

> Nonverbal communication of psychic states . . . in adult psychotherapy . . . is often overlooked. Patient and therapist are constantly communicating in facial expressions, physical gestures, vocal rhythms, and pauses and silences as well as even more subtle gestures such as the rustling of their clothes or a change of position. For example, a throat-clearing may communicate stress whereas leaning forward may communicate intensified interest: In a rather ordinary encounter, the therapist greeted her patient, a divorced middle-aged man, in the waiting room and walked with him into the office. The patient had not yet spoken, and his facial expression was unremarkable, but the therapist detected a change. "Something's up! Something good," she remarked. The patient's face relaxed into a grin. "I've met someone," he said. He told the story of his new romance, and the therapist wondered, but could not clarify, what alerted her to the presence of "something good." As the patient turned to say goodbye at the session's end, however, he made an almost-unnoticeable flourish with his head and shoulders. The therapist suddenly recognized that he had made the same gesture as he had stood aside for her to enter the office at the

beginning of the session. The affectively charged gesture, which she had not consciously noted before, had communicated his good news.

What is remarkable about such affectively charged gesture(s) is not only their evocative power, but the extent to which they are the basic stuff of the ongoing flux of everyday human contact. Usually, much of this goes on outside of explicit awareness: Brain responses to the observation of another's emotion displays may occur in time intervals much briefer than a second after the display is presented, too fast for the usual reflective processes to come into play. This is generally adaptive, since it allows for more complex, efficient communication and for urgent responses at times of distress or emerging danger. At other times, however, overly intense and/or contradictory social-affective inputs overwhelm the capacities of one or both members of the dyad. This may be especially likely in intimate, emotionally laden relationships like romances, domestic partnerships, parenting, and psychotherapy.

The comparisons between mother–infant interaction patterns leading to different attachment classification call clear attention to these differences. Even a few glances at the "split-screen" images evoke a powerful internal sense of the emotional impact of these brief dyadic exchanges.[5] That these frames reflect just a few seconds of interaction, at most, is a compelling demonstration of how the infant–parent matrix can induce the strongest emotions in those who take the time to observe it and offers an experiential window into understanding how such interactions can be so definitive in forming enduring structures of experience and behavior. Imagine watching one of the videos of the Disorganized (D) dyads in which a mother is frightening her baby when she or he is turning to her for comfort, or spending ninety minutes with such a mother and her baby, as many infant clinicians routinely do, or for that matter, watching them for three minutes in the supermarket aisle. Even more poignantly, imagine being the baby— lost, out-of-sync, frightened by the very person that you expect to protect you, who organizes your world more than anything else. (See Chapter 14.)

If we assume that these interaction patterns are characteristic of the observed dyads, then both our common intuition and clinical sense tell us that they will lead to habits of thinking and feeling that will be generalized elsewhere. We have long supposed that where nonrecognition and failure to comfort are typical, both infant and adult biobehavioral systems will be primed for disruption, distress, and danger elsewhere, and indeed this is what the research about disorganized attachment, trauma, and borderline psychopathology indicates. In this context, Beebe, Jaffe, and their colleagues' studies do two remarkable things at once: They provide empirical evidence that dyadic interaction patterns are influential in the formation of subsequent psychic structure, *and* they describe the details of such interactions. This is especially valuable in light of the extent to which the very short interaction processes are not immediately available to ordinary observation. Their written accounts may not adequately convey the power of the time-series analyses that their authors undertook: They studied very slowed down video of these interactions, sometimes to track gestures occurring at intervals as brief as one thirtieth of a single second. There is great power in watching these in a series of unfolding freeze frames, but when the movement and temporal dynamics are added, the effects are much more striking.

One direct effect of exposure to such material, in whatever form, is to sensitize the therapist to similar processes in the consulting room. Although we can't expect to keep up with their second-to-second flow, keeping the nonverbal, microanalytic dimension in mind draws the therapist's attention to meaningful gestures and moments that she or he might not otherwise realize were occurring. For example, I am now more likely to notice whether my patient looks at or away from me at the beginning of sessions, especially after a vacation or other similar disruption. I notice vocal rhythms, tones of voice, variations in skin tone, synchronies and asynchronies in movement, and so on. Sometimes this leads to an explicit comment on what I have observed; at other times, I privately try to make sense of what I have noticed and see whether those thoughts correlate with other observations or formulations. (Here, of course, I am making implicit use of an assumption that these micromoments are indicative of more general individual patterns of meaning-making, relating, defense, affect regulation, and the like. In practice, I regard these ideas as hypothetical even when I do talk about them; offering them, though, may lead to new information, including clarification of the emotional states that lay behind the gesture that I observed. In addition, the fact of the therapist making such observations may make the patient more aware of the therapist's commitment to understanding him.)

These observations are also helpful in thinking through my own emotional reactions to the patient, since they help me become aware of some of the specific pathways by which I have been influenced to feel whatever

I am feeling. In fact, I have come to make a kind of countertransference–transference intervention in which I try to tell the patient as specifically as possible about what she did that led to my talking about a particular idea or reacting in a particular way. (For example, I recently told a superficially curious patient that the way she drops her voice at the end of her questions gives me the feeling that she may mean something less cooperative than the apparent interest in hearing what I think.) This presents the usual danger of the therapist projecting his own projections back into the patient even when it seems more personal, but I have found that a reflective and judicious use of this approach can be quite helpful, including in some tight countertransference–transference binds. Patients have often heard bits of these kinds of accounts before, but creativity may be enhanced when they can be offered in the relatively nonpunitive atmosphere of the therapeutic relationship.

One of the strongest contributions for clinicians of microanalytic studies, then, is the exceptionally rich, detailed descriptions of dyadic interaction systems and their function and evolution; they delineate specific details of what is going on. For example, Beebe and her colleagues offer detailed accounts of head orientation, face-to-face interaction, gaze aversion, gaze/head orientation, stable versus unstable focus of attention on the mother's face (for the baby) or baby's face (for the mother). These can be well-observed in their well-illustrated *Mother–Infant Interaction Picture Book* (Beebe et al., 2017).

Here is their overview of "modalities of communication":

> We refine the study of the origins of attachment by examining separate modalities of communication: attention, affect, orientation and touch. Face-to-face communication generates multiple simultaneous emotional signals in numerous modalities . . . Redundancy and overlap facilitate selective attention, learning and memory . . . However, with disturbed communication, different modalities can convey discordant information, difficult to integrate into a coherent percept.
>
> (Beebe et al., 2010, p. 28)

Thus, rather than focus only on visual coordination between mother and baby, these authors analyzed several different communication modalities (worth mentioning again): attention, affect, touch, and spatial orientation. Further, they generated a set of "mother–infant 'modality pairings'" that are also worth repeating: "(1) infant gaze–mother gaze, (2) infant facial affect–mother facial affect, (3) infant vocal affect–mother facial affect, (4) infant engagement–mother engagement, (5) infant engagement–mother touch, (6) infant vocal affect–mother touch, (7) infant-initiated touch–mother touch, (8) infant head orientation–mother spatial orientation" (Beebe et al., 2010, pp. 33–34). Taken together, these evoke the experience-nearness of such microanalytic schemes, once some imaginative attention is paid to how it captures what occurs in ordinary conversation between adults as well as psychoanalytic interaction. All of this expands and refines the observational field, makes the research more robust on its face, and implicitly suggests a more elaborate and complete map of the nonverbal dimensions of therapist–patient interaction than might otherwise be offered.

Beebe and her colleagues' studies have much in common with other work that calls attention to how these processes are occurring over time. For example, Stern's (2004) microanalytic interview provides similar dimensionality from within the individual subjective experience of moment-to-moment perceptual flow. The temporal dimension of relating and meaning making has not been sufficiently explored, and yet is crucial to the development of the sense that the world is a predictable place where one's efforts can have an effect. (See Chapters 15 and 16; Stern, 2010.) Interpersonal interactions always take place over time, even when the time frames are very short: Descriptors that are already quite specific, such as "disruption and repair," "chase and dodge," and of course "contingency," become all the more vivid in light of this temporal orientation of such detailed accounts, which, after all, are presentations of lived experience in time.

These temporal process descriptors can be adapted for the working clinician's mindset much like those I mentioned earlier in the chapter. As do other colleagues influenced by infancy research, I often observe patterns of patient–therapist interaction that follow these interactive contours, as when, following an interpretation, I notice a sequence that seems like a chase-and-dodge (a description that sometimes seems more helpful and experience-near than the term *resistance*) or when the sense of a contingent call-and-response seems to suddenly give way to a choppy, incoherent set of monological gestures. In this second circumstance, I am drawn to recall, as precisely as possible, when the disruption began. While this might lead me to an effort to repair the break, it might well lead to an exploration of the discordant affect or meaning and/or even a non-reparative, further development of the non-contingent rhythm.

Therapists vary with regard to their tendencies in such situations. These differences seem partly to do with theoretical orientation: For example, interpretively oriented Freudians might be less likely to work to restore contingency than classical Kohutians. But other factors, like individual differences in character among therapists or even local variables like how the previous session had gone, are also quite significant.

One of the crucial findings of Jaffe, Beebe, and their colleagues' micro-analyses may shed some special light on this. At one time, they expected that the highest levels of contingency in the infant–mother interactions would be associated with secure attachment (Jaffe et al., 2001). Instead, they found much more complex patterns: High contingency is not in itself necessarily a desirable state of affairs in mother-infant interaction. In addition to being very important in itself, this finding suggests the possibility that there may be support for a number of different ways of negotiating the vicissitudes of the therapeutic relationship, such that various therapeutic approaches may lead to progressive change. Finding harmony is not necessarily the most important task for the therapist and patient; indeed, experiencing incoherence together might be a necessary step in exposing and resolving impediments to the patient's clarity and efficient use of her energy in following her own values. Such matters might be more situation-specific and dyad-specific than advocates of any single technical orientation may believe. Integrating infant research findings into psychotherapy practice need be less prescriptive than some might think.

Affect regulation in the caregiving interaction is currently emphasized throughout the infant developmental field. (See, for example, Schore, 1994; Tronick, 2007.) Moreover, the special place of the management of negative affect and heightened affect in the mother–infant relationship suggests parallels to psychotherapeutic processes, since therapists are typically most interested in the patient's intense, negative experiences, whether in the past or present. While some critics propose that psychodynamic therapists are overly interested in such painful feelings, it is often the case that these rightly command the greatest attention, since they can often not be circumvented by directions to shift attention elsewhere, as some of the more positivist therapeutic strategies suggest (e.g, Cognitive Behavioral Therapy). Following psychoanalysis, attachment theorists since Bowlby have seen both interpersonal and intrapersonal processes as oriented by attention to negative effects, especially fear-anxiety (see also Slade, 2014); they suggest that this is a bias of the human biopsychosocial system essential to species survival. With such an abundance of empirical, observational, and conceptual riches, Beebe and her colleagues do not overlook the extent to which affect is at the center of what is at issue in both the four-month mother–infant interactions and the attachment classifications themselves.

Overall, then, recent studies, including those of Beebe, Jaffe, and their colleagues, buttress the long-held intuition that effective, coherent coordination of individual and shared regulation of affect and attention in the social field in the care of very young infants provides for the most flexible and positive functioning in emotional relationships throughout the rest of the lifespan. There is an emerging synthesis of microanalytic infant–parent interaction research, current models of personality development and psychopathogenesis, and attachment theory and research presented in elegant and experience-near detail. They provide robust support for the complex creative application of developmental research to the theory and practice of psychodynamic psychotherapies.

Notes

1 This chapter was originally written as a commentary on research by Jaffe, Beebe, and their colleagues (2001) demonstrating that observations of patterns of contingency in microsecond interactions between infants and parents when the infant was four months of age could predict attachment classification at twelve months. This report links to other findings about continuities between very early caregiving and interaction patterns and later development, a few of which are considered suggestively in this chapter.
2 With regard to the special issues and controversies about the place of empirical scientific methods in relation to psychoanalysis, the short version of my own view is that the risks of dialogue with empiricism are worth taking when the analytic discourse method remains at the center of whatever syntheses may emerge.
3 As I have said, these are often drawn from different adjacent fields, including cognitive research, affect research, neuroscience, psychoanalysis and other psychotherapies, and trauma studies, as well as developmental research itself.
4 They also include a view of "the unconscious," but one that relies on broader and more complex conceptions of intrapersonal and interpersonal awareness than the traditional psychoanalytic emphasis on repression.
5 For example, two cameras simultaneously record the faces of a mother and baby interacting. The two videos are then streamed side by side.

Chapter 10

Theory IV

The move to the maternal: Gender, sexualities, and the Oedipus Complex in light of intersubjective developmental research

Since the Oedipal theory organizes many of the original psychoanalytic themes and controversies (see Chapters 1 and 2), we can now return to them in light of the contemporary perspectives. The relational approach dislocates the Oedipus Complex from the center of the analytic narrative.

The classical Freudian theories identify the Oedipal phase as the crucial phase for successful development. Its prominence is marked by the traditional delineation of development and psychopathology into "pre-Oedipal" and Oedipal: The absence of adequate Oedipal resolution is a fundamental developmental weakness, correlated with limited ego development, pathology organized around deficits rather than conflicts, and indications for technical compromises involving "support" rather than interpretation. Contemporary models, including many ego psychological models, have softened this distinction. But the Oedipal/pre-Oedipal dichotomy remains in common use, especially by contemporary Freudians. In addition, the Oedipal narrative has traditionally had a normative, proscriptive function: A particular form of Oedipal resolution—the heterosexual identification with the same-sex parent—has been treated as the desired outcome, with other outcomes regarded as pathological. (This is shifting some.)

Relational psychoanalysis, along with Self Psychological and Interpersonalist psychoanalysis, is less reliant on these formulations. This correlates with the assertion of the fundamental place of the relational motives and the marginalization of the irrational drives. Since the drive-oriented theories conceptualize the basic motives as asocial, if not anti-social, they require some set of developmental constructs like the Oedipus Complex to integrate the uncivilized, natural motivations into the social world. Hence, the Oedipus Complex is the moment in which the dual organizers of psychosocial life, gender and restraining authority, become part of the

DOI: 10.4324/9781003607328-13

personality. Maturity is fundamentally a matter of mastering the conflicts between the irrational, intrinsic, natural forces and the ordering requirements of social life.

The relational developmental models do not have the same need to rely on the Oedipal triangle to integrate the drives into the social world. The earliest and most basic motivations and states do not necessarily come into conflict with the social world as the child moves more fully into it. There is no special theoretical requirement for a transformational moment like the Oedipus Complex. Development is more continuous, organized around relationships, mostly in families, institutions, economies, and cultures, which usually (though not always) change gradually, rather than in the more definitively demarcated psychosexual stages of the Freudian models (even when their recognition of the ordinary blurring of those stages is taken into account).

The dislocation of the Oedipus Complex, the rejection of instinct theory and "the primitive infant": Implications for the analytic relationship and therapeutic action

Putting this another way, we might say that the emphasis on the centrality of cooperative social activity from infancy forward means that paternal authority is no longer the essential principle for social order, in that order no longer inheres in restraining the unruly drives. (See Chapters 1, 2, and 3.) Dislocating instinct theory and Oedipal hegemony thus opens psychoanalytic clinical theory to the fullest affirmation of a developmental approach to analytic change process. We can start at the beginning of life and go from there. From a social-power perspective, we might say that once the hierarchical bifurcation of paternal authority and maternal care dissipates, we are not obligated to see paternal authority, in its restrictive and oracular forms, as the marker of civilization and necessary order holding together what would otherwise lead the personality or the society to fall apart or descend into destructiveness.

There are implications here for how psychoanalytic therapeutic action and the analytic relationship are conceived. The traditional analytic method calls on the analyst to frustrate the patient's instinctual gratification so that she is driven to put forward her most inner fantasies, such that the analyst can then tell her what is most true about her. But if difficulties in reaching out toward others, rather than properly managing drives, are at the source of psychopathology, then there is no particular reason to assume that "analytic abstinence" will intensify the analytic experience or lead the analyst to more accurate understanding of the patient's isolated mind, as was expected according to the instinct-theory driven notion that instinctual energy drives emotional life. The analyst thus does not have to conform to the caricature of an oracular authority that follows a modified version of the paternal authority at the core of the Oedipal resolution, but rather can facilitate growth in the multiplicity of ways that parents, especially mothers, do. Instead, it is direct relationship that is most crucial to secure, vital, connected,[1] and effective living.

Decentering the Oedipus Complex and the constructivist conception of authority

The de-emphasis on the Oedipus Complex, then, correlates with the relational reconceptualization of the analyst's authority. The classical analytic conception of the analyst as the observer of emerging psychic facts, bearing the burden and discipline necessary for "objectivity," is rooted in and supported by the Oedipal narrative, which is thus simultaneously moral and developmental: Oedipal authority is paternal, oracular, and suppressive. Such authority exists by virtue of its moral necessity and its capacity to see the truth clearly. It is an inevitable necessity for individual and social order, whose absence or distortion manifests in social and/or psychological pathology. Freud (1913, 1930) was explicit about this in his social-theoretical works, like *Totem and Taboo* and *Civilization and Its Discontents*.

In the relational conceptualization, the analyst's authority is itself an emergent, contingent aspect of the analytic relationship, which is created and sustained in various configurations as part of the ongoing mutual influence process of the analytic relationship, and as such, is under ongoing "negotiation," both conscious and unconscious. The analyst's authority is not a given, but is derived from the transaction between analyst and patient. The analyst may indeed have substantial expertise, but the patient's interest and attribution of helpfulness and other meanings to this expertise may enhance its significance; alternatively, more negative attitudes about the analyst's competence, empathy, or good intentions may diminish the effect of the analyst's authority.[2] The decentering of the Oedipus Complex in the developmental narrative thus correlates with the constructivist-dialectical view of the analyst's authority and the mutual influence model drawn both from infancy research and the new "two-person" model of the analytic dyad.

Relationality, maternal authority, and the dynamics of attachment and recognition

The relational re-orientation thus implies that the analyst's power and authority are as much like the mother's as the father's. However, the broadest forms of developmental models do not rely on an alternative and perhaps equally caricatured image of the analyst as nurturant mother, simply providing care as never before, but instead, of the analyst as collaborator in discovering whatever potentials for growth may be available to the patient, in an effort rooted in what they are actually doing, which is something together (even when they are quite at odds or, perhaps worse, isolated from one another). There is an array of relationship characteristics that contribute to progressive growth and lively development, with manifestations and effects at multiple levels, from the brain, to the family, to the nation, and so on: care, attention, provision, recognition, protection, insight, emotional and physical responsiveness, mutual understanding, self- and other-knowledge, wisdom, and more.[3]

In the dyadic, transactional conception of early development, the mother's being a mother is itself dependent on the infant, at the most fundamental level, and within the intertwined dyad, is inseparable from the infant's influence. Again, this parallels the relational conception of the analyst's authority as co-created, further reflected in the concern that authoritarian analytic practice can itself be retraumatizing. Here, the links to feminism become more obvious, as contemporary developmental imagery affirms what has often been devalued as belonging to the marginalized feminine.

Integrating maternal subjectivity into developmental theory

Another effect of the mutual influence of feminism, infant observation research, and the relational approach to development is the recognition of the mother's subjectivity and individuality. Although the British object relations theorists recognized the essential place of the maternal function, they did not pay much attention to the specific psychology of the mother herself: Winnicott's (1956) extraordinary account of "primary maternal preoccupation" is an exception of sorts, since it investigates that phase of maternal psychology characterized by immersion into the maternal role. But even there, Winnicott did not take up the specific personality of each mother. Kohut (1977), Mahler (1972), and the developmental Ego Psychologists (Edgcumbe & Burgner, 1972; Hartmann, 1956) followed the same pattern, configuring the mother from the point of view of the child's developmental needs.

Feminist revisions of the analytic developmental accounts have more fully asserted the independent character of the mother. Chodorow's (1978) pathbreaking account of the intergenerational transmission of the mothering role provided a lucid description of the internal gratifications and compromises that were organized in the feminine identification with the maternal. Motherhood was no longer taken for granted, but was itself a developmental process with its own interiority. Many other contemporary accounts have taken the mother's subjectivity as an essential, rather than peripheral, part of the child development process. J. Benjamin (1988, 2004), drawing on Hegel (1977), has characterized dynamics of submission and dominance involved in the two-person negotiation of the infant's establishing his own subjectivity in relation to his dependence on the mother, and applied this to her interest in "doer/done-to" dynamics in psychoanalysis. Clinical infant observers, such as Fraiberg (Fraiberg et al., 1975) in her seminal "Ghosts in the Nursery" paper, developed complex accounts of how specific events in the parents' pasts led to quite specific parenting styles. Although this was most apparent when the parents' own histories were traumatic, the general principle of the intergenerational transmission of parenting style is now well established.

Polyphonic narratives of gender development and morality: Feminist and queer critiques of Oedipally oriented analysis and developmental models

This shift also synergizes with the feminist-postmodernist assertion of multiple narratives of gender and sexual orientation. Freud asserted that pre-Oedipal children were "polymorphously perverse," excited by the variety of sexual object choices. This was an opening toward a more tolerant view than the typical phallocentrism of Freud's era. But in its typical, if narrow, reading, the Oedipal theory affirmed the normative suppression of the variety of human sexual and affectionate possibilities, in service of a single, heterosexual object choice. Relationship-oriented theories are more sympathetic to alternate conceptions of gender and erotic patternings that construct gender and sexuality. Rather than treating sexuality as a primary, irreducible factor, relational motivational-developmental theory treats it as embedded in the interplay of a variety of affective and relational issues, such as security, excitement, pleasure and pain, delight and disgust. The move from the fixed psychosexual stage model with instincts being the primary motivators, to the greater role given to the social world in shaping development also provides for more room for a varied array of pathways for morality, gender, and sexual preference, as well as for the variety of developmental environments and relationships in families, cultures, and other situations.

In the late twentieth century and beyond, the broader social movements on behalf of women and gays have been instrumental in provoking shifts toward a more relationship-oriented, democratic, less sexist and homophobic orientation in psychoanalysis. This has proceeded almost simultaneously with the increasing presence of women and, more recently, lesbian and gay analysts in the field and its institutional hierarchies. The longstanding paternalistic hegemonies in analytic institutions have declined during these same decades. Increasingly, a more open and textured approach to sex and gender has found its way into psychoanalytic discourse, influenced by feminism, queer theory and other critical theories.[4] Here, the relational-developmental perspective also synergizes with the postmodern critique of psychoanalysis as a discourse that has been used to impose cultural discipline. (See, of course, Foucault, 1978, among many others.)

The Relational body

The Freudian theories (especially in Freud's original form) bring in the body through the instincts, as the pathway by which the physical begins to move into the mental world. This turns attention away from the lived experience of the body, as something known through the senses, in motion, in emotions, in general feelings of wellbeing and malaise, as well as in the ways that one is regarded by others. Relational-intersubjective theorizing features these direct experiences, as a core component of its approach to the relationship between the body and mental life.

The body is thus regarded as organized through relationships, rather than as autonomous and presocial. (See, for example, Aron & Anderson,

1998.) The body and the sense of self-with-others are fundamentally intertwined, evolving in each family and taking on the various constraints and opportunities offered in particular social situations and historical moments. This includes the idea that gender and sexuality are constructed in the transactions between individuals and culture, broadly and variably construed.

Notes

1 In the classical theory, the Sphinx and the seer Tiresias in the Sophocles play are prototypes of the analyst. When their vision is overturned or disregarded, violence and disorder ensue.
2 Sullivan (1953) suggested this insight when he took pains to justify the analyst's authority as a matter of his "expertise," rather than taking it for granted.
3 Here, then, the intersubjectivist-relational approach provides the clinical-metapsychological basis for the Middle Group's emphasis on combinations of contact and creativity at the core of what leads to change. My own reading of Winnicott has been much enriched by this approach.
4 A complete list of contributors would be very long, but notable voices in the Relational psychoanalytic movement include J. Benjamin (1988), Corbett (2009), Dimen and Goldner (1999), Elise (1997), Harris (1991), Mitchell (1975), and more recently, Guralnik and Simeon (2010), Hartman (2011) Rozmarin (2012), and Saketopoulou (2014), among many others. Other North American and Continental European analysts have also been influential.

Part III

Attachment and recognition in clinical process

Reflection, regulation, and emotional security

Attachment, reflectiveness, and "thinking" in therapeutic action

These next five chapters provide an orientation to the core theories of intersubjectivity and attachment and their basic interrelations, and then proceed to explore the links between mutual recognition processes, attachment security, the capacity for reflection, and vital intersubjective interchange, in both normal development and psychopathology. Overall, they integrate a more fully intersubjectivist perspective with the British object relations theories of Klein and the Middle Group, along with attachment theory and research.

The first two chapters offer "executive summaries" of intersubjectivity and attachment theory and research. I consider both as fundamental, intertwined motivation systems that organize personality and social interaction from the beginning of life onward. In reviewing intersubjectivity, I emphasize the inextricability of individuals with their partners in social relationships in both development and clinical process. I then review the historical evolution of attachment theory and research, from Bowlby's original proposal that proximity to responsive caregivers is a basic source of personal and interpersonal security, through Ainsworth's organized categories of secure and insecure attachment, to the current development of the Adult Attachment Interview and the Disorganized category. Core clinical applications are considered, to be elaborated in the subsequent chapters.

The third chapter integrates these conceptualizations with several of the broad themes that were introduced in the previous sections: object relations theories, attachment and mentalization, coordination and dyscoordination in parent–infant and therapist–patient interaction,

DOI: 10.4324/9781003607328-14

trauma theory, and others. I draw parallels between Bion's special use of the term *thinking* and the attachment theory emphasis on reflectiveness and the subsequent "mentalization" theory (Fonagy et al., 2002). Substantial empirical research is supporting the idea that deficits in reflective capacity and emotion regulation in infancy and childhood lead to serious difficulties in adulthood, especially following abuse and neglect. Thus, the broad analytic consensus that self-awareness is of great value finds renewed support in the developmental approach. From this platform, I continue the clinical application featured in Chapter 7.

I present a developmental perspective on psychotherapeutic change without a simple analogy between analytic work and re-parenting. To some extent, the interplay of self-reflection and the development of a more robust sense of intersubjectivity is featured, as I try to further clarify the mentalization concept. Overall, I show how a variety of therapeutic processes can be captured in a broad and inclusive developmental approach that reflects the intricate and often stressful ebbs and flows of ordinary analytic practice.

The last of this sequence of chapters, on projective identification and the intergenerational transmission of early trauma, applies this effort to the abusive interaction between a three-day-old boy and his father, who was himself physically abused as a young child. Rather than facilitating a reciprocal interaction in which the baby can feel protected and that he is having an effect on those around him, the father is imposing his own warded-off sense of being brutally controlled and punished onto his son. Since this kind of repetition follows the lines of the original Kleinian projective identification concept, I also work to show how psychic processes that have been largely discussed as fantasies can often actually be observed in detail and in real time, both in infancy and in adult interactions, including in psychotherapies. This serves another of my broad purposes, to reread the Kleinian ideas from an intersubjective perspective. Here, the themes of Chapter 13 are revisited in an even more painful situation.

Chapter 11

Intersubjectivity today

The orientation and the concept

Recent advances in developmental psychology, cognitive neuroscience, and parenting studies: The current context

Around the turn of the twenty-first century, developmental psychoanalysts and neuroscientists argued that there is an "intersubjective motivation system," as basic as the attachment or sexual motivations (Emde, 1988a; Stern, 2004; Tomasello, 1999; Trevarthen, 1993, 2000; among others): There are structures at every biopsychosocial level that prepare and organize human life in relationships with other people who recognize, respond, and communicate together—cells, brains, bodies, dyads, families, cultures. Emerging findings and concepts from apparently divergent fields began to move toward intersubjectivity theory, including approaching their empirical data from psychological, philosophical, and psychoanalytical perspectives. These include cognitive neuroscience, affect studies, developmental research, attachment theory, and ethology, as well as much of psychoanalysis. Many Independent Group writers anticipated this turn (see Laing, 1971, for one example), and Intersubjective Self Psychologists have also made central contributions (e.g., Stolorow et al., 1987).

A special section of *Psychoanalytic Dialogues* captured this moment. It included articles by Colwyn Trevarthen, one of the foremost of the original infant development researchers, Vittorio Gallese, one of the Italian research group that discovered mirror neurons, and Massimo Ammaniti and Cristina Trentini, leading child development researchers in Rome. All of these authors were European, elite, internationally known empirical researchers. But empirically methodologically sound as their work is, their intellectual and cultural disposition includes a basic affinity for both constructivist and intersubjectivist views. They want to know what the findings mean: Research

DOI: 10.4324/9781003607328-15

is a means to an end rather than an end in itself. In my introduction to these papers, I tried to summarize and amplify the implications of their different papers in that section. It offers a statement of some of the key dimensions of the intersubjective perspective, and thus, of my own basic orientation.

Colwyn Trevarthen: The intersubjective psychobiology of human meaning

Colwyn Trevarthen, an ethological psychologist at the University of Edinburgh, has distinguished himself for over four decades as one of the most inventive and rigorous explorers of infant development and its impli- cations. In the infant research world, he ranks with Bowlby, Brazelton, Emde, Sander, and Stern in breaking through misleading assumptions that had been held in their disciplines, to show what babies and parents really do. Trevarthen's (2009) paper begins almost as a ramble on human nature, leaving us wondering if we are going to get some homespun wisdom rather than the usual disciplinary paper. But it soon becomes clear that Trevarthen is instead taking the late-career liberty of saying what he thinks is most important, in the plainest language: that "our shared world . . . does depend on an intrinsically motivated *sympathy in action*, the 'feeling of company,' and upon creative pretense" (Trevarthen, 2009, p. 509, italics in original).

Trevarthen then goes beyond this basic postulate to present the radical idea that the bases of sociability, and hence human culture, lie in motor activity and musicality, by which he means not merely the usual blend of melody, harmony, and rhythm but the more basic patterning of shared, coor- dinated movements and sensations of all sorts, articulated over time and the interpersonal space. Just as Kerman (1994, p. 54) declared that "relational structure in music is created by sound in time," Trevarthen finds the essence of self-development in what emerges from moving and feeling with others over time, in embodied intersubjectivity (Merleau-Ponty, 1945/2002).

Mirror neurons and the foundations of intersubjectivity

Vittorio Gallese, of the University of Parma, is one of the original cog- nitive neuroscientific researchers into the phenomena of mirror neurons (Iacoboni, 2008; Rizzolatti et al., 1996). These are well described by Gallese (2009, p. 520): "Mirror neurons are premotor neurons that fire *both when an action is executed and when it is observed being performed by someone else"* (italics added). These remarkable findings have intrigued the intersubjectivist developmentalist community, including analysts, demonstrating that the registration of other people's experience is "wired" into brain structure, much like vision, hearing, or movement itself.

A neuroanatomical basis for empathy and identification thus appears in view, especially when mirror neurons are taken along with the already substantial attention to imitation, affective resonance, and the co-regulation of behavior and inner states. Further, the emerging model of mirror neuron functioning corresponds to a second feature of the intersubjective core of experience: As others are encountered, they are simultaneously taken as similar and different from oneself. For Gallese, as for the phenomenologists, these are inextricable: The encounter with the world *is* an encounter with the intersubjective.

In a similar resonance with the phenomenologists, Gallese stresses that personality and relatedness are rooted in the experience of one's own and others' bodies in time and space; he describes the fundamental basis of identification in the "embodied simulation" of the observed person's motions, affects, pain, and so on. Intersubjectivity is constituted at the very beginnings of perception and proprioception. Here the parallels to Trevarthen are clear: The basic elements of becoming oneself by being with others are, in the first place, movement, time, and space, all coordinated in social interaction. Subsequent developments, including language, theories of other minds, and the like, while significant, are not the primary core of personal and social meaning. Personality arises in our disposition to collaborate.

Echoes of Winnicott's (1958a, 1960b) radical emphasis on the dyadic, bodily origins of psychic life resound here, as such concepts as "psyche-soma," "going on being," and "the spontaneous gesture" can be clarified and elaborated when read along with this imaginative but nonetheless empirically rigorous research. In addition, the contemporary interest in the nonverbal, implicit, interactive dimensions of psychotherapy and psychoanalysis is well supported. (See, for example, Beebe et al., 2005; Damasio, 1999; Fosha, 2000; Knoblauch, 2000; Ogden et al., 2006; Stern, 2004; among many others.)

Parenting: Neuroscience, attachment, psychoanalys is

Massimo Ammaniti and Cristina Trentini (2009) work at the University of Rome. Ammaniti, a psychoanalyst and international leader in child psychiatry, has incorporated new developments in analysis and developmental research into an array of clinical and theoretical arenas, as he, Trentini, and other colleagues have carried out their own research. Their paper provides an encyclopedic review of research on parenting from the different fields that have studied it—affect research, attachment theory, mirror neuron research, neuroscience, parenting research, psychoanalysis— to show that parenting is a coherent system that draws on an array of inter-articulated subsystems at the levels of the brain, the emotions, cognition, dyadic interaction, attachment, and family life. They offer a panoramic view of the place of care, empathy, attachment, and recognition in this most basic form of human interrelatedness. The paper is a model multidisciplinary literature review that transcends the genre, creating a collage of hundreds of research studies to substantiate their strongest implications: The apparently disparate levels of the human biopsychosocial systems are best understood as part of integrated systems that support the species and the most tender, but complex and robust aspects of what makes us human. For Ammaniti and Trentini, that the intersubjective paradigm organizes such broad arrays of data substantiates the postulate of the fundamental intersubjective motivation system.

Analysts are often skeptical of empirical data, and "hard science" has often been taken as disconfirming psychoanalytic ideas. But the tide may be turning. The broad integrations presented in these papers correlate well with the relational-developmental psychoanalytic assertion of the central role of social relations in organizing psychic reality. Buttressed by fMRIs (functional magnetic resonance imaging), statistics, and publications in leading research journals, as well as conceptual and clinical analytic experience, they are fundamental, creative, generative, and holding up well over time. The notion that "life is with people" (Zborowski & Herzog, 1952) can no longer be taken as a mere sentiment or cultural style. It is a basic biopsychosocial fact.

Chapter 12

Attachment theory and research in context

Clinical implications

Attachment theory and research defined and reviewed

Although they are often used to connote the whole of the infancy research shift toward the primacy of relationships, the terms "attachment" and "attachment theory" more specifically refer to a particular body of theory and research that began with John Bowlby's (1969, 1980, 1988) seminal work of the first post-World War II decades. Drawing on primate research and direct observation of young children, he asserted that the child's tie to its parents or other caregivers is a primary, autonomous system, rather than secondary to the drives and phantasies that traditional Freudians had held to be the core motivations. He defined the primary attachment system as observable at approximately one year, including distress on separation, relief on reunion, and exploration from the attachment figure as a secure base (Bowlby, 1969, 1988). Bowlby went on to reformulate the analytic theories of separation and defense in accord with emerging regulatory systems models, stressing the importance of affects, especially fear (Bowlby, 1973, 1980). He also proposed that parental care is a core requirement for species reproduction, embedding social motivation in a broader evolutionary biological perspective. (See also Slavin & Kriegman, 1992.)

Subsequently, Mary Ainsworth (1978) developed the "strange situation," in which infants were briefly separated from their mothers and then reunited. (See www.youtube.com/watch?v=QTsewNrHUHU.) Ainsworth validated three specific attachment classifications: *secure* (B), *insecure/ avoidant* (A), and *insecure/resistant-ambivalent* (C). Securely attached infants show distress on separation, pleasure on reunion, and a quick return to exploration. Avoidant babies do not cry on separation, and avoid the parent on reunion, without showing anger. Resistant-ambivalent babies

DOI: 10.4324/9781003607328-16

are preoccupied with their parent, sometimes seeming angry; they don't settle down on reunion, and usually resume their focus on the parent, often crying. Ainsworth also demonstrated that attachment was a cross-cultural phenomenon. Her work led to a worldwide network of academic researchers constituting a formidable subfield of developmental psychology.

In the last decades, this group has shepherded "the move to the level of representation," the third phase of attachment theory. Following Bowlby's proposal, they described the "internal working models" of each attachment classification as stable representational structures that regulate the sense of personal security around proximity to familiar people. In a major breakthrough, Main and her colleagues (Main et al., 1985) developed the Adult Attachment Interview (AAI), a semi-structured interview, which classifies adults into groups correlated with the infant categories: *secure/autonomous*, *dismissing*, and *preoccupied*. Here, the sense of personal security is strongly correlated with the ability to *coherently reflect* on one's own memories and experience, rather than the actual historical events. This finding is particularly encouraging for psychoanalytic therapists, whose methods support this capacity, and links to the broad intersubjective emphasis on recognition processes. (See Chapter 13).

This is not to say that actual experience does not matter. Both retrospective and prospective studies correlating infant and adult attachment classifications provide support for the proposition that early interpersonal experience has enduring effects. Attachment researchers have reliably predicted the sense of security in adulthood, measured on the AAI, from attachment classification in the second year of life (Main, 2000; Main et al., 2005). In addition, AAI classifications of pre-partum mothers predict their toddlers' attachment classification. Taken together, these findings demonstrate the intergenerational transmission of personal security through parent–infant caregiving (van IJzendoorn, 1995). (See Chapter 9 for a more extensive discussion of such continuities.)

In addition, the current group of attachment researchers has validated a fourth classification, *disorganized/disoriented*, applied to infants, children, and adults with attachment organizations primarily characterized by mixtures of incoherence, fear, controlling behaviors, and the like. Disorganized attachment is strongly associated with both early relationship trauma and adult borderline psychopathology (Fonagy & Bateman, 2008; Main & Solomon, 1990). Findings from research in other areas—the study of long-term effects of early neglect, trauma, and maltreatment on the brain, and functional magnetic resonance imaging (fMRI) demonstrating patterns of brain dysfunction in adult disorders (see Hollander & Berlin, 2008, for a review)—suggest a convergence of attachment research and research in the neurosciences (Perry et al., 1995; Schore, 2003a; Van Der Kolk & Fisler, 1994).

Clinical applications of attachment theory

Both the attachment categories and the findings of the AAI are currently applied suggestively to child and adult psychotherapy. (See, for example, Lieberman et al., 2005; Schore, 2003b; Wallin, 2007.) Slade (2008) suggests that therapists can use knowledge of attachment categories to help understand how different patients construct their attachment to the therapist, usually in a suggestive rather than definitive way, and advises considering the countertransference in a similar light. Goldner (2014) has recently integrated the relational interest in countertransference in applying attachment theory to couples therapy. (See also Greenberg & Johnson, 1988.) Along with a broad application, Wallin (2007) suggests that therapists' awareness of their own attachment style will increase their understanding of their own emotional reactions and enhance therapeutic responsiveness.

For example, while a traditional psychoanalyst might focus on aggression in a patient's guarded and restrained presentation after a vacation, one following attachment theory might concentrate on the avoidant patient's tendency to detach to minimize the loss. Similarly, a patient who talked incessantly and mournfully about the same one-week vacation might be understood as protecting her sense of security through a preoccupied, ambivalently attached pattern. A securely attached person, on the other hand, might protest more directly (if at all), expressing anxiety, sadness, or anger about the interruption, and then proceeding. Often, such observations correspond with patients' reports of their relationships to their own parents and also to current attachment figures such as spouses and children.

Attachment, mentalization, and the link between security and vigorous subjectivity

Current attachment theory suggests that security in the presence of another—that is, secure attachment—is part of the same psychic process as the ability to understand the distinction between one's own mind and the external world (Fonagy & Target, 1996; Main, 1995). This is a dramatic innovation with rich and varied implications for the psychoanalytic views of psychopathology, clinical technique, and therapeutic action: It corresponds in focus remarkably closely to the everyday conduct of analysis, relying as it does on moment-to-moment efforts to understand the analysand's mind in an appropriately secure environment. In contrast, many other theories of therapeutic action require a kind of awkward translation from metapsychology to what analysts actually do. Inasmuch as current attachment researchers have now provided extensive empirical verification of their perspective, a quite encouraging and stimulating convergence of developmental research and basic psychoanalytic values is now available.

Many of these innovations rest on the AAI finding that it is the extent to which we can reflect coherently on our experiences that determines the level of security and organization in our psychic lives, more even than the experiences themselves. This discovery, in turn, links to a sophisticated and creative elaboration of the original attachment theory: The core emphasis on felt security in the presence of a reliable object is augmented by an account of the crucial developmental process by which a child comes to see beyond the immediate reality of her particular experience, grasping the distinction between that immediate experience and the mental state that underpins it. This process involves a number of essential capacities, including the ability to distinguish between one's own mind and the minds of others; to appreciate the distinction between intentions and effects; and to imagine that one's own experience of an external "reality" may be one among many. (See Bowlby, 1988). Fonagy and Target (Fonagy et al., 2002) have developed this extensively in their discussion of "mentalization." (See also Jurist et al., 2008.)

Overall, these are the underpinnings of an awareness of the distinction between one's own subjectivity and other people's. In thus acquiring "metacognition," the child comes to know that she has a mind of her own, in a world of her own that includes other people. This perspective overlaps with the established analytic developmental schemes that link the development of a subjective self to the simultaneous emergence of autonomy and relatedness, but it emphasizes recognition processes more than many of them. Chapter 13 is an elaboration of this, including convergences with other analytic theories, including Bion's (1962) concepts of "thinking" and "containment," and Winnicott's (1965a) ideas about "holding" and "transitional objects" (Seligman, 2000).

Reflective attention, relationship security, and therapeutic action

Thus, emerging attachment research, together with increasingly complex views of the therapeutic action of psychoanalysis, supports the current move toward a complex, multimodal model of the psychoanalytic situation, within which personal transformation is reached by a variety of pathways. Analysts, like parents, provide secure spaces for reflective and meaningful dialogues in which psychic structures can be elaborated and altered. But although communicative understanding is central to such development, it cannot be isolated from the emotionally laden interpersonal contexts within which it is achieved, just as analytic insight cannot be isolated from the analytic relationship.

This model departs from the ones that imply, at least in their more caricatured forms, that insight is the *sine qua non* of analytic change. But it differs from some other developmental models as well, in that it does not treat the analyst's efforts to understand as secondary to the reparative effects of analytic interactions. Understanding and interaction in psychoanalytic treatment are not opposed, but are part of a unified process. The established opposition between developmental and insight-based models of therapeutic action is thus rejected in favor of a more complex model stressing mutual regulation, recognition, and security in relationships.

Indeed, in both child development and psychoanalysis, the benign effort to communicate with and comprehend another person may be more important that the precise "accuracy" of the understanding itself. As I say elsewhere, understanding is not exactly *about* experience. It *is itself* an experience, and this experience involves the crucial presence of another person with whom one feels secure, in part by virtue of feeling understood by that person. Our sense of being safe with another person is synergistic with that person's efforts to understand us.

The everyday conduct of analysis is animated by analysts' elemental and uniquely intimate knowledge of the transformative potentials of this synergy. In confirming this from its own perspective, contemporary attachment research converges with psychoanalysis at a most crucial point.

Chapter 13

Recognition and reflection in infancy and psychotherapy

Convergences of attachment theory and psychoanalysis

This chapter develops the dialogue between object relations theories and current research about babies, especially attachment theory. Recognition and reflection have always been core values in everyday clinical work, but this central agreement has been obscured by the differences between the different analytic persuasions. Still, being understood and kept in mind by another person is seen as a crucial aspect of both child development and psychoanalyses. Reflective relationships have a number of essential progressive effects, including enhancing the senses of personal and interpersonal coherence and security, personal agency, the capacity to understand that other people have other minds, and that there is a separate "reality" in the world that has its own, more or less stable qualities; that is, "objectivity" (in other words, using Freud's terms, the acquisition of "the reality principle"). Self-reflection and recognition by others defines the space between separateness and relatedness.

Recognition and thinking are both content and process, at the vital intersection between the individual and the social surround. When these dynamics break down, internal and external space collapse, and there is an absence of vitality, agency, empathy, and the like. (See Chapters 15 and 16.) Within this framework, perspectives from different analytic persuasions can be brought into more contact: Bion's special conception of "thinking," for example, can be viewed as an implicit, self-reflective form of psychic organization, with commonalities with the attachment theory-based interest in psychological coherence and "mentalization," Winnicott's developmental model, especially concerning the transitional phase, and findings from the direct observation of infant–parent interaction.

From this perspective, the therapeutic action of developmentally oriented psychoanalytic psychotherapies reaches beyond the idea that this

DOI: 10.4324/9781003607328-17

approach is simply a matter of providing care that was not previously offered: Like parents, therapists help their patients grow in multiple ways. This is an application of a robust developmental perspective, both because of the parallels (complex as they are) with child–parent relationships as intricate and multifaceted systems and, more generally, because the therapeutic relationship is seen as a vehicle for forward-moving growth.

Bion: "Thinking" as an integrative developmental process

Bion, the most influential Kleinian after Mrs. Klein herself, proposed an extensive and profound psychoanalysis of attention and thinking. Bion's (1962) oft-noted, special use of the term "thinking" remains seminal and central today. For him, as for Freud (1911), *thinking* is a sophisticated developmental achievement, rooted in the capacity to tolerate frustration and live through adaptive mental process, rather than through action, pure phantasy, bodily states and somaticizations, raw emotions, and the like. For Bion, relationships are essential in transformations, both in child development and the analytic process. He advanced Klein's model by giving a more prominent account of how the mother tolerates and thus modifies the infant's most threatening projections, so as to enable the baby to reintroject them in a less primitive and thus more manageable way. Under such positive conditions, the infant reintrojects the modified bits of his primitive world so as to "think" for himself. Bion calls this transformation, "normal projective identification," and it is the prototype for the core developmental dynamic in Bionian theory: "container–contained."

Bion thus elaborated the ways by which the baby could find a way out of the originary instinctual binds of the paranoid-schizoid position. In contemporary terms, he highlights a kind of intersubjective-interpersonal dimension of developmental process that leads increasing coherence in development, along with increasing differentiation between the mother and the infant. Overall, his "theory of thinking" added a bold new dimension to the Kleinian account of the movement into the depressive position, in which she or he accepts the constraints of reality, including some frustration and separateness from the mother. Klein and her colleagues (Klein, 1940, 1946, 1975; Segal, 1957) had already linked the emergence into the world of relatedness with such integrations as mourning, the movement from part to whole objects, and the ability to use symbols and enter into vital intersubjective and verbal interchange. (Klein's, 1975, extraordinary essay, "Envy and Gratitude," remains one of the most eloquent and moving considerations of this transformation.) The analyst's containing and reprocessing the patient's projective identifications is the cornerstone of therapeutic action in contemporary Kleinian psychoanalysis. As Bion's work progressed, he (1967) presented an aesthetic of analysis as open, spacious and reaching toward the ineffable, illuminating deep, transformative potentials of attentive communication, including his description of the analyst's listening through reverie, and without memory or desire.

Pathological projective identification

In contrast to this "normal projective identification," Bion described forms of pathological projective identification in which the caregiver fails to transform the baby's destructive impulses, but instead re-presents them in their original dangerous, hateful, and disintegrative form. This leaves the child without any option but to try to get rid of these intolerable feelings; however, the re-projection onto the parent leads nowhere but to further intensification of the anxious, fragmented, incoherent state. A self-perpetuating, repetitive trap ensues, leading to potentially malignant and unstable psychological organizations, in which internal and external reality are confused, the inner senses of self and object are fragmented, and there is little or no sense of being separate yet related to someone who can pay attention to you (Rosenfeld, 1971; Steiner, 1987; see also Chapter 14). In Kleinian terms, the baby cannot "think," but instead is left stranded in the paranoid–schizoid position. This description, of course, captures something that is very familiar in an array of clinical situations, especially in certain kinds of transference–countertransference impasses, as well as in situations like those of Daniel and his father in Chapter 14.

Bion's model and the "observed infant": Limitations of the "normal projective identification" concept

Bion moved the original Kleinian model of infancy in an intersubjective direction by adding a place for the central role of relationships in the origin of reflective thought. However, despite its elaboration of an adaptive process, the concept of "normal" projective identification retains the original Kleinian allegiance to theory of the primitive, oral destructive drive, with the infant inevitably having to expel "bad" parts. I am persuaded by the infant observers' view that babies are prepared for a variety of affective responses and predisposed to initiate, respond to, and generally collaborate with caregiving, so as to create a basic sense of security. Babies come to experience biopsychosocial organization and agency without having to be extricated from innately potentiated catastrophic anxiety states. This perspective is also at the center of Winnicott's account of the extraordinary harmonies between the "good enough" mother and her baby.

Recognition, intersubjectivity, and reflective thinking in current attachment theory

Within the infancy research area, attachment theory has played a special role. Although it emerged from within psychoanalysis, it has developed at some distance from it. Attachment theory was traditionally viewed as at odds with the traditional analytic approaches: Bowlby's (1969) original models were sharply criticized by both Kleinian and Freudian analysts as inattentive to the internal world. Most attachment research has been based in the nonanalytic developmental psychology university centers.

Happily, this gap has narrowed. There has been an emerging consensus that the analytic establishment's original critiques of Bowlby were overzealous, at the same time that new developments in attachment theory are converging with the longstanding analytic interest in psychic organization and the reality sense, especially as related to infant development research. Although the new infancy research and attachment theory correspond closely, the former emphasizes the specific details and meanings of early interactions, while the latter stresses the general feeling of security and wellbeing that comes from reliable proximity to an attentive and protective caregiver. The infant interaction research depicts the development of a differentiated, related, intersubjective being in a field of objects, whether actual or internal.

The Adult Attachment Interview, metacognition, and mentalization

The current findings in attachment research contribute broadly to our thinking about the importance of recognition and being understood in both development and psychopathology. They also link to intersubjectivist insights about analytic theories of the self, the ego, and the therapeutic action of psychotherapy and psychoanalysis. Emerging findings correlate early infant–parent relationships, attachment classification, adult personality, and brain development. Links between emotion regulation, attachment, and personal security in infancy and adulthood have been clarified. (See, among others, Jurist et al., 2008; Main, 2000; and Seligman, 2012b.)

Drawing on philosophy, linguistics, and other developmental-psychological research, the contemporary attachment researchers have thus added a new emphasis in their developmental narrative: a crucial process in development where the child sees beyond the immediate reality of her particular experience and differentiates between that immediate experience and the mental state which underpins it. This "theory of other minds" involves a number of specific distinctions: between one's own mind and those of others; between intentions and effects; and the ability to imagine that one's own experience of an external "reality" may be one among many; that is, that one's thoughts are not the same as the objective world. The child is coming to know that she has a mind of her own, in a world of her own *with* other people, with other minds seeing the same world as she, but from a different perspective. Main (2000) has described such "metacognition"; Fonagy and his colleagues (1995) discuss "reflective functioning" and most extensively and influentially, "mentalization." Research using the Adult Attachment Interview (AAI) uses this exceptionally sophisticated research instrument (based on linguistically oriented, validated, reliable analyses) to demonstrate that the capacity for coherent reflection on our experiences determines the sense of security and organization, *to an even greater extent than the actual memories themselves.* Coherence and reflectiveness organize, and can even "override," troubling experiences, yielding a sense of personal and interpersonal security.

A key implication here is that the all-important senses of "objective reality," with others who nonetheless share that reality, are constituted in relationships, rather than being discovered, and that when such developments are impaired, basic psychopathology will likely ensue. There are correlations between developmental trauma, deficits in early affect regulation and recognition processes, and adult borderline personality disorder. These are, in turn, all correlated with disorganized attachment (Hesse & Main, 2000; Jurist et al., 2008; Main & Solomon, 1990; see also Chapters 9 and 12). Many of the precursors of dissociation can be seen in infants classified disorganized, including gaze aversion, freezing, and acute detachment from caregivers (Fraiberg, 1982; Jaffe et al., 2001; Beebe et al., 2010; see also Chapter 14).

The link between being understood and the sense of coherence and security in personality organization is thus explicated. Thinking reflectively and making meanings that make sense are a crucial aspect of feeling secure, and deficits in these developments will lead to difficulties in living. Put in Freud's (1911, 1914a) language: Attachment theory has moved from a theory of the anaclitic to engage two of the other central psychic domains: the narcissistic and the "reality principle."

As I have said, the current generation of attachment theorists organizes their field's history in three phases: Bowlby's original attachment model, which focused on proximity to the attachment figure; Ainsworth's subsequent empirical validation, leading to the secure/insecure categories; and the current phase, called the "move to the level of representation," which extends Bowlby's "internal working models of attachment" from something like companionship, to link to representation, recognition processes, self-organization, and intersubjective relatedness. In addition, the new "disorganized" category links the field to dysfunctional parenting, trauma, and other forms of psychopathology in a way which had not been possible before.[1]

Attachment theory and infant interaction research

This also moves attachment theory into greater harmony with other major currents in infant development research. These have emphasized the active, mutual influence of parents and infants in early dyadic interactions; these dynamics have not been featured in attachment theory, although they are of course implied there. Stern's (1985) conceptualization of affect attunement, for example, describes the infant developing her own subjective self as she has the experience of being known in the mind of the parent, whose recognition is *simultaneously a representation and transformation* of the infant's experience. (There are echoes of Bion here, but in a more fully developmentally and relationship-oriented model.) Contrary to the common impression that attunement is a virtual reproduction of the experience of the one to whom the "attuner" is "attuning," Stern is careful to stress that the moment of attunement rests on the simultaneity of sameness and difference between the two minds of the infant and parent. His emphasis on attunements occurring across sensory modalities, as when the running toddler falls suddenly (a motor event) and the mother says, "Oops!"

(a vocal-auditory event), demonstrates how the linked vitality and coherence of the two-person field depends on communication between different minds "marking" their difference while getting in touch. (See also Fonagy et al., 2002.) The rising and falling volume of the "ooOPs!" has a similar contour to the pace of the baby's running and sudden fall, but in a different register, paralleling the similarity and difference between the baby's and mother's subjective positions.

Something crucial has been added to attachment theory: It is not just the child's proximity to the caregiver, but also the caregiver's understanding of both the child's specific experiences and also seeing her as separate but connected. Overall, the description of attachment is rendered more complex and located not just in attachment per se, but also in the dialectics and dynamics of recognition and intersubjectivity. (See, among many, Benjamin, 1995; Hegel, 1977; Lyons-Ruth, 2006; Ogden, 1986, 1992; and Sander, 2002.) Stern's approach illuminates the dialectic-dialogical roots of intersubjectivity, reading infant–parent interactions along the lines of such dialectics as being understood *by someone else*, the vitality of communication as it depends on living with the otherness of another, speaking for yourself in languages that have been established collectively over historical time, the longing for completeness that can only be fulfilled by other people especially in romantic and erotic love, and more (cf. Lacan, 1949).

Relationships to other analytic theories

Many established analytic developmental schemes feature the child's mourning of the early dependence on the responsive mother, including internalization of that object relation to support a transformation toward a more self-sufficient internal world. These include Freud's (1923) account of identification as an adaptation to frustration, Klein's (1940) views of the emergence into the depressive position, and lucidly, Mahler's (Mahler et al., 1975) "separation/individuation" theory, and beyond. The more fully intersubjective, bidirectional perspective both extends and synergizes with this approach. In some sense, the attachment-mentalization perspective adds a new capacity to the catalog of ego capacities, encompassing attachment security, affect regulation, and the development of an (inter) subjective self in the coherence of being understood. Here, the emergence of secondary process and the development of object relations are linked with infancy research.

Winnicott's (1958b) developmental model is built around the creative possibilities and risks that arise in this most basic matrix. Winnicott's vivid and immediate picture of the infant's absolute dependence on the mother is fundamentally relational, as it includes an acute sense of its bodily roots. (It is simultaneously and inextricably physiological and psychological.) An account of the infant's progress from the "subjective object" phase toward "object usage" follows the evolution of the emergence of intersubjectivity in and from the mother–infant matrix. In the first phase ("the subjective object"), the baby's subjectivity is at first immersed in the maternal *environment*, then configured in the intermediate transitional space, an area where the separateness of the object, whether a person or otherwise, is subsumed to the paradox of the "not-me possession." Winnicott saw the prototypes of such processes in how a child's play creates (with persons, in toys, and in other transitional objects) a medium in which to express inner states in an external arena that is nonetheless of the self. This establishes a psychic-relational field where the subject/object distinction is enlivening, but not noticed. Finally, in the phase of "object usage," a fuller individuation is added to these. All of these forms of intersubjectivity remain essential throughout the life cycle.

Although less definitively than Winnicott, Bion also moves the original Kleinian model of infancy in an intersubjective direction by adding a place for the central role of relationships in the origin of reflective thought. Contemporary Kleinians, like Britton (1992, 1999) and Caper (1997), have extended this to emphasize the recognition that others have minds of their own and that facts differ from subjective beliefs. As I have said, my own view is that Bion's model is strengthened when freed from the "death instinct" and the image of the primitive infant. By seeing themselves as seen in the minds of others, children come to feel affective vitality, inner coherence and value, and that it is possible to be one's own self as one is understood by and connected to others. Contemporary Bionian field theorists, such as Civitarese and Ferro (2012), have taken Bion's work in this direction.

Contemporary analysts who have drawn on Hegelian phenomenological and hermeneutic philosophy along with intersubjective infancy research, have advanced related ideas (e.g., J. Benjamin, 1988; Ogden, 1994a, 1994b; Stolorow et al., 2002; and Trevarthen, 2009; among others). Much of this resonates with such classic analytic writers as Sullivan, (1953), Kohut, (1977), and, in a different way, Lacan, (1949); Laing, (1961) and Laplanche, (1999).

A number of crucial papers of Freud's (1911, 1917a, for example) and others in his early circle, such as Ferenczi (1949b), can be approached in a vital, contemporary manner from this vantage point (as Bion did). This overall approach comprises a Hegelian-phenomenological-dialectical reading of psychoanalysis: Transformation through relationships (animate and inanimate) is at the center of Hegel's (1977) philosophy of mind (Kojève, 1969). Overall, these convergences suggest possibilities for synthesis between the apparently divergent "one-person" and "two-person" models.

Clinical implications: Reflection, metacognition, coherence, and the objectivity of reality in psychopathology and the analytic relationship

Analysis as an arrangement for careful reflection

Developmental and clinical thinking converge here: It is not only what the parent understands about the child that is most important, but the effort to understand, in itself. Similarly, it is not exactly what the analyst understands, but that the analysand feels known. The analyst's particular theoretical persuasion may not be as important as its adherents think; rather, it is her way of conducting herself. Process often matters more than content. (Relational analysts and Bionian field theorists, like Civitarese and Ferro, 2012, elaborate similar views.)

Psychoanalyses are social arrangements between two people, with roles and rules that enhance and protect reflectiveness and empathy. The analyst generally maintains a commitment to paying thoughtful attention on the analysand's behalf, which will be shared, more or less, with the patient, depending on an array of feelings and behaviors. The analyst's commitment to paying attention is a set point to maintain a particular dyadic relationship form, dedicated to reflection (at least, at first, on the analyst's side). As it proceeds, this relationship format potentiates various transformative relationship dynamics (Chapter 17; Seligman, 2014a).

The attachment researchers' emphasis on reflective process supports psychoanalytic therapists' confidence in what we do: Solid empirical research showing that how people think about themselves is central to mental health. This is indeed what analysts do: Our "product" is thinking things through. This orientation crosses the various analytic persuasions, supporting the hope that people change when they can think about themselves in the context of a secure relationship. Fewer mediating concepts are required here than with most conventional accounts of therapeutic change. This approach can be explicitly explained to patients, especially in initial consultations.

Monitoring thinking: Mentalization in psychopathology and psychotherapy

Attention to analysands' patterns of thinking, reality, and subjectivity can improve everyday clinical practice, both in assessing personality organization and the moment-to-moment fluxes of mentalization in the hours. As many have noted, a prominent feature of posttraumatic states is that reflection is precluded by overwhelming painful emotions, mind-breaking incoherences, and/or prohibitions against knowing what is going on that were part of the original traumatic situation. These forms of thinking shape the ongoing residua of the trauma, and thus often must be taken up before the content can be considered. Difficulties in affect regulation and in distinguishing the internal and external worlds are mutually reinforcing. In this sense, the oft-noted analytic split-mindedness involves empathy for the analysand's (and analyst's) non-self-reflective states of mind, while also remaining embedded in other "realities." (See, for example, Modell, 1990; Schafer, 1983.) Both analytic and nonanalytic therapies have been conceptualized this way, especially for posttraumatic and borderline conditions, including dialectical behavioral therapy (Linehan et al., 1999), mentalization-based (Fonagy and Bateman, 2008) and transference-focused therapies (Clarkin et al., 2006). Fonagy & Bateman (2008, p. 160) have summarized: "All moderately effective current therapies for BPD are able to present a view of the internal world of the patient that is stable, coherent, can be clearly perceived, and they may be adopted as the reflective part of the self (the self-image of the patient's mind)."

Difficulties in thinking in borderline, narcissistic, and posttraumatic states

From different perspectives, the attachment researchers and contemporary analysts note how more disorganized and posttraumatic patients take their subjective experience as the only "reality"; for them, the mental state of the moment is the only one. Under such psychic conditions, trusting oneself or anyone else is difficult because there isn't a sense of things persisting beyond the moment, and there is no reliable sense that psychic reality is only that, which makes bad feelings especially problematic. In this regard, Fonagy and his colleagues (2002) have made a useful observation about splitting and projection. Under the "meta-assumption" that fantasies and feelings are as real as other people, painful experiences cannot be conceived as something just in the mind; they are in fact hyperreal and cannot be contained as subjective experience. These distinctions are irrelevant at such moments.

Thus, as has been noted, they have to be relocated outward. This, in turn, reinforces the paranoid states, with a persistent sense of the external world as dangerous, but also as depended upon to take on the projections, with the aforementioned splitting and projection necessary to preserve psychic equilibrium in the face of overwhelming affects and phantasies. (This is a strong interpretation of the rich Kleinian interpretation of the "paranoid-schizoid" position.) Such projections may well further reinforce paranoid states, as the external world appears to be highly dangerous. At the same time, as he is left with his dependent feelings, the patient may experience himself as especially vulnerable to the power of the analyst, whose help he needs so badly. The patient also needs the relationship with the analyst to provide an object for the projected psychic dangers. A vicious cycle may ensue, in which the attachment intensifies the sense of fear and danger, which intensifies the dependent feelings, and so on. Involvement with a therapist may be increasingly dangerous as contact and closeness increases. In addition, anxieties about the exposure of underlying states of disintegration or loss of reality are also mobilized. With patients who have been traumatized, especially those with disorganized attachments, there is already a predisposition to link attachment and insoluble fear (Hesse & Main, 2000).

"Narcissistic resistances" and the breakdown of metacognition/mentalization

Patients are thus more likely to be frightened, and to react with anger, when they are deficient in self-reflective functioning. At least intermittently, they cannot imagine any alternative explanation of their subjective (if actually reified) realities. Further, any suggestion that there might be alternative perspectives may seem like abandonment, disrupting the implicit assumption that everyone sees the world in the same way. It might also feel like an accusation that the patient is unable to grasp reality. The malignancy of this projection is amplified by the projective paranoid–dependent dynamic just described. Even "accurate" interpretations can lead to fearful self-protectively aggressive reactions. The "resistance" is often to the otherness of the analyst's mind rather than the content of the interpretation. I am here elaborating clinical suggestions made in the last chapter, in further case examples.

Premature interpretation in the absence of metacognition

In such situations, the danger of considering alternative views of "reality" must be taken up first. Premature interpretations can amplify the patient's sense of danger, deprivation, despair, and rage when they overestimate the extent to which reflection is possible. Risks include malignant regressions, disruptions, or compensatory solutions, including pseudo-compliance and "false self" identifications with analysis, such as precocious use of pseudo-psychological language. The self-protective and fearful sources of such enraged or withdrawing responses should be considered: Life without metacognition is risky. Shifts into and out of metacognition should be observed, with interpretation most likely to work when the patient begins to shift from concretization to mentalization. Even when interpretation is precluded, such understanding can help with countertransference feelings of being stranded with helplessness, frustration, and guilt.

In some such circumstances, the implicit challenge (however subtle) of an interpretation may also be taken as an accusation that the patient is "crazy," or at least has defective judgment about what is real. In this way, as in others, the emerging sense of threat both amplifies and is amplified by internal, persecutory objects, and a vicious cycle can ensue. Projective identifications and other maneuvers often externalize the persecutory phantasies, which may in turn be further amplified by the responsive, if potentially destructive, actions of the analyst. Sometimes, a persistent sense of grievance will be reinforced.

Case illustration: Jacob

Jacob, a 47-year-old, was a partner in a business consulting firm. Despite his professional success, Jacob typically felt mistreated at work, complaining about colleagues, clients, and others who "did not give him his due."

He came to therapy as he had been asked to withdraw from an account with which he had been associated for some time. When I tried to inquire about whether he could use some help restraining the anger, which was apparently leading to such difficulties, Jacob felt misunderstood and blamed: He would become irritated, if not enraged, about my efforts to attend to whatever role his psychology might play in his disappointments. "It's not about me," he would declare. "I was mistreated! That's what happened." Here, he could not think about his own behavior along with his hurt feelings. Only one of these "realities" could exist at any given moment; the others had to be projected with force and certainty.

This pattern asserted itself with vigor in relation to my not replying to Jacob's texts while on vacation. Even as he understood the professional limitations involved here, Jacob insisted that I was being irresponsible and self-centered. He could not tolerate that our relationship might have limitations and that I had requirements of my own, and his feeling that I was negligent and considered him unworthy could not be considered as anything other than actual. Angrily denouncing my interpretations of these feelings of deprivation and rage, Jacob accused me of using the analytic role to protect myself. He could not conceive that my attention to his agonies might be a reflection of at least some helpful analytic interest, reflecting his difficulties with self-reflective functioning. Jacob was compelled by an aggrieved, projective worldview—necessary, he believed, for his feelings to be taken seriously. (With similar psychic circularity, the mother of a fifteen-month-old, whose toddler had become anxious in response to her overly rigorous toileting requirements said, "There can't be any problem here, since my mother did this for me.")

Eventually, as I communicated my growing understanding that he was taking transference interpretations as challenges to his fragile sense of authority of his own thinking, Jacob could briefly consider more complex sources of his suffering that included his own psychology *along with* the actions of others. Over an extended period, these interpretations led him to recall how his parents' very antagonistic divorce when he was five left him profoundly ignored. His mother left the family to pursue a relationship with a wealthy man, eventually marrying and starting another family, moving to another city and rarely seeing him. He could now consider, if only briefly, that some of his anger and dismissal of me "had something to do" with those past experiences. This reflected the beginnings of a gradual emergence of a capacity to differentiate his own emotions and fantasies from the actions and attitudes of the people around him.

Transference as a failure of metacognition

An emphasis on the patient's capacity for reflectiveness can clarify an ambiguity about the concept of transference. While the classical conception of transference treats it as a matter of regression, projection, and distortion, many contemporary analysts regard transference as plausible, both because the analysand notices (indeed, may be hyperalert to) the actual analyst. In addition, the analyst may be pressured to act so as to reproduce the very relational patterns that also constitute the transference. Transference is sometimes characterized as selective (in)attention, as part of an interactional matrix which must be considered along with the intrapsychic dimension.

This challenge to the traditional conception of transference has left a gap in clinical theorizing. Many clarifications have, of course, been offered. These clarifications may be enhanced and nuanced by conceptualizing transference reactions of various sorts as *impairments of metacognition.* In its pure forms, the transference state does not afford the usual mental procedures for correcting "misperceptions." In the grip of the transference, patients take their subjective experience as if it were "real," no matter what information they may have about the "actual" analyst. In the transference neurosis, the theory of other minds no longer applies; the analyst is thus engaged with an unusual state of mind in which reflective functioning has been eclipsed by other mental trends. Greenson's (1967) list of the prominent markers of transference—inappropriateness, intensity, capriciousness, tenacity, and ambivalence—captures this state of psychic affairs from another perspective. It is not that the patient doesn't know the other facts about the analyst; it's just that he can't think about it.

All this echoes the Kleinian emphasis on the ubiquity of "primitive" states, the absence of reflective thinking, and projective identification in the transference, in the paranoid-schizoid position, in all patients (e.g., Joseph, 1985). By thinking of the absence of "objectivity" as an aspect of a psychic state, we can better conceptualize this aspect of transference as a metacognitive variant from its other conditions: distortion, projection, desire, developmental possibility, and so on. *Transference* is here a state of mind that lacks coherence, both internally and with the "actual" situation. This is not a basically cognitive matter: Powerful affects, fantasies, and internal representations can usefully be conceptualized in terms of coherence/incoherence without sacrificing their vividness and inherent intrapsychic and interpersonal pressure.

An analysand responded to the analyst's inquiring about his doubts about the analysis by insisting that the analyst wanted to "keep him here" because of his own financial need. Although the fee was already reduced and the analysand knew that the analyst was busy, this belief prevailed. As the hour proceeded, he oscillated between suspicious anger and briefly considering that his suspicions were based on his own feelings, rather than the analyst's actual motivations.

Personality organization and misrecognition in "higher functioning" cases

In "higher functioning" personalities, failures of recognition and mentalization also come into play. Self-reflective functioning may be inconsistent, varying across emotional and interpersonal situations. At times, an apparent composure and adaptive ways of living obscure more traumatic and dissociative psychological structures. "Ordinary" life tasks go along well enough, but certain situations evoke strong affects, especially anxiety, that preclude thinking about meanings other than the one that first floods the mind.

A neurotic patient presented a persecutory view of his boss: He would say, "The boss is out to get me," although just a moment before, he had presented extensive evidence that this view was not plausible. He was oscillating from believing that his subjective reality was absolutely true, to thinking in other terms. At times, he was able to notice the discrepancy between his fearful views and the information that he had presented, but not at others. In other words, his metacognitive capacity was intermittent.

Case illustration: Jennifer

Here is another example. Jennifer, a woman in her thirties, was a high school teacher and a concerned and thoughtful mother. However, within the sessions, she would be suspicious and provocative, and would spend long periods of time detached, if not silent. She presented a dissociated state in which she felt simultaneously detached and flooded by thoughts about which she did not feel able to speak, however much she wished to.

In the course of a long analysis, it became increasingly clear that Jennifer felt both terrified and disorganized by the analyst's interest, which she also badly wanted. She could describe how this might have evoked child-hood traumata of the witnessing of two terrible crimes of violence and early difficulties with a sexually intrusive neighbor, but these memories seemed to be quite detached and dissociated from her current experiences in therapy and in her marriage, which was similarly markedly ambivalent. On two occasions, she interrupted the analysis for avowedly practical reasons. When she returned after an absence of several months, she could acknowledge that there were powerful emotional currents that had driven her. But she then left again in a similar way, only to return again, finally settling into a more reflective position.

This evolution illustrates the emergence of mentalization. At first, Jennifer's own psychic reality was hardly affected by information other than her own intense emotional reactions. Later, she could begin to differentiate between her automatic projections and alternate realities, realizing that her internal world and external actualities were not equivalent.

Extreme failures of metacognition: When people are like things

Although they are apparent in neurotic situations, such difficulties are often more prominent in borderline and other characterological organizations, especially following traumatic abuse and/or neglect. Without the transaction between attentive people who care about each other's minds and bodies, there can hardly be a sense of the difference between people and things. This is chilling to watch in early infant–parent interactions, as is well-known to infant mental health specialists and infant observers, who have seen it lead to a variety of acutely dissociated and otherwise disorganized states, including deadness and utterly detached flatness, as well as addiction and sociopathy. (See, for example, Chapter 15.)

The Public Defender asked me to interview a convicted murderer, a 26-year-old man who had brutally killed a former employer, so as to provide a psychological appeal to the jury in the death penalty phase of his trial. He was not psychotic and was only marginally under the influence of drugs at the time of the murders. What was most apparent in interviews with key people from the first twenty years of his life, including his parents, was that nobody had the feeling that emotions, psychic reality, or subjectivity overall had any special meaning. This helped clarify how this man could kill: He lacked a grasp of what distinguishes people from other objects. (See Chapter 15.)

Therapeutic action and the aesthetics of psychoanalysis

What is provided here, then, is a basic psychoanalytic aesthetic of active absorption in the patient's psyche, spanning the theoretical persuasions. Analysts provide steady availability of our minds (and hearts), often with great effort and amidst substantial pressure. From the classical perspectives, this engagement potentiates the emergence of the analysand's unconscious. The interactionist-relationalist innovation features other forms of participation, affirming interaction and the analyst's personal contribution to countertransference. Still, a basic framework spans the perspectives. The dynamic transaction between reflection and strong affects, between awareness and nonawareness, between the analyst's thoughtfulness and the pressures that arise in the analytic relationship, is crucial to constituting its unique transformative potentials (Chapter 17; Seligman, 2014a).

Emphasizing reflection does not imply that insight is the only form of analytic change, nor does it relegate the analyst's understanding as secondary to interactions. Understanding and interaction are not opposed, but part of a single process. The emphasis on the analyst's reflectiveness supports a complex, multimodal model of analysis' mutative action. In addition to the direct effects of recognition processes, personal change can occur through a variety of pathways, under the special conditions of the reflectively oriented relationship system: insight, disconfirmation of expectations, new developmental opportunities, and empathic responsiveness, among others. There is an analogy between infant and child development and analytic therapeutic action, but one that does not rest solely on the idea that the therapist is simply providing care that was not previously offered. Like parents, therapists help their patients grow in innumerable ways.

Understanding is not only *about* experience, it is itself an experience, as I have said: Psychic security and organization are synergistic with recognition. In many respects, this corresponds to the direct experience of conducting analysis, just as of taking care of infants. The analyst might be likened to a mother with a distressed baby, who can do the wrong thing if she just ignores the distress, but can do many things to help. Similarly, there are many procedures and languages by which analysts facilitate change. The array of "right" things is constrained by many factors, especially contact with the patient's inner world. But within these constraints, it is not simply *what* is understood and recognized, but that someone reasonable is paying attention so as to understand. Again, as with parents and infants, all of this is intertwined with shared physical and emotional presence.

This is not to renovate the caricature of the "neutral" analyst. The analyst's understanding, whatever her model, is constituted in an actively constructed and evolving social relationship rather than a straightforward search for something pre-existing in the patient's mind: As many have noted, understanding an idea can change the very nature of the idea itself. Further, the emphasis on understanding does not discount the inevitability of analysts acting with patients, nor need it displace the emphasis on unconscious thinking. Observing the ongoing variations in the patient's metacognitive functioning synergizes with the emergence of previously unthought ideas—both those repressed or otherwise unthinkable in implicit or dissociative formats like somaticization and nonreflective enactment. Generally, analytic interactions may be differentiated between those potentiating and those diminishing reflection, as one of the central ways in which they promote growth.

Reflection, attachment, and therapeutic action

From the perspective of the dynamics of recognition and reflective thinking, psychoanalyses are dyadic social systems with specific procedures in place that support reflection and recognition: The analyst is afforded special opportunities for thinking, amidst many other feelings and behaviors. If we approach questions of clinical method from this point of view, some implicit commonalities between apparently divergent techniques may emerge. Different analytic schools emphasize, or at least are more explicit in describing one or another of these various dynamics, but varied accounts of therapeutic action converge with regard to the centrality of reflective thinking in the analytic dyad. The analyst's commitment to reflection creates a certain kind of relationship that enables mutative action along the multiple lines of which we are increasingly aware: Understanding is a kind of relationship, and indeed, understanding and being understood within relationships—thinking together with someone—is a relationship form with especially transformative potentials. As one senior classical analyst put it, when "two people get together to think about one of them, some-thing good is likely to happen" (Herbert Lehmann, personal communica-tion, 1997). In the moment-to-moment flux of everyday practice, even as they rely on the particular languages of the different persuasions, analysts pay careful attention to whether and how the analyst and analysand reflect on whatever is going on, how this may be communicated, and with what senses of safety or anxiety.

From a variety of perspectives, there is thus an affirmation for the direct activity of analytic work, the effort to understand someone, as *in itself* of the most basic and profound importance. This is an application of a fully developmental perspective, both because of the parallels (complex as they are) with child–parent relationships and more generally, because the therapeutic relationship is seen as a vehicle for forward-moving growth. Psychoanalysis offers a sophisticated conceptual language to talk about all the varied forms of consciousness and unconsciousness, connection and disconnection, attention and inattention, feeling and nonfeeling, noticing and not noticing (and more) that characterize how people put their worlds together in their minds and in their social worlds: Thinking along these lines, psychoanalysts are well justified in claiming to have a more sophis-ticated conceptual language in these areas than any other discipline.

Note

1 The "D" category was developed in the same group at the University of California, Berkeley, as the Adult Attachment Interview, under the leadership of Mary Main.

Chapter 14

Infant–parent interactions, phantasies, and an "internal two-person psychology"

Kleinian and intersubjective views of projective identification and the intergenerational transmission of trauma

In this chapter, I show how intersubjective infant research and modern Kleinian thinking can be brought together to yield a strong psychoanalytic model of psychic life oriented in a theory of internal two-person structures. I borrow from the observationally oriented infant researchers' emphasis on interaction processes to look at two different fathers interacting with their babies, Jamal Jr. and Daniel. Jamal Jr.'s father is generally responsive, while Daniel's manhandles him, at three days of age; in so doing, he is re-enacting his own father's treatment of him. I invite the reader to make the plausible assumption that these observed interactions would, if generalized, affect the development of their unfolding psychology.

This leads toward a new perspective on the concept of projective identification as an asymmetrical, coercive form of relating, that does not rely on metapsychological assumptions about universal phantasies or an innate destructive instinct. At the same time, although I emphasize the contribution of actual experiences to the various forms of two-person psychic structure and interpersonal interaction, I do not mean to imply that internal mental structures reproduce reality in some virtual way or that we can easily predict how particular events will lead to particular outcomes over the course of development. I hope to leave room for the bidirectional mediations between the internal world and actual events, over time, whether in the mind of the infant, child, adult, or psychoanalytic patient.

Such internal psychological structures, along with the processes by which they become part of the personality, are substantially outside awareness. I draw on ideas such as Bowlby's (1973) "internal working models" and Stern's (1985) "representations of interactions which have been generalized," anticipating the more current interest in "implicit relational knowing" (Boston Change Process Study Group, 2010). As they develop, these

DOI: 10.4324/9781003607328-18

internal working models are individual, idiosyncratic, and in that sense, distinctively of the internal world. This said, they are not straightforward representations of an external relationship; instead, they show some of the qualities of internality and autonomy from current experience most commonly associated with the "psychic reality" of the classical analysts, both Freudian and Kleinian, and thus depart from a tendency in some of the relational approaches.

A revised conceptualization of the Kleinian idea of phantasy offers pathways for this integration. That concept of phantasy refers to overarching mental structures that organize both psychic and interpersonal activity, along with having the distinctive qualities of unconsciousness and imperviousness to actuality. Keeping this in mind, I read the basic phantasy concept in light of a "two-person," self-with-object approach, which is not inconsistent with much of the Kleinian project (especially once the role of the innate destructive instincts is deemphasized). I am working toward conceptualizing internal, two-person psychic structures in a way that differs from the Freudian–Kleinian models in that their development gives the social environment substantial weight from the beginning and is intrinsically intersubjective, but that also retains much of the radical and private subjectivity of those conceptions of the relative independence of "psychic reality" from the outside world.

My overall effort, then, is to, first, integrate the concept of unconscious phantasy as a basic psychic format with the infant observers' models of internal two-person "working models" organized around and regulating affects, bodily states, and relational scenarios and expectancies; and second, to give actual events a greater role in the development of these structures over childhood into adulthood. I propose that this offers a way to eliminate the faulty and mystifying vestiges of the dual-drive model while preserving the most crucial aspects of the phantasy-based approach. I also believe that this approach provides a more effective, accurate, and experience-near model of the place of the body in phantasy by emphasizing actual bodily affective-relational experience rather than reifying the body, as do the cruder forms of instinct theory, as something outside the mind that enters it in the form of instinctual principles or energies.

As I reject the classical instinct theory, I also reject the link between infancy and what has been called "primitive," and instead, point toward the link between psychic disorganization and trauma, especially in early development. This means that some children and adults will have chaotic inner lives, while others will not: The baby's psychological organization depends on her circumstances, as well as her innate endowment. I take my hypothetical but plausible speculations about Daniel to suggest that the projective identification format itself is not a universal feature of the infant's psychic life, but instead takes shape depending on the different experiences between baby and caregivers in which the baby's emergent sense of self is handled so as to configure the basic ground of subject, objects, and intersubjectivity.

The concept of projective identification

Klein transformed psychoanalysis by insisting on the primary role of self and object organizations within the earliest psychic reality. The crucial imagery for this movement was the infant's phantasies and internal object relations that organized the libidinal (life) and destructive (death) instincts. Klein's infant handles the anxiety of inevitable inner destructiveness by fantasizing its expulsion into the object. The baby's psychic life is thus characterized by oscillations, from self to object, in the "location" of anxieties and psychic valences such as goodness and badness, all driven by instinctual, bodily based phantasies. This account is consistent with Freud's original idea that very early psychic life is organized around oral configurations as well as the life and death instincts. Thus, splitting and projective identification were the crucial organizers of mental life in the earliest phases of development (see Chapter 3).

As a cornerstone of the extraordinary contemporary Kleinian clinical literature (Klein, 1946; Ogden, 1982; Spillius, 1988; Steiner, 1993; among others), the concept captures important elements of countertransference–transference experience, particularly those vexing moments when the therapist feels pressured and even coerced, consciously or unconsciously, to take on feelings or entire roles that seem inauthentic or unacceptable—moments when we feel especially unable to find a way to live within the transference–countertransference field and still be true to ourselves—on the patient's side of this same transaction. Relational analysts have relied on and extended the projective identification idea in describing such moments, also including an affirmative exploration of how analysts' own psychologies are implicated in their reactions to patients' projections, especially in impasses.

In my own experience of discussing "projective identification" with students and colleagues, I have seen as much imprecision as enthusiasm.

The concept is sometimes used to encompass all of countertransference or, at least, all situations in which the therapist believes that he or she feels something like what the patient is feeling. The boundary between projective identification and empathy can become quite vague; a countertransference feeling might be called "empathy" when it feels good and "projective identification" when it feels bad or at least alien. One colleague joked that anxious therapists refer to projective identification instead of saying, "The Devil made me do it!" (Robin Silverman, personal communication, 1997).

Despite these problems, the robust and evocative power of the projective identification concept compels us to make efforts to use it as fully and thoughtfully as possible.

Re-conceptualizing phantasy with infant observation research

In Kleinian psychoanalysis, "*ph*antasy" refers to the most basic psychic element, at the threshold between mental life and the bodily based instincts. Phantasies are pre-symbolic and not primarily in the form of images (as in the usual "*f*antasy"), but rather, something like presences or internal relational forms. *The New Dictionary of Kleinian Thought* (Spillius et al., 2011, p. 3) defines *phantasy* thus:

> In Kleinian theory unconscious phantasies underlie every mental process and accompany all mental activity. They are the mental representation of those somatic events in the body that comprise the instincts, and are physical sensations interpreted as relationships of both libidinal and aggressive impulses and also of defence mechanisms against those impulses.

I have found this concept indispensable in directing attention to powerful and deep internal and external relationship patterns that would otherwise remain in the shadows. But I also believe that it can benefit from a critical integration with the intersubjectively oriented, direct observation of infants and parents interacting that emerged in the last decades of the twentieth century. Some of the more cumbersome and controversial assumptions of the Kleinian image of the infant and the emphasis on instincts are not necessary to create a strong account that captures most of what is best in their conceptualization of phantasy. When these assumptions are set aside, the most important elements of the powerful Kleinian orientation can be clarified and strengthened. At the same time, when taken up in light of the Kleinian primary process, internal object-oriented sensibility, the intersubjective-Relational approaches can become more engaged with the irrational, driven, and often confused and confusing challenges that present themselves. More broadly, this synthesis advances the much-needed development of clinical-theoretical approaches that integrate the strengths of established one-person psychologies with emerging two-person approaches: This is one of the central tasks of this book. By directly observing the details of infant–parent interactions and then returning to the Kleinian concepts, rather than starting from the concepts and trying to push the observations into them, we can generate approaches that are more precise and immediate without losing explanatory depth and power. This approach to the Kleinian models has much in common with the Middle Group's strong revision of them. Although this is left implicit here, I hope that some of that resonance will come through.

In this chapter, I work to augment the Kleinian phantasy orientation with two aspects of the contemporary, intersubjectivist reading of infant observation research: (1) new understandings about how nonverbal patternings in early dyadic interactions express and shape internal structures of meaning in preverbal, affective, chorographic, and kinesthetic dimensions of self-with-other experience; and (2) the image of the infant–parent dyad as a two-person, mutual influence, mutual regulation system. This also follows the expanded conceptualization of "the unconscious."

Observing infant–parent interactions

Jamal and his father

Direct and evocative images of infants and their parents in motion and feeling together can illuminate both the overall structure and moment-to-moment details of prerepresentational interactional process. Here is an account of a few minutes of interaction in which a six-month-old boy, Jamal Jr., and his father, Jamal Sr., play together, first while the baby is in his father's arms and then as they are both lying on the floor, mostly facing one another. The overall tone is loving and animated, even somewhat hyper, as Jamal Sr. revs Jamal Jr. up a bit. The father and son are quite fond of each other; there are frequent exchanges of gazes, an affectionate lilt to the father's vocalizations, and he waits for little Jamal to finish whatever he is doing before taking another initiative or picking him up. For example, he lets him carefully look over and feel the rug fibers before engaging Jamal Jr. in play grabbing a candy box. When Jamal Sr. does pick up his son, there is a comfortable and shared relaxation.

Yet, there is also some sense that the father is leading the son too fast, revving him up too much, and setting expectations too high. For example, when initiating the candy box play, Jamal Sr. places the box out of his son's reach, and the baby has to strain to crawl for it; Jamal Sr. does not help Jamal Jr. here, even though he seems to see that strain. Some might feel that there is an undercurrent of challenging teasing. But when the infant does get to the box, his dad applauds him, and they are elated together.

Meanwhile, Jamal Jr.'s mother can be heard saying that her boy prefers her husband these days, with pride and warmth, and that she is not surprised, as she wished for a girl. After a few moments, Jamal Sr. leaves after letting his son know that he will be going, saying an affectionate goodbye. Jamal Jr. follows his father out of the room with his eyes, looks at the candy box, looks back at the door, and then settles in to play with the box.

Many issues can be discussed here: the separation; the mother's comments about wanting a girl; the cultural dimension, inasmuch as this is an African American family; the father's motivations to have his son be like him; and so on. Many of these broad issues can be seen in the details of the nonverbal patterning of affection and influence between father and son. This includes, for example, the various emotions, the pacing, and the role of bodily effort and bodily contact, all with their impact on Jamal Jr.'s sense of his own body, including his strain, his sense of accomplishment, and his comfort in his father's presence. Preverbal antecedents of his sense of himself as a gendered boy are also in play here. Overall, the influence is asymmetrical, with the father taking the lead most of the time, although he does usually notice his son's cues.

The whole interaction has a very affectionate tone, even as Jamal Sr. seems, at least to some, to push too hard and overlook the little boy's inner experience. This is the way that the elder Jamal loves his son: He is proud and awfully pleased that his son loves him and looks up to him. This joining is supported by the mother, too; she seems to take for granted that Jamal Sr. is grooming Jamal Jr. to take after him. Assuming that this is a typical interaction, young Jamal might well continue to become like his father and will be admired for it; he is being encouraged to idealize and identify with his father.

This situation involves a particular configuration of the parents' (and especially the father's) internal expectations, ideals, wishes, self-images, and so on—a configuration that interacts with the baby's constitutional givens (e.g., an apparent motor competence), along with what he has already come to enjoy and how he has already come to experience himself. All of this is expressed in an observable form of relating between father and son, with distinctive rhythms, tonalities, and choreography. For young Jamal, being with father also means being like father, including feeling pushed and revved up somewhat; this way of being is also basic to how the elder Jamal feels, both to himself and to others. In another affective atmosphere, this experience might feel uncomfortably imposing and demanding to Jamal Jr., but the cheerfully proud and affectionate cadences of his father lead one to imagine that the boy might come to see being pushed a bit, as well as pushing people a bit, as part of a congenial form of getting along.

However well this ultimately works for little Jamal, this perspective gives us a window into how it feels to be this baby. Looking at this couple, we get a sense of how much these patterns are registered at unspoken levels of how it feels to be oneself in one's body (for example, how it feels to use one's muscles) and how it feels to be oneself with someone else. Interpersonal expectancies and senses of self are not explicit here, but lived through in various interaction patterns—whether others' cues will be followed and at what pace, when one chooses to listen and when to speak, and so on and so on. Such as these experiences are repeated and generalized, they are quite likely to remain implicit and prereflective (not in awareness but not repressed) and located in physical and affective registers (rather than narratively coherent verbal forms). Various conceptual languages and contributions from several disciplines have been used to describe how self-experience and interpersonal interactions are organized according to generalized representations of relationships (Stern, 1985), affective patternings (e.g., Demos, 1988; Emde, 1983), internal working models (Bowlby, 1988) and "implicit relational knowing" (Boston Change Process Study Group, 2010; Lyons-Ruth & Boston Change Process Study Group, 1998) that regulate what individuals do with others and what they expect from them.

Nonverbal dimensions of the construction and contours of meaning in dyadic interactional fields

This vignette and discussion illustrate how infant researchers' microanalytic concepts can clarify both broad contours of psychic structures and fine details of both psychic structure and clinical process. This can be helpful in clinical work with adults and older children, too. Various types of interactive sequences and patterns have been described, including affect attunement (Stern, 1985), rupture and repair (Tronick, 2007), chase and dodge (Beebe & Lachmann, 1988, 2002), reciprocity, rhythmicity, contingency, affect, arousal, attachment, relational expectancies, meaning-making (Tronick, 2005), and the like. (See Chapters 6 and 8.) These novel observations help us become more aware of broad, nonverbal, affectively and narratively organized interactional "formats" in psychic structure and therapeutic interaction, through which intersubjectivity is created and structured. In this chapter, I approach projective identification as such a nonverbal, prerepresentational format for organizing intersubjective experience.

Since these nonverbal patternings are largely implicit, they are often outside reflective awareness. They thus have this in common with the Kleinian phantasies. Both are unconscious by virtue of their particular form, rather than by having been repressed. (See Chapter 6 and 7.) In addition, both approaches depict basic psychic organizers at the "psyche-soma" level (Winnicott, 1949) that influence all of psychic life, especially in regard to emotionally relevant relationships.

Coercive parent–infant interactions and projective identification

I now turn to the intergenerational transmission of abuse trauma, in order to focus on projective identification.

Daniel and his father

A three-day-old, Daniel, and his father are observed just before their discharge from the newborn nursery. This father had been repeatedly physically abused as a child and had abused his previous children, which finally resulted in their removal from his care. In this brief episode, he holds his baby very awkwardly, just below his neck, and forcefully brings the neonate's face close to his own with a frightening look and a loud vocal tone that somehow seems to convey some tenderness along with much anxiety. Next, the father tries to force Daniel to drink from a bottle of water while the baby desperately shows that he is satiated, first by not sucking, then by keeping his mouth closed and tensing up his whole body, and finally going limp. During this sequence, the father rebuffs efforts by his wife and a therapist observer to get him to notice Daniel's resistance to his brutal ministrations, remaining oblivious to his son's repeated reactions. The father again looms in his son's face, calls him "Chump!" and pugilistically says, "Do you want to tell me about it?" He hoists Daniel high up in the air, as if he were roughhousing with a much older boy. Finally, as the baby seems to collapse into a droopy, withdrawn state, the father exclaims, "That's enough of your garbage!"

This is very disturbing. In part, this reflects the extent to which we are prepared to read the infant as a comprehensible signaller, even at three days, and we are blatantly disturbed when the father overrides these cues with his own malevolent attributions. This is not to say that the baby is self-conscious or signalling with a sense of agency. Indeed, to whatever extent this kind of interaction will become characteristic of his interpersonal experience, this boy will feel that helplessness and ineffectuality are fundamental modes of self-experience.[1]

In an extended infant–parent psychotherapy, this father became aware of how helpless he had felt as a child, especially when he was beaten by his own father, along with how much having his own children reminded him of this. In his own way, the father was inducing a feeling in his son that he was not able to tolerate in himself, intensified as the infant's presence evoked that feeling in him. In watching the details of the interaction, we can see how the infant is pressured to feel helpless, through interactions that are essentially nonverbal and prerepresentational. This also includes an agonizing sense of Daniel's bodily experience—prodded, tossed about, and deprived of any sense of comfort and control.

Clinical implications: Viewing adults' "projective identifications" as repetitions of coercive relationships in early childhood

Under the coercive conditions that Daniel's father inflicts on him (as in many traumatizing situations), Daniel is permitted only one possible way to interrelate. There are no "open spaces" (Sander, 2002) in which he can get a sense of his own agency and subjectivity. At three days, he is already deprived of the chance to feel how his own signals can have effects and can be rendered meaningful by a caregiver's contingent, understanding, and appreciative responses: He cannot rest long enough to feel that what is happening to him could be otherwise. Daniel is forced to become the receptacle-object for his father's most painful unthought experiences—the site of the identification that his father has inflicted on him. In a sense, he will have no self of his own, or, perhaps more exactly, he will have a nonsubjective self without any self-reflective awareness, a self-as-object-to-his-father. The potential for a vital interchange between self and other has been obviated, if not annihilated. We are witnessing the blockage or collapse of intersubjectivity that follows from the compelled identificative compliance with his father's traumatizing projective identification (e.g., Davies & Frawley, 1994; Grotstein, 1994, 1995).

Daniel's father, then, shows an acute deficit in the development of self-reflexiveness. He has hardly any awareness of what he is expressing, what his son is feeling, or where he is coming from. (Perhaps it would be better to say "when he is coming from," if we think of him as reenacting—rather than remembering—his own experience with his father.) As with Daniel and his father, parents who have been thus traumatized will themselves often pressure their own children to experience internal images of self and others of which they are not aware, through coercive patterns of highly asymmetrical influence in actual interactions, such that the infants identify with parts of their parents' experiences about which the parents cannot think (Fraiberg, 1982; Seligman, 1994).There is something like a displacement here, within a dissociative field.

In addition, especially in older children, any demonstrations to the abusers that things could be thought otherwise may be brushed aside or even suppressed, on pain of loss of whatever relational comfort is available, and sometimes in response to threats of violence or other more explicit forms of coercion. Overall, the children are precluded from reflecting on their inner states of mind or about what is actually happening to them, and instead come to feel that the experiences that they are having are just how the world works. Such internal working models function without being subject to reflection and the sense that there can be alternative ways of behaving and relating. They are at the basic ground of experience but cannot be thought about. This formulation shares the dimensions of peremptory drivenness and nonawareness with the Kleinian phantasies and other unconscious phenomena in the traditional Freudian models, but it gives more weight to traumatic relationships and how they shape experience. (Echoes of Ferenczi's, 1949b, p. 225, "confusion of tongues" can be heard here.)

Indeed, this is what people with a prevalence of such experiences in their childhood will demonstrate when the analyst suggests, through interpretation or other verbal interventions, that the affective world could be otherwise; with such "concrete" patients, it is often only action that can gradually provide the sense that things can actually be different. In the midst of pathological projective identification dynamics in both development and psychotherapy, reflection on the situation is impossible. As many have written, this is not a matter of repression but of the dissociative impossibility of thinking about what is going on, at all, except in dissociated or otherwise alienated forms.

This elaborates my observation about how premature interpretations sometimes reflect insufficient appreciation of how inarticulate or constrained the patient is in trying to think and speak about the experience in a meaningful way. Analysts sometimes underestimate patients' limits with regard to intersubjectivity, agency, and introspection. Inasmuch as many patients cannot actually reflect on the reflective language that is offered, there may be an experience of being told that one is actually feeling something that one does not know about—that one does not actually know one's own mind. This parallels another aspect of traumatization, one in which the victim's basic sense of reality is undermined. (Another factor here is that analysts sometimes want to offer their analysands something like what they were offered in their own analyses, as well as what has been most idealized in their training.)

When patients with such experiences treat their analysts as they have been treated, they may still feel (*at the same moment*) that they are being treated that way themselves. Pathological projective identification is an unstable and unsuccessful defense; since it is organized around oscillations of self and object positions, it leads to its own repetition, as with Daniel and his father or the more strained moments of the clinical vignette above. Traumatized patients cannot know that they are doing any of this any more than Daniel's father knew what he was actually doing or perhaps any more than Daniel could have been aware of what was happening to him, because such nonawareness is itself part of the psychic state that is being reproduced. Furthermore, such nonawareness may be protected by a variety of defensive processes, such as splitting, denial, and dissociation. To put this another way: Therapists sometimes confound dissociation with other forms of defense.

The patient may be initiating "projective identification" in the analysis, but this apparent act of illusory agency may be little more than a desperate attempt to avoid the even more unbearable psychic possibilities, including loss of the entire relationship and the sense of desperate frustration and isolated and overwhelming helplessness that are at the core of his or her experience, much as they were for Daniel and, ultimately, his father. Patients are always attempting to make their analytic therapist into someone other than who he or she usually is, someone whom they hope for, and someone whom they fear. This is often one of the underlying conditions of transference, and it is one of the essential clinical facts that give the projective identification concept its appeal. Indeed, the contemporary Kleinians have made one of their most distinctive contributions in seeing this type of influence process as ubiquitous in analyses rather than as restricted to treatments of more disturbed patients. But when this perspective is used without subtlety, so as to overattribute negative or destructive motivation locating them within the patient, perception can turn into persecution, and therapeutic opportunities may go awry. This is a common problem with interpretation in work with traumatized, "borderline" patients, which often goes unnoticed.

Such difficulties appear in less extreme forms with patients whose traumatic experiences have not been so intense. In most analyses, analysands push the analyst to behave, feel, and identify in specific ways that feel coercive and alien; this quality is, in some sense, part of every transference situation, especially negative transferences. In addition, of course, the analyst is also influenced to become someone whom the patient needs. These different influence patterns present themselves in almost infinitely varied and blended forms. The Relational and Kleinian literatures are both very attentive to all of this, especially when the Kleinian literature is augmented with Bion's (1962) innovative readings of the projective identification concept (e.g., Britton, 1992; Joseph, 1988; Spillius, 1988), as I've elaborated in Chapter 13.

One analyst found himself stymied by a female patient who frequently characterized him as cruel and withholding, although he experienced himself as earnestly trying to be supportive. At one point, he was persistent in trying to help her talk about her feelings about his impending vacation and in trying to communicate how her affect went flat when she said that he "was entitled to take some time off" and that she was glad for him. His subsequent efforts to be empathetic with her distress, now about her irritation with his persistence, were generally ineffective, as the patient would take them as condescending, and his interpretations of the projective and defensive aspects of her criticisms were even more provocative for her, as the patient took them as attacks that confirmed her view of the analyst as using pseudotechnique to humiliate her. As she confronted him, he offered that her comments had a "grain of truth," but he could not empathize with her saying that he was being sadistic (although he usually took his patients' descriptions of him seriously).

In this atmosphere, it was useful for the analyst to describe the details of how such interactions would proceed to leave him feeling that he could not possibly respond to his patient's criticisms: If he agreed that he was being cruel, he would be confessing to a crime that he did not feel that he had committed; but if he tried to explain how he saw things differently, he would indeed be acting so as to lead the patient to feel attacked. As this description corresponded, in more or less specific detail, with the patient's treatment at the hands of her very critical and sometimes unreasonable mother, she became more able to reflect on the situation and make some links to the past.

At the same time that they supported self-reflection for the patient, these links also helped the analyst feel less controlled and relieved some of his own guilt and anger. He was thus better able to create an atmosphere in which the patient's attributions could be handled differently from how the patient had been able to handle them when similar assaults were inflicted on her as a child. In addition, this process offered a glimmer of enhanced reflectiveness about the prototraumatic situation that was becoming reproduced in the analytic relationship. The analyst and patient were, together, finding a way to extricate themselves from the shared experience of coercive attribution without perspective that was indeed characteristic of this patient's childhood relationships.[2]

"Technique" and the repetition of the trauma in the therapist–patient interaction

There are substantial pitfalls in overlooking the subtleties of such processes: The precocious and overgeneralizing interpretation of the patient's inferred inner states (especially of negative motives) overlooks the actual psychic organization of the patient and substitutes an experience-distant formulation. This can, from the point of view of the patient's subjective experience, actually repeat the original trauma of coercive attribution. Such approaches often overestimate the patient's own agency in creating the coercion—without speaking to the desperate and inarticulate sense of being coerced, which is actually at the heart of the patient's experience. As I said, premature interpretations might confirm the patient's fear of being dominated by a needed object who has superior power who is also attributing negative motives.

This is further complicated by the way that a patient's coercive behavior may engender frustration and even hostility in the analyst, even when the patient is not feeling hostile or at least not experiencing the hostility. Following the Kleinian formulation, therapists sometimes presume that their own hostile feelings are evidence of the patient's having transferred a feeling onto the analyst—that is, that the patient actually feels such a feeling, if unconsciously. But this position may instead reflect a misconstruction on the part of the analyst, who has added something derived from her own feeling of having been offended and misrecognized and having her own expectations of the analytic situation violated. But the patient may be desperately protecting herself in the only way that she knows. This is not the same as the Kleinian notion that the patient is "putting feelings into the analyst." When the analyst simply attributes the hostile feeling to the patient, rather than seeing it as a newly constructed outcome of an intersubjective situation, the interpretation may indeed not only be premature but may actually be incorrect, and the patient may again experience misattribution. Here again, a less inferential and attributive approach may be more helpful.

Integrating infant–parent observation research and Kleinian concepts

The concept of projective identification as an essentially internal phantasy is thus recast in intersubjective terms as describing a particular procedural format at the most basic levels of self object organization—a particular way of organizing the senses of self and intersubjectivity, with particular features. The projective identification concept here captures a particular form of asymmetrical influence, with both internal-structural and behavioral-communicational aspects, in which one person pressures another to experience as part of herself something that the first person cannot accept within his own self-experience. If this sounds confusing, that is because it is: It reflects an inner state of confusion about boundaries and interpersonal space. This is illustrated in the extreme in Daniel's father's way of constructing the flux of self and other in the interplay of the internal and external worlds, which is, paradoxically but typically, fluid and rigid at the same time. There is constant chaos and agony in his procedures for organizing which feelings and attributes "belong" to himself and which to others, as in the paranoid-schizoid position.

The Kleinian perspective, in turn, adds to the intersubjectivist infant researchers' perspective. The concept of the internal phantasy in an internally driven psychic world captures the repetitive pressure and compulsion that is so obvious here, along with the destructiveness that is so striking in this father's blatant overriding of his son's cues, as well as the crucial dimensions of unconsciousness and the sense of being a fundamental overarching psychic principle. Integrating these perspectives, we can think of the Kleinian psychology of the internal object world as an account of a specific kind of caregiving relationship, where the internal world of one person eclipses the actuality of the other. However, neither projective identification nor the paranoid-schizoid position is the universal starting point of object relations.

This critical synthesis with the contemporary infant researchers' emphasis on the social, dialogical nature of the baby's world calls for a more open and varied model of these vicissitudes than is often offered, at least in the more tradition-bound of the Kleinian accounts: Contra Klein, it is not all infants who suffer from the absence of intersubjective vitality and the terrors of omnipotent destructiveness and deprivation; the imagery of the desperate world of the instincts is not universal. Instead, it is one of many forms of configuring intersubjective relationship space. Others might be more reciprocal, symmetrical, empathic, low key, and so on. Aron (1990), for example, has described the usual psychoanalytic therapeutic arrangement as reciprocal but asymmetrical.

Kleinian metapsychology and developmental narrative as overgeneralization

The Kleinian image of an intrinsically "primitive" infant, organized around projection as the compelled pathway to cope with life-threatening anxieties, can now be reconceptualized as describing object relations under conditions of stress and strain, rather than as the infant's usual format for linking to her objects, whether internal or external. The idea that projective identification is the basic mode of infantile object relations overgeneralizes post-traumatic mental organization, illuminating dimensions of such situations but also obscuring important features there and elsewhere. The classical account of infantile projective identification makes too much of retrospective inferences drawn from the analysis of older children and adults, especially those who have been traumatized.

When the parents' influence is especially forceful and one-sided, without regard for the child's inner experiences or external cues, the controlling projective identification format may well become most dominant in the child's personality and likely will be passed on to the next generation in an inflexible way. Indeed, parents are always influencing their infants and attributing meanings to them, and so there will always be a dynamic interplay of parental projection and the infant's attributes. But often, other kinds of forms of intersubjectivity will be more central, at the most basic, unconscious levels of dyadic intrapsychic organization and from the beginning of development. Projective identification as a peremptory form of ridding oneself of intolerable feelings will not be the central mode of psychic organization, even in earliest infancy, when things have gone well enough. Even when they haven't, there may be other ways of organizing the senses of self-with-others to handle the emerging anxiety. The Kleinian metapsychology universalizes with the turbulence and destructiveness of the instinctual world and the nonreality orientation of the originary mind.

Psychoanalytic instinct theory and the infant's bodily experience

The Kleinian metapsychology anchors its theory of unconscious phantasy in the hypothetical world of the basic, irreducible, and "primitive" oral evacuative and incorporative phantasy structure of the infant psyche. This underestimates the importance of actual early experiences at the most basic levels of the psyche and in the earliest moments of development, many of which are quite protective, cooperative, and reciprocal, full of positive affect. As much as I admire the Kleinian depth and power, I find its picture of the infant to be far from what actual babies are going through—consciously or unconsciously, in reality or phantasy.

In the response to these criticisms, defenders of the traditional instinct theories argue that they have the special virtue of capturing something about the bedrock importance of the physical-bodily realm for both infants and adults. Integrating the traditional emphasis on phantasy with direct observational approaches to infancy offers a powerful response to these objections, as the direct observation approach is so attentive to concrete and vivid interactional processes that occur at the most basic psychophysical levels: affects; kinesthetic, proprioceptive, and other bodily experiences; rhythms; synchronies and asynchronies; and other details of interaction sequences. Building a theory of phantasy that includes these elements clarifies a burdensome ambiguity in the Kleinian concepts and, indeed, in most of the "classical" models by untethering the questionable assumptions of instinct theory from the essential goal of keeping bodily experience at the center of the analytic discourse. (This also leads to a different look for core concepts such as "the id.") Susan Isaacs' (1948) brilliant, seminal Kleinian paper on "the nature and function of phantasy" suggests such a direction, but it is also limited by her allegiance to the Freud–Klein metapsychology and the limited research of its time.

This approach also responds to problems with the evolution of the projective identification concept that have been raised both inside and outside the Kleinian community. In her review of the projective identification concept, Spillius (1988, pp. 84–85) wrote:

> Klein was punctilious in specifying the exact physical means by which a projection was being effected and into which part of the recipient's body. Even the original definition specifies "together with these harmful excrements, expelled in hatred, split off parts of the ego are also projected onto the mother, or, as I would rather call it, into the mother" (Klein, 1946), thus making it clear that the excretory organs are the executive agents of the projection . . . Gradually, however, many analysts have come to speak and think of projection by the mind of the projector into the mind of the recipient without specifying the physical basis of the phantasy, unless it is particularly obtrusive.

Spillius here does note the concretization of the psychosexual stage theory in the original Kleinian approach, but doesn't consider the possibility of looking elsewhere to see "the physical basis of the phantasy." I am arguing that looking at the actual transmission processes in infant–parent interactions can help fill this gap and point the way to an intersubjectively oriented view of both infancy and transference–countertransference that is both more comprehensive and experience-near.

Accounts of bodily experience should indeed be included at the center of both developmental and clinical theory, but they should emphasize the entire sense of the body rather than configurations centered on particular zones or arbitrarily privileged physical states such as unpleasant tension. Moving away from the vestiges of the drive-instinct model's caricature of bodily experience would open more space for the rich and immediate accounts of the crucial role of the body in personal and social experience, as is illustrated in the extreme in the overall sense of having one's body become the object of someone else's force, which is so apparent in the way that Daniel is handled by his father (Seligman, 1996). (See Salo & Paul, 2017, for a similar approach to infantile sexuality.) As I have said, the account of identification as a two-person process that is simultaneously interactional and intrapsychic is more powerful than those vestigial narratives supported by oral ingestive metaphors, like incorporation and metabolism.

A direct, observational approach to the body and the baby can break through the traditional position that locates bodily experience in the "one-person" realm and social experience in the "two-person" arena. Social experience is bodily, and bodily experience is social.

Rethinking identification and projective identification from the intersubjective perspective: Internal nonverbal interaction patterns in self-with-object structures

The infant–father interactions described here include specific, observable details of interaction processes by which inner states actually come to be expressed and communicated in the intersubjective/interpersonal arena. With this in mind, we can now approach projection and identification as "two-person" phenomena that we can describe in detail and in real time. The most obvious element of Daniel's situation in the infant–parent interaction is the brutal projective-attributive behavior of the father: He coercively overrides his son's cues, he treats him with hostility while feeling that he loves him; he treats him like a thing without agency, and so on. In doing this, he externalizes and actualizes his own helpless, hostile, depleted "bad" self and object representations, attributing them to his son, putting them into action without any reflective thought.

Identification as a two-person phenomenon

This nonreflective, coercive, asymmetrical pattern between Daniel and his father could be described as a "relationship format," a particular "form of intersubjectivity." As I have said, there are many other such formats, including the somewhat more reciprocal but still asymmetrical pattern of Jamal Sr. and Jamal Jr. or, alternatively, an even more reciprocal pattern in yet another infant–parent interaction. (See the vignette of Rebecca in Chapter 15 for an example.)

Classical theory treats identification as a standard format, but I want to emphasize that *each person's identification with whichever other person has its own distinctive relational dimensions, specific to that relationship*, including both its actual and imaginative dimensions that are not matters of content. In the case of Daniel and his father, there is a particular kind of identification process, agonizingly characterized by controlling projection; this differs from other forms of identification (e.g., Jamal Jr.'s). This perspective elaborates and is indebted to, but differs somewhat from, that of Sandler (1987), Sandler and Rosenblatt (1962), and Schafer (1968).

Projective identification as a two-person phenomenon

Daniel has no choice but to "identify" with those relational-emotional states that his father keeps out of his own awareness in thoughtlessly inflicting them on his son, including the sense of helplessness: As he comes to take on helplessness as a characteristic mode of experience and relating, he might well, also becoming like his father, come to feel that the only way to get through this to a sense of interpersonal contact and effectiveness would be to forcefully, even violently, override others' attempts to influence and control him, as this would have been the only way to make his wishes felt with his father. From another perspective, we would see him thus adopt his father's implicit relational strategies or "inner working models"— organizing his relationships, at the unconscious, preverbal level, along the affective-relational principle that the only way to make a difference in the world is to push as hard as you can, relying on intensity to overcome the unthought sense of pervasive helplessness. (See Bollas, 1987.)

This development would, then, *constitute an "identification" with both sides of the father's internal self and object world*: Daniel, like his father, might become the abuser of the father's own dyadic "abuser-abused" internal role relationship, but he would simultaneously be taking on the abused, helpless self as well. This identification, then, is with a dyadic relationship system rather than with a single role or, to put it another way, as an orientation of one's subjectivity *within* a self-with-other relationship dyad characterized by oscillation between one position and the other. This perspective applies the contemporary notion that internal object configurations are organized dyadically and as something like fields. This applies to the Kleinian account of the ubiquity of projection, introjection, and identification in the internal object world.

"Identification with the aggressor" as an intersubjective/ interactional concept

This general approach can be further illustrated in an effort to clarify the specific term, "identification with the aggressor," which was proposed by Ferenczi (1949a), extended by Anna Freud (1936), and was used so eloquently by Fraiberg et al. (1975) in regard to the intergenerational transmission of trauma, as well as more generally. Under such conditions, identification with the abusive aggressor is a reproduction of a relational process rather than just of an object representation alone. Daniel's identification with his father as aggressor involves this *internalization of the entire dyadic projective identificatory process*. Under such conditions, the particular nature of the identification-with-the-aggressor process is best described in terms of an internal dyadic model defined by its inescapability and coercive dyadic contours, rather than the traditional conceptualization in which the image of the aggressor is psychically relocated in the self. Identification with the aggressor does not do away with the victimized self; it projectively dislocates it.

To the substantial extent that Daniel's experience with his father is organized around the two-person relationship of abuser–abused, with its peremptory affective intensity, Daniel would experience the two sides of the two-person interaction as comprising the universe of possible relational patterns. Under such constraint and without the benefit of reflective thinking that can conceive of alternatives, the controlling position might "settle in" so as to prevent the even more overwhelming sense of helplessness of which an infant like Daniel can hardly become aware. This sense of helpless inevitability without reflection has been vividly described by, for example, Bion (1962), who writes of a sense of "nameless dread," and by the attachment theorist Mary Main (1995), who writes of "fear without solution." It is, of course, one of the essential features of traumatic states, and the process thus described is one of the central mechanisms in the intergenerational transmission of trauma, as has been noted. (See, for example, Fraiberg et al., 1975.)

Toward a contemporary integration

Overall, this approach is consistent with many of the points emerging in the exceptionally sophisticated Kleinian literature on transference and countertransference, in the contemporary relational-intersubjective theory in general, and in the burgeoning clinical and neurodevelopmental literature on trauma. The contemporary Kleinians are among the most acute analytic observers of the intricate interrelation of the intrapsychic and transference–countertransference fields; thus, there is greater overlap with the emerging intersubjective paradigms than is often realized. The analytic situation is set up to amplify patients' efforts to influence their therapists to feel and act so as to experience and enact their internal worlds. Kleinian analysts have been especially sensitive to the extent to which such pressure is one of the underlying conditions of transference in general and have used the projective identification concept as one of the cornerstones of this realization. When we delink the image of the infant from analogies with psychic primitivity, severe psychopathology, and endogenous instincts, what remains in the Kleinian lexicon comprises an extraordinarily rich and surprisingly experience-near set of descriptors of dyadic interaction in general and of the special kinds of interactions and peculiar patterns of dyadic influence that take place in analytic relationships in particular.

Notes

1 I emphasize that I am thinking hypothetically about potential developmental outcomes in order to explore how we might think about the effect of such treatment on an infant, rather than offering any predictions or predictive formulae about the effects of a single relationship. See Chapter 9, however, for an account of some of the increasingly strong research about such continuities.
2 Crastnopol's (2015) account of micro-trauma is relevant here.

Part IV

Vitality, activity, and communication in development and psychotherapy

Vitality and vacuity in the subjective experience of time and other forms of meaning and movement

These chapters explore core personal experiences like vitality and effectiveness, the personal senses of the future and the past, and the connection to one's body and mind as separate but related. This lively way of being in the world originates in infancy and is apparent in infant observation research. Thinking about vitality offers a compelling platform for psychodynamic theory and clinical practice.

In the first of these two chapters, I explore how the personal sense of time—temporality—is organized and experienced in different clinical situations. I use examples from infancy observations to draw links between caregivers' response to infants' capacities for motor activity and emotional communication and the development of the senses of personal security, vital intersubjectivity, and the feeling of a meaningful self and an open future. My approach links moment-to-moment interactions with these highly personal core experiences of what it feels like to live in the world. The accretion of "micro" interactions reflects and sustains the "macro" structures that analysts usually describe.

With this in mind, I propose a dimension of psychopathology that I call "disorders of temporality." One group of these involves the blurring of past and present, especially following trauma. Much of the chapter, though, is concerned with a basic deficit in the sense of time that can be observed, when a patient presents without the hope that new experiences can emerge, however fitfully. I suggest parallels between such psychological situations and the experiences of an infant with a chronically unresponsive parent. There, emotional and interpersonal vacuity is more prominent than the underlying vitality that

DOI: 10.4324/9781003607328-19

enlivens collaborating, loving, and caring interpersonal relationships, work, interests, etc.

The second chapter is an expanded version of a review of Daniel Stern's final book, *Forms of Vitality*. Beginning in the 1970s, Stern was one of the first to observe the details of infant–parent interaction, looking through the lens of his own experience in dance and other art forms that involved people communicating and moving through time and space to evoke strong emotions and meanings. Uniquely able to integrate an aesthetic orientation with psychoanalytic and psychiatric mindedness, he extended this vision to psychotherapy, both with infants and parents and adults. In addition, he was seriously involved with both phenomenological philosophy and the array of scientific findings from adjacent fields, including cognitive and developmental neuroscience and affect research.

Stern was always very interested in *form*, and he was unparalleled among the "baby watchers" at bringing forth the choreographic immediacy of dyadic social processes. Here, I read his project as a synthesis of these different influences to root analytic theory in *lived experience*, in both mental imagery and feeling and as bodily movement. His conceptualization of "vitality forms" is a general formulation that can be applied to movement, to music, to how emotions contour as they become more or less intense over short (or long) time intervals, to social interaction, as well as to psychotherapy process. It refers to a dimension of experience that is *both* experienced and observable, often both in the individual and social realms. This multiplicity of applications and contexts suggests great power to this approach.

In these chapters, I suggest a direction for updating and reconfiguring the original Freudian instinct-energy model, rooting it in the direct experience of an embodied mind rather than in a force that comes from somewhere other than the lived experience of the body itself. Like Stern, I start by imagining the infant building a world with such core dimensions as movement, emotion, heat and cold, light and dark, presence and absence, contact and effectiveness (or their opposites), in relations with actual objects, especially other people— all taking place in the evolving senses of space and time. Critics of relationship-oriented approaches in analysis have criticized them for "losing the body," claiming that the instinct theory protects analysis from losing the body in its theory. On the contrary, I believe that it devalues it, since the corporeal body is manifest and available from infancy forward, known subjectively and observable to others—both consciously and unconsciously. Taken together, these core experiences comprise a basic sense of subjectivity and intersubjectivity as a lively way of being in the world. In this re-orientation, the original "libido" concept becomes a matter of the lived experience of being an energetic and connected person, rather than as sexual energy to be discharged or bound. (I believe that a similar theme runs strongly through Winnicott's work.)

Chapter 15

Coming to life in time

Temporality, early deprivation, and the sense
of a lively future

Temporality: The time sense at the core
of personal experience

Time is at the center of psychoanalysis. Analyses sort out the present from the
past. Repetition and reconstruction, and progression and development, in their
various forms, are at the core of case formulation and technique. We conven-
tionally think of time as something uniform, to be represented or expressed
directly—a series of nows (the Greek term, *chronos*, applies here, as in the
chronometric movement of the forward-moving hands or digits of a clock).
But from the psychoanalyst's perspective, the sense of time is a deeply personal phenomenon, as it goes by more or less quickly and spaciously in different situations, at different ages and stages of the life cycle, whether we're
bored or engaged, in pain or having a good time, neurotic or psychotic, and
so on. (Here, the Greek *kairos* applies.) Memory and history, linking the past
and present, take so many forms and feelings—seen or concealed, felt or submerged, imagined, felt emotionally, encoded narratively, and on and on in so
many different ways—all appearing in intricate mixtures and again, shifting
from moment to moment and venue to venue. Philosophers use the term *temporality* to capture this underlying sense of time, as opposed to the everyday
notion of time as a flow of instants succeeding one another.

Hans Loewald (1980, pp. 144–145), in his neglected essay on the experience of time, described the special way that time presents itself to the
analyst:

> When we consider time as psychoanalysts . . . we encounter time in
> psychic life primarily as linking activity in which what we call past,
> present, and future are woven into a nexus . . . there is no irrevers-
> ibility on a linear continuum, as in the common concept of time as

DOI: 10.4324/9781003607328-20

a succession, but a reciprocal relationship whereby one time mode cannot be experienced or thought without the other and whereby they continually modify each other.

Freud's contemporary Marcel Proust (2002) showed how both the "now" and the "then" exist together in the same moment. The classic moment there occurs when the taste of the Madeleine cookie transports Marcel to his childhood and spurs the rest of the seven-volume narrative, *In Search of Lost Time*. Proust's monumental work is, of course, an extraordinarily textured and layered tour of the present dissolving into past, perception floating in memory which in turn saturates the present. It is the exemplary twentieth century study of temporality and its vicissitudes, creating an incomparably delicate and sensuously rich flow of space and time.

In "Combray," the chapter that amounts to an overture for his fabulously extended excursion through time, Proust wrote about the floating liminality that lies behind ordinary time:

A sleeping man holds in a circle around him the sequence of the hours, the order of the years and worlds. He consults them instinctively as he wakes and reads in a second the point on the earth he occupies, the time that has elapsed before his waking; but their ranks can be mixed up, broken. If toward morning, after a bout of insomnia, sleep overcomes him as he is reading, in a position quite different from the one in which he usually sleeps, his raised arm alone is enough to stop the sun and make it retreat, and in the first minute of his waking, he will no longer know what time it is, he will think he has only just gone to bed. If he dozes off in a position still more displaced and divergent, after dinner sitting in an armchair for instance, then the confusion among the disordered worlds will be complete, the magic armchair will send him traveling at top speed through time and space, and, at the moment of opening his eyelids, he will believe he went to bed several months earlier in another country.

(Proust, 2002, p. 5)

Tamsin Shaw (2013, p. 231) captured this elusive complexity in a few words:

Human consciousness differentiates past, present and future, wresting them from the moment. "This differentiation is the *flash of light*. . .

And it is only now, after this burst of light, that the atmosphere that protects human life can be called a *cloud."*

Historical time

Temporality in collective life is as multi-dimensional as in the personal, if not more so; archaeologists and historians (like neuroscientists and analysts) are well aware of the fluidity of time. But all of this is also visible (if often hidden in plain sight) in everyday situations: Each life unfolds in personal, cultural, and historical moments that organize and impose temporality in distinctive ways. I wrote the first draft of this chapter in view of the Old City of Jerusalem; there, within one square mile, are the remains of the Western Wall of the more than 2000-year-old Holy Temple of the Jews, the sites of Jesus' Crucifixion and Resurrection, Mohammed's ascent to Heaven, and the Crusaders' routes (later trod by the Arab League in 1948 and then by the Israeli Defense Forces when they entered the city after their victory in the 1967 "Six-Day War"). And, just steps away, you can also buy Rihanna CDs, iPhones, Armani eyeglass frames, and your favorite team t-shirt in Hebrew characters. Visiting the Old City is to enter a vertigo not unlike the Freudian topographic unconscious, archaeologically layered, or rather, pre-archaeologically disorganized. The first-timer in such dense environments who knows the history is visiting places that he remembers but has never seen, as if in a dream, but now in an actual place where the present and the past mingle and compel the future, lived out today. I have heard this in accounts of first-time visitors to the Parthenon: As it is shockingly new, it's oddly familiar, as if seen many times before, since it's simulated in all the thousands of neo-classical buildings with columns, pediments, and the like, to be found everywhere from Washington to Shanghai.

Psychoanalysts' attention to temporality

Psychoanalysis deconstructs the ordinary sense of time as a sequence of "nows" following one another in a more or less linear sequence, showing that this is not the only form of temporality. Loewald (1980, p. 143) characterized the place of time in analysis this way: "When we consider time as psychoanalysts, the concept of time as duration, objectively observed or subjectively experienced, loses much of its relevance . . . Past, present, and future present themselves in psychic life not primarily as one preceding the other, but as modes of time which determine and shape each other . . ." Arlow (1986, p. 507) echoed this: "Psychoanalysis is fundamentally related to time because it is an effort to understand how disturbances in the present are determined by events in the past . . . Psychoanalysis more than any other discipline sheds light on the coexistence of past, present, and future, thinking." The array of psychoanalytic writing on this subject is too extensive to review here.

The analytic setting, then, dislocates the usual social and language arrangements that structure the ordinary sense of time and facilitates the sliding movement of past and present over and into one another. Each analysis is "perched on the pyramid of the past" (Proust, cited by Merleau-Ponty, 2012/1945). Our cherished interpretive strategies turn the present into the past and back again; we cultivate the ubiquity of memory in coloring current knowledge; we allow ourselves in the transference to serve in effigy for the most important personal-historical figures; we approach the patient's world as if it were a dream that might contain all the currents of past, present, and even future as if they could all occupy the same place and time. Freud (1911) asserts that a radical disorientation from the manifest linearity of temporality is at the core of each person's mental life, when he defines the *primary* process as beyond ordinary time, with memory and perception mingling without distinction. (See Chapter 1.) Dreams, fantasies, and transferences are the most striking examples of this. The distinctive differences between different patients' experiences of the "same" analyst reflect the central and ubiquitous presence of the past in every analytic hour.

Baranger and Baranger (2008, p. 800) put it this way:

> The temporal aspect of the [analytic] field is nothing like the time experienced in everyday situations. The time of the analysis is simultaneously a present, a past and a future. It is a present as a new situation, a relationship with a person who adopts an attitude essentially different from that of the objects of the patient's history, but is at the same time past, since it is managed in a way which permits the patient the free repetition of all the conflicting situations of his or her history. It is this temporal ambiguity, the mixture of present, past and future, that permits patients not only to become aware of their history but also to modify it retroactively. This history is a gross weight, with its series of traumatisms and damaging situations that have been given once and

for all, until re-experiencing them in the state of temporal ambiguity permits the patients to take them on again with new meaning. The patients know they had a difficult birth, suffered hunger when a tiny baby, had a wet nurse, etc. But these traumatic situations can now be experienced not as unchangeable deadweight with an attitude of resignation, if they are taken up again, worked through and reintegrated into a different temporal perspective.

Limitations in psychoanalytic approaches to time

Many of our core psychoanalytic narratives can freeze the ambiguities of temporality, to the extent they present the past and present as distinctive; that is, by overstating the ordinary sequentiality in which the present comes later than the past. Sensitive as psychoanalytic traditions and theories may be to personal history and its vicissitudes, psychoanalysts nonetheless tend to use spatial metaphors more than temporal ones—separations, fragments, attachments, *objects*. Even the postmodernist theory of multiple selves configures them as having some form and temporal dimension, with past events leading to a present, however distorted. Thus, we usually presume a certain kind of temporal order, buried as it may be, and try to conceptualize a retrospective (backward-flowing) narrative about our patient's lives and difficulties in service of our effort to help them establish a forward-flowing way of living.

In these and other ways, then, analysts sometimes overlook specific variations of temporality in each case, rather than considering the idiosyncratic forms of temporality with which we all live: We take temporality for granted, mistaking it as an invariant given. Despite the contributions already noted, it may be fair to say that the sense of time has not gotten as much attention as other similarly fundamental domains. Loewald's (1980, p. 138) comment of over forty years ago may well remain relevant today: "[P]sychoanalytic contributions dealing with the subject are sparse, although there has been some increase in recent years."

Temporality, intentionality, and intersubjectivity: Extending into the world of human relationships

Phenomenological philosophy points toward the essential role that temporality plays in how it feels to have an adequate relationship to the world:

Time is at the very core of Being itself. (See, in the most prominent example, Heidegger, 1962.) Temporality is thus linked to "intentionality," the sense of having "a direction toward an object" (Crane, 1995, p. 412), of having a world of objects and presences which are *there*, in the most basic sense. Applying this at the level of the body and the lived experiences of self and others in the interpersonal world, we can say that subjectivity and intersubjectivity are similarly bound up with temporality and intentionality: A person who responds to and extends the communicative possibilities of another person's gestures gives that person the sense that she exists in a broader field of time, space, movement, feeling, and ultimately meaning. We learn about meaning in relationship—both in the sense that being physically alive is significant, and about communication as something that has to do with letting someone else know what we mean. Representation and, eventually, language and culture arise in such relational-intersubjective matrices. This is true whether we are talking about a mother and an infant, a patient and an analyst, or two friends in conversation.

Intersubjectivity and the personal sense of temporality: Illustrations in infant–parent interaction

Psychoanalysts who have studied early development have specified such dynamics, emphasizing core needs, emotions, and interpersonal interaction and companionship overall.

Babies seem to be immersed in their environments, whether feeding, playing, sleeping, or looking, listening, and moving around. More obviously than older children and adults, infants live through direct sensorimotor engagements; observing babies opens a window onto such core dimensions of experiencing. In this way, infant observation resonates with a phenomenonological perspective: "For Heidegger," as Michael Levin (personal communication, 2010) wrote, "human beings are in and *of* our worlds on the deepest level . . ." Merleau-Ponty (2004, 1945/2012) stressed the importance of direct perceptual and motor engagement in giving rise to mental life. For him, temporality, intentionality, and subjectivity, and intersubjectivity are all dependent on the embodied origins of the mind.

In general, having one's actions (including one's needs and emotions) recognized and seeing that they have effects is crucial to the sense of lively being-in-the-world. These gestures are fundamentally emergent from the infant's bodily experience, of affects, psychophysiological states, movement, and the like. When they are recognized and responded to by another person, they are extended into the interpersonal world, as they are extended in the broader, more vital contours of space and especially, of time: When someone keeps the dialogue going, whether around a baby's hand gesture or distressed cry or an adult analysand's (more or less hopeful) wish to be understood, it feels like the moment keeps going, rather than, at its worst, just collapsing. Bollas (1987) has captured this in conceptualizing "the *transformational object*" as the form for a primary, vitalizing relationship. Overall, then, interpersonal responsiveness supports the development of sense of individual meaning and agency in relation to other people; that is, intersubjectivity and subjectivity.

The more or less robust senses of temporality and intentionality are inevitably a part of this: When the baby's interaction partner responds to her initial gesture (whether emotion, motion, physical state such as hunger or being hot or cold, and more), the instant is extended into and over time. Ideally, the caregiver's response keeps things going or changes the baby's situation for the better, so that a sense of continuity is preserved amidst the flux of change. This is at the core of the robust temporal sense: Ricoeur (1988, p. 70) captures the emergence of the future-sense in the "unity of coming-towards, having-been and making-present." Ordinarily, then, the caregiver's responses to the infant's gestures give the baby compelling evidence of her effect on the world. Without really anticipating it going somewhere, the infant extends himself into his not yet defined surround—say, by moving his head up to encounter a gaze, or lifting a hand without imagining what will happen next, or by making a crying sound that flows automatically from some inner distress, or whatever. When the attentive caregiver notices and responds, that extension is essentially transformed, over time and space, into something that gives the baby the feeling of a world of time and space, in which something that she has done has led to something else occurring that has followed it, in a communicative intention: The simultaneous, intertwined core of *intersubjectivity*, *intentionality*, and *temporality* come into being. Here, mother and infant co-create a coherent self-with-other in a receptive world, which is discovered as it is created and identified with in the same dyadic action-moment. In bodily activity, the two elements of physical space and the extension of time are intertwined and occur and develop in concert, all so as to lead to the coherence and effectiveness of the sense of self with objects, enduring over time, when things are going well enough.

Going-on-being, the responsive environment, and the development of temporality and vitality

Winnicott (1958b) captured this fundamental process in his accounts of "going-on-being" and its evolution into the potential space that gives rise to culture. Imagine a two-month-old baby waking up from a nap, opening his eyes, and turning his head to the side, something which he has only recently become able to do. As he turns, his mother notices the turning, and moves her face into his visual field in synchrony with his left to right turn (though hers is right to left from her perspective), intensifying her smile as she matches his direction. The baby then smiles (also something that he is just beginning to do with any sense of initiative), and his mom makes a thrilled noise, thrilling him. This sequence may go on for a while. In Winnicottian terms, the baby's spontaneous gestures (opening his eyes, turning his head, smiling) become something more then they are. Daniel Stern (2010) has described the life-shaping effects of these transactions in conceptualizing "forms of vitality." (See Chapter 16.)

The elaboration of such sequences, as they are repeated thousands of times, creates and sustains a sense of time, linking time, movement, gesture, and emotion so as to enhance (indeed create) the baby's feeling of being effective and linked to her objects (here, the most crucial object, her mother). In such moments, the sense of time is intertwined with intersubjective vitality. If the mother had not matched the baby's initial gesture (the turning head), the forward flow of time may well not be vitalized.

Infant–parent interaction and the development of the sense of a lively future

These dynamics can be illustrated and clarified through some descriptions of infant–parent interactions. A video vignette of a mother, Ms. A, and her three-month-old baby, Rebecca, shows how responsive interactions shape the sense of a forward-moving future. After the first part of an initial interview in a nonclinical situation during which Rebecca was in her mother's arms, the observer invites the mother to set her on the floor. As Ms. A catches Rebecca's attention by talking in a sing-song voice, Rebecca starts to move her foot back and forth in time to her mother's vocal rhythm. Noticing this, Ms. A lightly places her hand on Rebecca's foot, allowing it to be guided by her infant's movements. Here, she extends the movement, which is already part of a proto-conversation conducted through auditory, affective, and motor pathways. The movement is turned into an even more meaningful gesture, part of a pattern of communicative meaning in the intersubjective field, lengthening it and extending it in time and space. These extensions include both the physical space, which has been expanded by the addition of the mother's hand, and the relational space and time of the added link between the mother and baby at the point of the harmonizing moving foot and hand.

But when these most basic responses are absent, or the caregiver frightens the baby or imposes her will or projections onto her, things can go quite badly. A chronic, inner listlessness can set in, with emotional deadness, chaos, helplessness, and even a state of ongoing psychic emergency. The gestures stay without response, frozen in non-time and hence becoming nothing, and leaving the child with a deadened object and without an intersubjective self. Only as sensation, motion, and feeling are passed between people does space get its contours in the flux of time. The unresponsive caregiver doesn't only leave the self starving, but without a life in time.

This is well-illustrated in another caregiver–infant interaction. Twenty-two-month-old Claudia is examining blocks on a table while her mother, Jackie, sits behind her, chatting idly with the interviewer or vacantly staring into space for brief moments. Except for her moving lips and occasional head movements, the mother is more or less immobile. Claudia seems to be looking for something to do, but she just shifts her attention from one block to another, picking one up, setting it down, and doing the same with another one. Finally, she finds a small toy car that grabs her interest, and she tentatively pivots and holds it up toward her mother. But Jackie merely glances at her for just a fraction of a second, and then returns to her earlier routine, all but ignoring Claudia. Claudia keeps trying, presenting the car again, gently pushing up against her mom's legs, but to no avail. Jackie continues her bland, immobile conversation with the interviewer without any meaningful acknowledgement of Claudia.

Here, a bid that might have turned into a moment, or process, of shared attention and affective exchange is instead left as next to nothing. Jackie's nonresponsiveness leaves Claudia without a sense of how such bids, as extensions into an intersubjective-interpersonal space, offer the potential for turning into intentionality that links to concrete objects and other people, so as to yield a sense of being effective, of living in animated time and space. But when these possibilities are denied, flatness and despair are the remaining outcomes. Rather than a sense of time moving forward, there is stasis. As I will elaborate, this is not the confusion of the present with a torturous past that is commonly addressed in our theories about repetition in psychopathogenesis. Rather, this is the stasis of a non-vitalized present that never gives way to the emergent future, as the body in motion and affect don't responses that mark them as a part of a sequence in time.

There is a varied array of compensatory "strategies" for this kind of lifelessness, well-described in much of the analytic literature. Examples include interpersonal relationships of all sorts: somaticizations, including physical pain, drugs, bodily illnesses, and others, frantic or manic interests and activities, professional and other ambitions, and even psychotic symptomatology. Bion's (1965) conceptualization of "Beta elements," which take the place of more organized experiencing, captures a range of these phenomena. Winnicott (1960b) proposes the concept of the "false self" to describe ways of living that preserve a semblance of individuality and presence in the face of challenging environmental conditions in infancy; he specifies the mother's part in these conditions as her failure to respond to the infant's spontaneous gestures.

Disorders of temporality

Once temporality becomes central to our attention, it is hard to imagine an analytic case that does not involve fissures and failures in regard to how past, present, and future are interrelated. Baranger and Baranger (2008, p. 800) highlight the extent to which every analysis is an analysis of temporality:

> Most often, patients come to analysis because they feel they have no future. They were prisoners of their neurosis, with no prospect of at least being released from this imprisonment . . . The attempt to have an analysis often indicates a last attempt to re-open the future and re-orient existence . . . Under these conditions, the dialectical process of the constitution of the past and the future on the basis of the present can be freed to some extent.

Overall, I propose to use the term "disorders of temporality" to capture some of more problematic configurations of the sense of time, as an aspect of experience, that lie at the very core of our relations to the world. Along such lines, Loewald (1980, p. 140) proposed that we consider the

> reciprocal relations between past, present and future as active modes of psychic life . . . as we discern them in our psychoanalytic work, for instance, in the play of transference, in the impact of unconscious and conscious remembering and anticipating in the present, in the interplay between primitive (stemming from the past) and higher-order ("present") motivations.

There appear to be more or less specific variations in the difficulties in how patients experience the relationship between past, present, and future, as well as time itself. It might well be useful to generate a more extended catalog of these. But for now, I will try to delineate two broad types, so as to suggest how we might begin to think along these lines and to illustrate my perspective: In the first, the past and present are melded together; I propose to call these, at least for now, "*disorders of simultaneity.*"

Most of what follows, however, is concerned with "*disorders of subsequency,*" more essential deficits in the core sense of time in the intersubjective field. Here, the feeling of the future unfolding in a forward-moving way, different from the present, is itself constrained. There are difficulties in the fabric of temporality itself, where there is a limited sense of a future that can be different from the past and the present; in this situation, at the implicit levels of affective-relational engagement that frame intersubjectivity, past, present, and future don't mean much. There is a sense that things don't really change, such that the underlying (if often inconspicuous) sense of the world is quite flat and without the sense that whatever one does can make any difference. This was illustrated in describing Claudia's flatness when Jackie ignored her interests, emotions, and bids for attention, leaving her with the sense that nothing that she does really matters, without the feeling of the vital interchange that occurs when others recognize you as a center of initiative and agency (Slavin, 2016).

Disorders of simultaneity: Posttraumatic fixation in developmental-historical time

The first pattern in which the past and present are blurred is the most extensively discussed in the classic analytic accounts, where the repeated but often unprocessed past eclipses the experience of the present. As

I described in Chapter 1, Freud's theories of neurosis formulated the effects of trauma in fixing unconscious motivation on overwhelming psychological situations from the past which have persisted into the present, unresolved. Instead, they are anticipated and frightening, as defensive efforts of different sorts get underway to avoid the imminent threat of repetition.

Freud, of course, found his first key to psychopathology in the trouble arising when the past has been so unbearable that it persists inexorably, overwhelming the present and blocking the novelty of the future. This is the classic post-traumatic condition of repetition, with its *excess of simultaneity over subsequency*. Ideally, the "present" is experienced as something separate from the past; in other words, the reality of "now" is implicitly distinguished from memory. *But the post-traumatic subject does not experience the trauma as something which has happened in the past but will not happen now.* Instead, she or he is caught in an endless loop in which two events far removed in ordinary time-space—one "past" and one "present"—are confounded, such that the unmanageable event is anticipated in any situation that evokes its specter in memory. Such processes are at the core of both symptoms and transferences: The symptom covers up the wounds of the past while repeating them, while the transference reveals them more openly, albeit out of the patient's awareness. Both formations render the present and past as simultaneous; the influence of history has both hypertrophied *and* dissociated, rather than integrated.

From this perspective, analytic work rescues the present and future from the problematic past, whatever form recovery takes. As many contemporary historical critics have said (especially those influenced by psychoanalysis), this predicament afflicts culture and politics as well as the intrapsychic world. (See, among others, Caruth, 1995; Faimberg, 1988; and LaCapra, 2001.) For example, during the same visit to Israel that I mentioned, many analytic colleagues suggested that both Israeli Jews and Palestinians were caught in post-traumatic thinking, with the Jews seeing the present through the template of the Holocaust and the Palestinians through the lens of their harsh treatment at the hands of the Israeli government.

Multi-directional influence in the temporal-historical field: "Afterwardsness"

Freud also showed how the present can reconfigure or even define the past, as current experience can actually change memory. Trauma recasts itself by recasting the present, just as memory recasts the past through its emerging templates and metaphors. Similarly, emerging events alter the perception of those that went before them. This is the famous *Nachträglichkeit*. Each person and each generation make their own version of the "historical" past,[1] just as each person's current situation and emerging development affect her "life story." Trauma is painfully effective in configuring and reconfiguring both the past and the present in its frightening image. Thus, it also colors and even obliterates the possibilities offered by the emerging future.[2]

This all suggests a further dynamic element of temporality that is more ordinary than the post-traumatic: that one's sense of the past is typically affected by the present. This is obvious at the global level, at which, say, a nation reshapes its account of its history in a way that gets many citizens thinking and feeling, changing their identifications. It's also at work on smaller scales: As you read this, what you read next will affect how you experience what you are reading right now. Then, this "now" will not be the same then as it is now, both because of its emergent "pastness" (it won't be a "now" anymore; it will be a "then") and because its meaning will change as it is assimilated to what else came before and after, including a long time ago. Current neuroscientific and psychological research on memory as well as on trauma confirms this, conceptualizing memory as a fluid, dynamic system affected by an array of environmental and physiological circumstances rather than a mechanism for veridical reproduction of past moments.

Fear of breakdown: It's actually happening now! (Even though I may not have noticed it then)

A second variation resembles the first, but differs in ways which have important clinical implications. Some patients experience the traumatic event as if it were actually happening in the present moment, rather than expecting it to happen.

Winnicott (1963) elaborated a particular, very valuable application of this understanding. In his paper, "Fear of Breakdown," he directed attention to a deep experience of helplessness and of temporal disorientation, since, from the patient's point of view, the terrible thing is going on *right now*. Here, the trauma feels like it is actually underway, now (rather than being anticipated). This thus involves a second sense of fear

212 Relationships in development

and additional helplessness, in that the fear of the impending trauma is coupled with the simultaneous experience of the recurrence of what is so frightening. Further, the entire psychic situation is terribly disorienting, as past, present, and future are confused, which exacerbates the potential for breakdown. For example, when I told a patient that I thought she was afraid of my dying after she got angry at me, just as her mother had in a tragic, traumatic coincidence that occurred when she was a young child, she forcefully corrected me: "No! You don't understand. You *are* dying!"

Such situations can be especially difficult as they often involve a history of dissociation in the face of the trauma, such that the overwhelming memory has, in some sense, never been rendered into memory. This may involve a complex relation to the events, in which the trauma itself was never actually admitted into experience, but instead was dissociated at the time at which it occurred, and is still being experienced, but in dissociated modes. The "breakdown" is current at the same time that it fills the mind-body with great turbulence. Winnicott (1974, pp. 104–105) summarized this:

> I have attempted to show that fear of breakdown can be a fear of a past event that has not yet been experienced. The need to experience it is equivalent to a need to remember in terms of the analysis of psychoneurotics . . . There are moments, according to my experience, when a patient needs to be told that the breakdown, a fear of which destroys his or her life, *has already been*. It is a fact that is carried round hidden away in the unconscious. The unconscious here is not exactly the repressed unconscious of psychoneurosis, nor is it the unconscious of Freud's formulation of the part of the psyche that is very close to neurophysiological functioning . . . In this special context the unconscious means that the ego integration is not able to encompass something. The ego is too immature to gather all the phenomena into the area of personal omnipotence.
>
> It must be asked here: Why does the patient go on being worried by this that belongs to the past? The answer must be that the original experience of primitive agony cannot get into the past tense unless the ego can first gather it into its own present time experience and into omnipotent control now (assuming the auxiliary ego-supporting function of the mother (analyst)).

> (Italics in original)

In these clinical situations, then, the overwhelming situation was never actually *experienced*, even as it was happening in a raw and compelling way. Winnicott stresses a dissociative dynamic, in which the overwhelming experience cannot be thought of *having occurred*, even as it is going on in the present. Rather than being retained as a memory, albeit in some unconscious form, it is both imminent and absent.

Subsequency and its vicissitudes: The unresponsive object and the vacuity of the future

I would like to focus now, however, on difficulties in the fabric of time itself. It isn't just that the future, like the present, cannot be different from the awful past, but that the future as a category of experience has hardly any dimensionality at all: *Temporality itself is collapsed, obscured, or absent, not only by the persistence of a terrible past, but by the mangling or deprivation of the possibility of an orderly flow of events in the meaningful emotional and interpersonal area.* This is of course not a matter of chronology, but rather a disorder of temporal sequentiality as a basic principle of the subjective sense of self.

This *form of living in time* links to a basic fault in lively intersubjectivity— a vacuum in the usual senses of self-coherence and agency, a deficit in "intentionality" in the field of relationships and emotions. Beyond ordinary hopelessness, a kind of undifferentiated sense of things and people may settle in; a feeling that things just don't change lies at the base of everyday experience. This seems to parallel the image of an infant whose parent ignores her interests, emotions, and bids for attention, leaving her with the sense that nothing that she does really matters, without the feeling of the vital interchange that occurs when others recognize you so as to offer a world in which what you care about matters and has an effect.

In evoking the images of Claudia and emotionally deprived infants in general, I mean to suggest, at least, that such experiences are often observable in patients with chronic histories of trauma and/or neglect. In some respects, these types of timelessness can be seen on quasi-representational repetitions of, on the one hand, the senses of endless, unpunctuated time and space so common in children whose needs for social interaction and basic care are not met. Alternatively, chaos and overwhelmingly confusing experiences that may well ensue when the outside world is not mediated by an attentive person who looks after the baby's states of mind, body, and social connectedness. This may be especially difficult when the family surround is unpredictable or assaultive, but even "ordinary" environments can be quite baffling and confusing to a child when no one makes any effort to help them make sense.

These unusual forms of temporality are often not so obvious in analyses. At times, what seems like depression may actually present a more encompassing sense that "things are just not moving forward," as one of my patients recently reported, which translated into a pervasive hopelessness that anything at all could make a difference. A sense of grim sameness may haunt the patient's life and/or the analytic hours. Some treatments unfold with a chronic sense of meaninglessness, boredom, and even desolation; at times, such feelings ensue even when the verbal narrative is apparently intriguing and coherent. The analyst may lose interest and even become sleepy, sometimes inexplicably; in many such situations, I have searched for an underlying dissociation, decisive detachment, and related forms of psychotic-like process, only to find instead a more diffuse and blank state, characterized by something like gray bleakness rather than primitive fantasy (cf. Green's (1973/1999) "blank (or white) psychosis," or Kristeva's (1989) "black sun").

In another variation, patients rely on an idealized image of the analyst and the analytic relationship. At first, this may seem like a promising basis for a developmentally progressive supportive attachment that can provide a basis for new experiences and internal structures. But as chronological time goes on, nothing deep happens. The idealized relationship is protected at great cost: It must be eternal, undisturbed by the realities of space, and perhaps most of all, time. (See Loewald, 1980, again.) Vacations, ends of the hour, knowledge of the analyst's family members, colleagues, interests, and even changes in the furniture in the consulting room are disturbing, as they pose threats to the matrix of timeless connection. Such fantasies may reflect idealizations of implicit memories of the lived experience of endless time with a depressed, largely unresponsive parent, stretching out like a desolate road without directional signs or even mile markers to punctuate the days where not very much lively or meaningful has happened. By idealizing, even enshrining this experience, those limited shreds of close time with that caregiver can be preserved and elevated. But they still disclose a world where even frustration is mostly absent, since the usual rhythms of gesture or need leading to response were obscure, if notable at all. There are many other variations on these themes, which may often be understood as compensations or defenses against terrible psychic calamities and the like.

Clinical illustration and implications: Samuel

This conceptualization of "disorders of subsequency" may be further elaborated with a clinical illustration. Samuel was the fourth of five children, born in quick succession to a depressed single mother, in a tough, poor Latino neighborhood in the United States. His mother was intermittently attentive, barely managing to keep up with everything. While with him, I often pictured a baby whose cries were dismissed or ignored. He recalled falling down the stairs in his apartment building as a toddler. No one came, and finally he crawled up the steps, knees scraped and arms bruised, only to be told what a clumsy kid he was. Even when he had a few minutes of his mother's time, she would drift off: Watching a baseball game on TV, he was elated when she shared his pleasure in a player from their home country. But after that enthusiastic moment, she left the room without any explanation at all. Similarly, his older siblings' harsh bullying was never acknowledged. When he was abused by the parish priest, all his mother could say was, "Father Patrick is a good man."

Even as my empathy with the awful things that happened to Samuel helped him, something else seemed fundamental: He really didn't have a sense of a future, in the sense of a *new present that could be different by virtue of not having happened yet*. This, then, was a deficit of *subsequency*, rather than of repetition: He didn't really expect that he could have an effect where it mattered most, so why should he feel that anything would ever change? All of this raised such essential questions as, "How can you love anyone if you don't live in the time of memory and hope? How can you be anywhere at all without someone who embodies, 'You are here with me being with you'?"

Dramatic disillusionment following the failure of idealizations

Samuel came for analysis in his late thirties in a depressive crisis precipitated by a profound disillusionment. He had done well enough at school to finish college and law school, having compensated for his deprivation by a precocious reliance on his disembodied intelligence. He had idealized his legal ambitions as a redeeming arena in which he could find some recognition and his wish to fight for justice, unconsciously hoping to find a way to redeem the grievances of his own childhood. But, as he found himself limited by the realities of his profession and his own character, he came to analysis as the last hope for something which would transform his life, especially as he had few meaningful personal relationships.

In the earliest phases of analysis, we saw some halting progress and an apparent alliance, although Samuel could become profoundly disorganized and anxious. However, in the face of vacations, ordinary empathic failures and other signs of my individuality, he feared that analysis was not the panacea that he hoped for, and he would become acutely detached, preoccupied, and/or terrified. He would succumb to a pervasive sense of helplessness, disillusionment, and despair that encompassed everything. Samuel had been surviving on whatever imaginary self-created dreams of a future he had been able to sustain. He managed by relying on a world of pseudo-hopeful objects and a false self in fantasized future. This took tremendous energy; it wasn't real temporality, just an idealization of the future as object that filled the vacuums with which he would otherwise be living.

Once the idealized objects failed him, he simply could not sustain these illusions. Now he was left with the unresponsive object, bereft of movement in time and space. When analysis, real, connected, and effective as it might be, fell short of transformative redemption, reality caved in on him toward increasing collapse. There could be no extension, all was lost, and there was nothing and no temporality. The possibility of something real that I might offer in understanding his past could not find a corresponding form in Samuel's subjectivity, and nightmares of devastated landscapes, frozen, flooding rivers, and terrifying attackers emerged relentlessly. Improving professional opportunities, which might have once seemed to be fulfillments, now felt like empty holes that would just lead to oblivion.

Analyst and patient living in two different worlds

Now, Samuel would sit with a frozen stillness, some combination of fear and despair. Even when I would say things that conveyed an understanding of his emotional pain, and the emptiness that came with it, he would continue to feel, as much as I understood, that I lived in a different world. At first, I believed that the differences were matters of class, of ethnicity, of the fact that I had a family and a career that seemed to be going well, and these of course mattered very much. But beyond this, we were basically different in how we inhabit the world of temporality, intentionality, and intersubjectivity. Our senses of what is involved in time were more different than I had initially realized.

The ordinary disruptions of the analytic matrix, even those as "minimal" as the ends of the hours, may be so difficult for some patients, since they signal the inexorable return of the unresponsive object, which after all is not an object at all but a dead space, without temporality or vitality. The patient is left with an awful dissonance between two worlds, one with a future and the expectation of meaning, and one with nothing there. This can have the additional effect of making him feel "crazy," in that he is living in a fundamentally inconsistent and unpredictable universe. This should not be mistaken for a pure regression, but is instead seen as "incoherence breakdown" set in motion by the progressive potentials of the analytic relationship. The protective dissociation may be falling apart.

It helped Samuel when I could let him know that I understood this: I was confident about "going-on-being," and he was not. This provided an experience of which he had been deprived in both the distant and recent past: I seemed to understand something about what it meant to be him that had not been otherwise appreciated. I want to stress that this was *emotionally and formally prior to whatever content we might otherwise be talking about.*

Understanding failures at the inner core helps the analyst think: Countertransference with the non-temporalizing object

Also, this kind of thinking helped with an unusual countertransference that emerges in this situation, by giving me a way to think about how I took on the futility and despair that was engrossing us. I like to feel that I am more or less prepared to empathize with and tolerate terrible feelings about what has happened to some of my patients, but it's been harder to find the words and inner pictures for a more pervasive feeling of quiet oblivion that just seems to go on and exist at some impenetrable level that sits below everything. Thinking about what really forms a moment of intersubjectivity in time and motion helps the analyst make herself available to the patient's inner world, however it is or is not presenting itself. This can help turn despair into a gesture that might not have existed as such yet. Moments of intentionality can take hold, and a bit of meaning is created.

The analyst's dedicated attention and the patient's senses of temporality, intentionality, and intersubjectivity: The value of the analyst's not coming to conclusions

The special role of the analyst's dedicated attention also takes on greater meaning here: Instead of coming to a conclusion, the analyst makes herself available to the patient's proto-gestures, in whatever form, and to be disposed to mark them, also in whatever way. Even simple responses, like shaking one's head or making complementary vocalizations (even the infamous "uh-huh"), can extend the patient who has lived with unresponsive objects into time that *leads somewhere*. Recognition sustains the time sense as it sustains intersubjectivity. Having a future and living intersubjectively go together.

This elaborates Winnicott's (1965b) idea of the "spontaneous gesture." Here, Winnicott saw how the baby would make a move into an undefined space, spontaneous inasmuch as it was unplanned, unselfconscious, and at its core, unintentional. The outcome is unanticipated by the baby, but when it finds a contingent response in the surround, the original gesture becomes something meaningful and intentional, even if this outcome was not anticipated by the baby. The mother's total immersion in the neonate's world (her "primary maternal preoccupation") is the precondition for this kind of development. Rebecca's mother made her attention and affective and motor responsiveness available in such as a way to "find herself" naturally grasping and wiggling her baby's toes. Similarly, the attentive analyst positions herself to make such natural moves by making herself available as a general object of intentionality and extension in whatever mode—emotional, nonverbal, explicitly interpretive, making practical arrangements, listening, other actions, and so on.

Overall, then, we can think of the whole field of mutual interaction as contributing to the development of the subject. This of course includes the handling of the patient's most intense and intolerable emotions. Some may think of this in terms of "projective identification." But much of this does not feel alienated or so emotionally intense; rather, it is part of the quotidian business of everyday analysis. Psychoanalysts may not be sufficiently interested in the gradual effects of the sustained analytic work, as we are, especially in our literature, most compelled by the high-intensity, dramatic, decisive moments.

Life in time begins when there is another person there, one who has kept the space open enough that there is room to move. When that other person takes up the move, does a little something with it, maybe not too much, then we learn, in a kind of afterwardness, how the gesture can become communication, and part of the extension of time. Sometimes patients are just putting things out there, not even really expecting or even hoping that the analyst can help, whether with excruciating feelings or by marking the moment in time and extending it. If the analyst can manage to do this, something creative may go on; if not, things can feel like they are going nowhere. It would be like having a musical instrument without any music to play. It's just noise: sometimes cacophony, sometimes like scraping and screeching, sometimes just white noise or dead silence.

A note on termination

We hope for mourning in termination, but it doesn't always happen. Attention to the development of temporality suggests another dimension of what really happens sometimes. Whether the patient has mourned the previously unrealized past, and/or developed a new quantum of temporality and intentionality, hence learning to be a subject, we can only hope that she leaves the analysis with a sense that the future is there, that she lives in a temporal world in which extension is possible, where time moves into something that is open even as history exerts its inevitable influence. Coming to live in unfolding time is a great benefit of many analyses.

Notes

1 Walter Benjamin (1968, p. 261)wrote: "History is the subject of a structure whose site is not homogeneous, empty time, but time filled by the presence of the now."
2 Halberstam (2005) and others, writing about "queer time," have suggested that some kinds of posttraumatic situations can open opportunities for getting beyond the constraining and exclusive structures that conventional cultures offer.

Chapter 16

Forms of vitality and other integrations

Daniel Stern's contribution to the psychoanalytic core[1]

From its beginnings, psychoanalysis has located itself in relation to the broadest array of sources, ranging from the fine arts, through politics, culture, and history, to the natural and social sciences. Shifts in scientific paradigms, especially in physics and neurobiology, have undercut some of the assumptions on which the original Freudian metapsychology was based, and philosophical and political currents, from hermeneutics and feminism, for example, have dislocated some of the original methodological certainties. Not surprisingly, Freud was explicit about the value of consilience with other fields, especially the natural and physical science. Two developmentalists tackling broader questions, Erikson and Winnicott, have been among the handful of Freud's most eloquent successors in this regard: As I have said, developmental thinking lends itself to such applications to basic questions, since it looks at whole persons and also at very young ones, who are often thought of as offering clues to the question of what is most fundamental in human motivation and organization.

Among contemporary psychoanalysts and child psychiatrists, Daniel Stern was in the forefront of this project. Most psychoanalysts think of him as a leading developmentalist, rather than as a cutting-edge metapsychologist. But when taken as a whole, Stern's work proposes a more general, clinically resonant, flexible, analytic model of mental life rooted in direct contact with lived experience, based in the actual body, emotions, and what is happening moment-to-moment both within and between minds. This all leads to lively meaning-making and meaning-processing, integrating life processes from basic levels as small as cells and neurotransmitters, through intermediate processes such as movement and emotions, to collective social and cultural forms such as language and the arts. His project draws directly on the contemporary scientific disciplines closest to

DOI: 10.4324/9781003607328-21

psychoanalysis: neuroscience, developmental and cognitive psychology, philosophy, and the arts.

Stern was one of the very first to look directly at infants and their caregivers; as an analyst, he applied what he saw to the core questions of psychoanalytic theory and clinical work. In an early, highly original paper, Stern (1971) used frame-by-frame analysis of films to study the different interaction patterns between a mother and each of her three-and-a-half-month-old twins; this was a breakthrough of both insight and research tactics. Stern saw a world of meaning and emotion in the split-second choreography of caregiving. Along with a handful of path-breaking colleagues like Sander, Brazelton, Bruner, Emde, Greenspan, Korner, and Trevarthen, he brought forward the world of meaning and emotion that was communicated and constructed through the nonverbal activity of bodies moving together, especially as sights, sounds, tastes, and touch came into play. For those of us reading this for the first time, a world that had seemed just beyond our conceptual grasp came into focus, as it now seemed possible to observe and describe something we had known was going on (not only between mothers and babies but in the formation of psychic structure and in psychoanalytic hours), but whose form we hadn't yet grasped. Such work anticipated and supported the turn to a more intersubjective view in psychoanalysis and in other fields (including neuroscience and infant developmental psychology as a whole). In addition, the split-screen, frame-by-frame analysis of infant-parent interaction inaugurated a research technique that is taken for granted today, applied to social interactions of all sorts, including psychoanalytic sessions, couples, and police interrogations, and augmented by advanced technologies that can isolate moments as brief as hundredths of a second. (Stern began with film.)

Stern's first book, *The First Relationship* (1977), remains the definitive report of the first phase of infant interaction research into the evocative details of how babies and their parents shape a web of increasingly complex and meaningful dialogue from the first moments of life onward. In *The Interpersonal World of the Infant* (1985), he took this original project further to question and revise an array of basic analytic assumptions, both about development and about how mental life gets constructed. Transforming psychoanalytic developmental theory as it did, this book was one of the most important psychoanalytic books of the 1980s. The underestimated *Diary of a Baby* (1990), an attempt to imagine how a baby would describe his experience if he could put it into words, remains the best account of the inner world of infants in either the academic or the popular literature, and was a Book of the Month Club alternate selection. *The Motherhood Constellation* (1995) is the authoritative psychodynamic synthesis of maternal psychology and infant-parent psychotherapy. Bold, brilliant, innovative, and directly useful, *The Present Moment in Psychotherapy and Everyday Life* (2004) synthesized cognitive neuroscience, phenomenological philosophy, and developmental research to propose a new theory of therapeutic action that has garnered wide interest. And the work of the Boston Change Process Study Group (2010), of which Stern was a principal, is widely regarded as one of the most important applications of developmental and neuroscientific research to psychodynamic and psychoanalytic clinical theory. Since its publication, the paper laying out the group's central argument (Stern et al., 1998) has been one of the most commonly cited psychoanalytic articles.

Stern's final book, *Forms of Vitality: Exploring Dynamic Experience in Psychology, the Arts, Psychotherapy, and Development* (2010), secured his position as one of our most original, integrative, and rigorous theorists. True to his psychoanalytic roots, Stern was concerned with what actually constitutes the "bedrock" of experience, both conscious and unconscious: He proposes that the concept of "dynamic vitality forms" provides the basis for a deep and comprehensive model that stays close to what actually goes on in people's minds, though not always in reflective awareness. Stern was always one of the most cosmopolitan analytic writers, and here he is at his most ambitious. He features the many sources that have inspired him to go beyond analysis in order to reconfigure it: his unique knowledge and feeling for babies applied in order to access core dimensions of adult experience and psychic structure; his affinity for continental European philosophy, especially phenomenology; his longtime engagement with the performing arts (especially dance); and the recent application of affective and cognitive neuroscience and other research to the study of psychological and psychoanalytic models of development.

Stern had a special feel for how these apparently divergent sources can be synthesized. He was a brilliant, nonlinear thinker, able to move gracefully from the arts to the sciences with no loss of rigor. (The sciences in which he was interested rely on nonlinear dynamic systems theories.) Although he keeps his analytic sources in the background, he is in a vigorous dialogue with them in what finally is an imaginative reconstruction of the dynamic and topographic models consistent with Freud's original purposes. (Stern was aleady a central contributor to today's rethinking of the genetic and developmental perspectives.) *Forms of Vitality* is a twenty-first-century fulfillment of Freud's seminal "project" of applying neuroscience to describe how the bodily systems link with the world to bring about mental life.

Stern (2010, p. 8) begins the book with an introduction to the concept of vitality forms, definitively declaring that "dynamic forms of vitality are the most fundamental forms of all felt experience when dealing with other humans in motion." These are basic gestalts integrating sensorimotor perception and self-awareness into elements of consciousness, moving through space and time as they occur in the mind. They are mental phenomena, not simply units of sensation, since they have already undergone transformation and integration into these higher-level formats; that is, they are "not directly based on physical nature" (2010, p. 30). Dedicated to getting directly at what really goes on in the mind, Stern explains that vitality forms link five dynamic qualities together: "movement, time, force, space, and intention/directionality [which] taken together give rise to the experience of vitality" (2010, p. 4). Elaborating this, Stern provides a list of thirty-three words that describe different vitality forms, reminding us that these are just a few of many; they include "exploding," "surging," "tentative," and "languorous" (2010, p. 8).

A graphic representation of some of these different forms is then presented (one that will be familiar to Stern's readers), with intensity as the vertical axis and time the horizontal: *Exploding*, for example, is represented by a steep, climbing curve representing a rapid increase in intensity; *fading* is a less steep, downward sloping line; and *pulsing*, of course, has a bumpy contour undulating with more or less regular patterns of rise and fall. These words and images show the extent to which Stern considers motion in time to be the crucial element of the vitality forms. (See Chapter 15; also Chapter 11.) I want to stress again that he is interested in the inner experience of movement, both one's own and that of others, rather than movement as an objective event. The dynamic vitality forms are a kind of mental energetic, bearing the subjective experience of motion, intensity, and force over time and space. An extended quotation from Stern's comment on this list captures his perspective:

> Most of the words are adverbs or adjectives. The items in it are not emotions. They are not motivational states. They are not pure

perceptions. They are not sensations in the strict sense, as they have no modality. They are not acts, as they have no goal state and no specific means. They fall in between the cracks—in movement—with a temporal contour, and a sense of aliveness, of going somewhere. They do not belong to any particular content. They are more form than content. They concern the "How," the manner, and the style, not the "What" or the "Why" . . . dynamic forms of vitality are the most fundamental of all felt experience when dealing with other humans in motion.

(Stern, 2010, p. 8)

Stern thus offers his most explicit move toward joining the extended and painstaking project of finding useful links between developmental, cognitive, and neuroscientific research and lived experience. His deliberate and experience-near approach avoids many of the pitfalls of this effort (which are especially familiar to analysts) and so offers substantial promise of clarifying some of our knottier theoretical and clinical confusions. For example, he reports recent research showing that some sensory neurons respond to multiple sensory inputs at the same time, buttressing the view that it is the properties common to the different sensory modalities (e.g., intensity, force, and temporality) that give rise to the core components of experience.

With regard to the centrality of movement, Stern offers an array of sources. Not surprisingly, recent research on mirror neurons in the motor cortex is prominent, but its implications are not exaggerated, and it is presented as one among many data sources pointing in the same direction. As I reviewed in Chapter 11, Vittorio Gallese (2009), one of the principal researchers in this area, focuses on the internal experience of movement, first the proprioceptive sense of feeling one's own motions, and then the correlated experience of observing those of others, which he describes as "embodied simulation," a kind of motor empathy of the sort one might feel when watching someone else stand up, which engenders a parallel sensation in the observer even if the observer remains seated. With a wider frame of reference, Colwyn Trevarthen (2009, pp. 508–509), one of the most respected and brilliant of all developmental researchers, echoes Stern's basic framework, writing that:

Sympathetic movements of human bodies, driven by spontaneous oscillations of energy in human brains, share *prospective intelligence*. . . Our gestures and expressions of face and voice communicate to other minds the anticipated and imagined events in a creative "flow" that feeds dreams and memories . . . and that animates conversation for practical cooperation, for friendship and teaching, as well as for psychotherapy.

Overall, then, Stern is interested in getting to the bottom of how people think, of what constitutes lived experience. His debt to the phenomenological philosophers who championed this approach, like Husserl, Merleau-Ponty, and Susanne Langer, is apparent throughout. In addition, the book includes a valuable chapter on the time-based arts—dance, music, film, and theater—especially works that call attention to the beauty and formal elegance of movements, gestures, and moments. Aesthetics have always been an inspiration for Stern, but here he is most extensive in presenting the artistic sources of his acute feeling for the choreography and cadence of infant-parent interactions, especially his knowledge of dance technique and its written language, Labanotation, and his personal relationships with the late Jerome Robbins, the eminent choreographer, and Robert Wilson, the avant-garde theater director.

Like his rich observations of infant–parent interactions and of psychotherapy, Stern's research on the details of consciousness relies on the concept of "present moments," which he studied through microanalysis of people's accounts of very brief time intervals (a few seconds to a few minutes). For example, one subject's interview about his brief breakfast took several hours to complete, as he recalled a flow of associations, bodily experiences, sights and sounds, memories, intentions, fantasies, images, and so on. (Analysts, of course, will not be surprised that every moment contains so much mental activity and meaning.)

In this book, as elsewhere, Stern (2010, pp. 135–136) applies this microanalytic approach to clinical practice. He suggests that analysts' attention should become more microscopic, since "vitality forms are realized at 'the local level,'" and since such small "units of meaning" as "gestures, expressions, spoken phrases, or the emergence of a thought usually last between 1 and 10 seconds." Attention to such moments of meaning may often provide more direct access to patients' experience of both present and past than larger-scale attention to verbal or narrative themes. He notes that memories are often organized around feelings and vitality forms, and that core intrapsychic structures are presented at the local level in homologous patterns of thought and social interaction in short time intervals. As in *The*

Present Moment, Stern follows the phenomenological view that the world can be seen in "a Grain of Sand" (William Blake, quoted in Stern, 2004).

Similarly, and consistent with his view that mental life is rooted in the world of dynamic interactions with objects, especially other people, Stern emphasizes that personal meanings are best articulated in the intersubjective context and that spontaneous "interpsychic" interactions offer the best chance for meaningful psychic change. Further recasting analytic concepts, he offers a convincing analysis of identification and empathy as substantially nonverbal processes mediated by basic human capacities to "share or interchange experience" (2010, p. 140) through interpersonal body-mind transactions. He brings this to life with a description of the "basic therapeutic methods" of "improvisation music therapy" (Wigram, quoted in Stern, 2010): "Mirroring, imitating and copying"; "matching"; "empathic improvisation"; "grounding, holding, and containing"; "dialoguing" (2010, p. 139). These specific descriptors are then embedded in terms more familiar to analysts, including object choice, emotional investment, excitation, and arousal. (Arousal is especially important in Stern's conception of vitality.)

Overall, then, Stern's conceptualizations of vitality forms lead him toward a thoroughgoing interest in the emergence of the intrapsychic through the intersubjective and interpersonal fields, and to value aliveness and spontaneity in facilitating therapeutic change. Here he has much in common with generations of analytic innovators, especially from the American Relational and British Independent Groups. He concludes the book with a report of a study by Heller and Haynal (1997), who found that while neither therapists nor experimental judges examining videotaped facial expressions of suicidal patients could predict whether they would make another attempt, the same judges could make significant predictions when studying the faces of the *treating therapists*: "Something in the patients' behavior must have evoked forms of vitality in the therapists that let them know (unconsciously). . . Perhaps I am taking a step too far. However, the overreach attests to the clinical possibilities that invite exploration when vitality forms are brought to the fore . . ." (Stern, 2010, p. 148).

This new approach to consciousness and psychic structure will of course evoke the question of how to conceptualize unconscious mental processes. Stern follows the contemporary move toward a broad approach to this problem, one that includes patterns of action and feeling that may not be noticed or reflected on, even when not repressed. While the best-known example of such unconscious knowledge may be the "implicit relational knowing" proposed by Stern and his colleagues in the Boston Change Process Study Group (2010; Lyons-Ruth & The Boston Change Process Study Group, 1998), he refers to other models as well, including the concepts of procedural knowledge (Clyman, 1991) and dissociation (Bromberg, 1998; Freud, 1938). Although this view of unconscious processes includes the network of relations with external objects and especially other people, it does not exclude the intrapersonal solipsistic forms organized by repression that may be more familiar to most analysts.

Throughout much of the book, complex resonances to basic issues in psychoanalytic theory are not far from view. Stern (2010, p. 6) quotes Einstein, who when "asked whether he thought in words or pictures . . . answered, 'Neither, I think in terms of forces and volumes moving in time and space.'" For Stern, this response illustrates "a physicist's language of 'dynamics,' the process of change or rapid evolution of forces in motion." Freud's models of the mind, of course, turned on psychophysical dynamics conceived as forces and further conceptualized as they emerge in mental space and time. Taken in this light, the entire conceptualization of vitality forms may be taken as a translation of the notion of an energic, dynamic "life instinct," updated in light of today's neurobiology. It is not hard to imagine that Freud would have welcomed such an effort to bring his models into line with developments in the same sciences with which he sought consilience for psychoanalysis when he first proposed it: physics, biology, and especially brain science, such as it was.

Indeed, it is here that Stern makes his radical departure from the conventional theories of instincts and mental topography. Along with Freud, he locates the body at the center of his model, but this body is not one that propels forces into the perceptual field to be organized into primitive pre-thoughts. Instead, it is an active player in the origin of mental life from its beginnings, in a psychosomatic matrix of coordinated sensation and movement that constitutes experience, such that experience is organized around the dynamics of force and energy. Thus, mental life is fundamentally constituted in activity and interaction with objects, both animate and inanimate. Stern's earlier interest in the social origins of mental life both anticipates and follows from this model, since other people are the most interesting of all objects, uniquely able to move and feel responsively so as to sustain, reflect, and amplify one's own movements and feelings to extend them into time and space. Stern's final book, *Forms of Vitality*, is thus a synthesis of Stern's interest in intersubjective models of early development, the basic sensorimotor origins of consciousness, and his more recent proposal for a basic intersubjective motivation system.

All of this may seem quite controversial, if not heretical, especially to those not immersed in the contemporary trends that Stern both spearheaded and relied on. However, psychoanalysis will reach its fullest potentials by adapting heartily and flexibly to the surrounding arts and sciences. Retaining core assumptions originating in scientific models over a century old violates both common sense and Freud's (1895) own intentions in his original "Project for a Scientific Psychology." Contemporary psychoanalysis holds the promise of integrating the broadest array of knowledge from the neurosciences, developmental and social psychology, and its own 100 years of thoughtful immersion in minds of all sorts, a legacy that is uniquely ours to claim. Daniel Stern's contribution to this project should not be underestimated.

Note

1 Portions of this chapter were originally written as a review of Daniel Stern's last book, *Forms of Vitality* (Seligman, 2011). It has been expanded here as a more general discussion of the implications of his applications of infancy research to psychoanalysis. Here, I've reviewed Stern's work as moving from his breakthrough observations of babies to a radical and substantial update of Freud's basic motivational models.

Part V

Awareness, confusion, and uncertainty

Nonlinear dynamics in everyday practice

The first of these chapters builds on my engagement with nonlinear dynamic systems (NLDS) theories, beginning with the broad observation that both analysts and patients tolerate a great deal of anxiety and uncertainty in their everyday practice. One of the most distinctive and appealing features of psychoanalytic thinking is its focus on mental processes that defy categorization and linear explanation. Analytic therapists find meaning in apparently disordered communication, and embrace the unexpected twists and turns that emerge from intimate attention to the ordinary complexities of everyday life. Like child care, psychoanalysis is frequently uncomfortable, unpredictable, and "messy." In agreeing to analytic work, the patient agrees to tolerate this kind of experience, believing that it will help her. In the context of the special analytic relationship and the analyst's dedication to paying attention to what is going on, the engagement with indeterminacy is a central element of what potentiates change. These are hallmarks of a psychoanalytic sensibility that spans various theoretical persuasions.

Drawing on a developmental perspective augmented by (NLDS) theories and a phenomenological perspective, I consider some of the similarities between maternal preoccupation and the analyst's reflective concentration as a change factor in the analytic field. Analysts' ability to refrain from action offers a pathway that implicitly disrupts established patterns of feeling and relating that have been repeated by patients, as part of closed systems that can now be opened up at a thoughtful and mutually regulated pace. This links to the integration of attachment theory, infancy interaction research, and Bionian theories of "thinking" that I offered in Chapters 13 and 14.

DOI: 10.4324/9781003607328-22

The first chapter in this section was written as part of a suite of papers exploring the possibilities of integrating insights from the traditional Freudian traditions into the emerging Relational turn. The different papers, by Steven Cooper, Ken Corbett, and Adrienne Harris, along with my contribution, converged in wondering whether the well-justified enthusiasm for interaction among Relationalists has led to some unnecessary devaluing of the opportunities offered by analysts' special aptitude for an open, quiet, focused mind in the midst of intense emotional and interpersonal activity.

The second of these chapters is an orientation to NLDS theory, making a case that it is a basic scientific framework to undergird contemporary analytic thinking—both clinical and conceptual, as well as linking analysis to current developments in an array of relevant sciences. This does not, however, fall into a positivist trap that "science" is the final arbiter of truth or epistemological value. The nonlinear systems approach embodies the same sensibilities as analysis: It emphasizes shifting patterns, complexity, flux and flow, the interplay of ambiguity and order, stability and instability, and the natural value of uncertainty and generative chaos. I have tried to trace such complex turns as I have presented case vignettes over the course of the book, offering a more direct clinical window into the same sensibility.

I hope that this chapter makes systems theory available in an intuitive, experience-near way, so as to offer a language and an imagery that underlie everyday clinical thinking. When taken that way, its metaphors and aesthetics can help analysts become more precise, spacious, and immediate about basic assumptions that tend to be taken for granted. As an overarching model for psychodynamic thinking, the nonlinear dynamic approaches offer a broad envelope that allows for links with other disciplines while preserving the psychoanalytic affinity for complexity and even mystery. In some ways, importing NLDS into analytic metapsychology extends the Ego Psychologists' ambition to build a comprehensive model that would unify analysis internally as well as with adjacent fields. The dynamic systems models, however, avoid much of the overly theory-driven rigidities of those earlier attempts.

The third chapter continues this broad integrative project through Louis Sander's bold syntheses of infant observation research, NLDS theories, and current biology, physics, and other "hard" sciences. He thus rethought the psychoanalytic approach to psychic structure, motivation, and therapeutic action, and updated Freud's project of linking psychoanalysis with scientific paradigms, but without reductionism, epistemological naiveté, or an implicit anti-psychological attitude. Sander emphasized the dynamic relationships between elements in systems. He drew parallels between the different levels of the functioning of natural systems, starting with the basic "biological" level of cells and organs and moving toward the psychic and interpersonal phenomena that are of greatest interest to psychoanalysts. He thus opened a window toward a broad and inclusive "relational metapsychology." Sander was among the very first psychoanalysts to look carefully at very early infant development, and he is revered by generations of developmentally oriented analysts and developmental researchers, upon whom he exerted a profound and lasting influence.

Chapter 17

Feeling puzzled while paying attention

The analytic mindset as an agent of therapeutic change

This chapter starts with a broad observation of what goes on in the analytic relationship, as it is actually lived every day: The analyst is usually paying careful attention to the patient. This fundamental fact is often overlooked, despite wide agreement about how important it is. Surprisingly, Relational analysts may be among those suffering from this "inattention to attention," especially as we have featured the analyst's interactive participation. More generally, while this perspective may seem obvious to many, it is often subordinated to the persistent pressures of analytic clinical work and institutional cultures. Many psychoanalytic metapsychologies and clinical presentations operate at some distance from a comprehensive account of the concrete, specific activities that constitute everyday practice.

A second part of the everyday activity of analyst and the patient is that both tolerate a great deal of anxiety and uncertainty. Psychoanalytic practice is frequently uncomfortable, unpredictable and "messy," as the systems theorists would say. Indeed, the patient agrees to tolerate this kind of experience, believing that it will help her change. In the context of the special analytic relationship and the analyst's dedication to paying attention to what is going on, the engagement with indeterminacy is a central element of what potentiates change.

The creative role of the analyst's chronic puzzlement: The central role of chaos in the analyst's experience

A puzzled and uncertain mood and mindset are familiar in most of our everyday work, often in the background. Although they are sometimes viewed as impediments, these feelings are actually at the core of analytic

DOI: 10.4324/9781003607328-23

progress. One source of this is the elusive and enigmatic nature of the mind, especially when viewed through the analytic prism. But if we look to the dynamic systems theories, we see uncertainty as a reflection of the transformational, chaotic nature of the analytic process: *The analyst may well be puzzled when in touch with potential change.*

Several factors may be involved in the frequency with which these states occur, varying within and across cases. Generally, unprocessed, intense, painful emotions are central and disorganizing. In addition, as such feelings are generally not explicit and thus often present in the analytic field in a barely perceptible form, they remain unacknowledged while nonetheless driving the situation. The analyst may find herself struggling with ideas and emotional states that seem sudden, unbidden, inarticulate, forbidden, out of sync, all while the patient may be more or less somewhere else. In addition, the ubiquity of projection, identification, and empathy make it difficult to sort out who is leading whom to feel what. Furthermore, that transference and countertransference do not always unfold synchronously makes all of this more puzzling, even when the analyst and patient are in communicative contact.

Another factor for the chronicity of the unsteady mood is that change in psychoanalysis is frequently incremental and uneven, becoming apparent only over extended periods of time. One sign of the importance of the ongoing immersion in uncertainty comes when colleagues in case consultation groups who hear one another's cases periodically are more aware of shifts than the therapists themselves. The presenters are just going along, but their colleagues see the emergence of something new. There is a tendency to get used to what is going on, to habituate, that may subtly occlude the analyst's vision. In systems terms, routine analytic work involves building more complex, inclusive structures over time, with all the ebbs and flows, fluxes and shifts that are involved in such changes.

Noting the gradual and routine dimension of analytic change points to what might be a misleading aspect of some Relational case reports, as I mentioned. By highlighting pivotal, even sensational, affectively charged, transformative enactments, these may distract attention from the central place of incremental, messy working through of indeterminacy in analysis. Some traditional analysts have taken this to mean that Relational analysts in general somehow do not have a subtle grasp of analytic process, but this is usually a partisan misunderstanding: There is no shortage of case reports in the classical analytic literature that focus on a moment where the analyst makes a crucial interpretation to the patient, or finds the clue to a stalemate in some newly understood bit of projective identification, rather than grasping the vague unfolding of something substantially less defined.[1]

There are a number of general problems that are in play here. Analysts tend to emphasize those moments that confirm or at least illustrate our own preferred concepts. There is something to be said for this approach: We follow our own theories in conducting treatments and will therefore be likely to create interactions that enact those theories and/or to read our interactions along such lines (Seligman, 2006). But this may also lead us to overlook some of the more quotidian aspects of how our everyday activity is more central to change than we have realized.

Affirming uncertainty as a source of dynamic change

Life along these fault lines is therefore basic to the everyday work life of the practicing analyst. When we are on our game, we react differently from most people going about their business: In ordinary situations, most of us may well be motivated to reduce uncertainty, to resolve matters, and to habituate to others and to our own experience, both with others and also intrapsychically. There may be some costs to this, but it is often valuable in getting things done and even in providing a sense of ongoing security.

But one of the distinctive properties of the analytic situation, oriented to change as it is, is that such resolutions are not sought in the short run, and probably not in the middle run, either. Psychoanalysis has a different "set point" with regard to anxiety and uncertainty. The interest in the internal world moves the focus away from the effect on actual objects and toward empty, open space and time. "Good analysts" may well be biased toward postponing resolution until the potentials for effective change have emerged: This is supported by openness and optimism that things can work out for the best, even in the face of suffering. This hopefulness is paradoxical, since it rests on an interest in that same suffering (Mitchell, 1993).

Diagnosis of whatever sort is often influential in affecting how much anxiety is tolerated: With more severe personality organizations, therapists are more likely to regulate or constrain anxiety and uncertainty, all things being equal. In addition, each analyst's clinical theoretical orientation influences how various moments are understood, negotiated, and so on. The analyst's persuasion affects where she directs her attention and how she organizes her experience, which may be even more important than her specific interventions over the course of the treatment. For example, contemporary Freudians are more likely to think in terms of structural conflict than about trauma (all things being equal). Inasmuch as structural formulations have a more formally definite quality than those about trauma, the analyst who thinks in such terms is more likely to have a less turbulent, anxious, and indeterminate frame in mind when she listens to the patient and to herself. Personality and generational differences will also be very much involved here, too.[2]

The sense of certainty, or at least of competence, that is offered by identifications with one or another analytic grouping and its ideas may buffer the analyst against her own anxiety in the face of the ubiquitous indeterminacy of analytic work, especially inasmuch as analysis is so personal, private, and dyad specific, so as to limit the possibilities for more "objective" markers of what to do next. This is not to say that some of us do not take too long to work toward resolving uncertainty. Still, I think that the more general problem is impatience with uncertainty, which then ends up closing down the analytic space. Here are some examples: premature interpretations, especially of the transference; premature reassurances; using frustration as a platform for technique that is actually there to help the analyst know how to behave; so-called "policies" about problematic aspects of the analytic relationship such as fees and missed appointments; and reflexive (*as opposed to reflective*) self-disclosure. We might say that such maneuvers are distractions, instead promoting inattention to the core anxieties and other difficult feelings.

Both new analysts and those who are too loyal to their own version of technique are especially prone to such pitfalls. Often, they are motivated by the analyst's wish to be someone who knows what is going on, or by a misreading of anxiety as a condition that ought to be resolved, which masks the analyst's intolerance of it. In service of these motivations, clinical theoretical positions are invoked, but this kind of thing often relies on idealization of theories and groups, along with the precocity that can go along with it. Analyst's specific concerns about professional identity are often in play: For example, some of us will do what we think is expected of us by certain colleagues, real and imagined, so that we feel a comforting identification with a group or set of ideas that we value, and thus less beleaguered by loneliness and fears of inferiority. Sometimes a fantasized competitive edge over certain real or imagined colleagues is sought. In addition to all this, of course, the countertransference pressures are very substantial.

I have recently been consulted by a quite sensitive therapist, Tim, who is beginning analytic training. The talk at his training program emphasizes transference, as is appropriate, but it sounds to me like this is applied overzealously. In any case, Tim feels pressured to talk to his patient about his own feelings, quite early in the treatment and early in hours, before anything real gets going with this quite detached woman. For example, when the analysand began an hour talking about her girlfriend wanting expensive gifts, Tim immediately said something about his fee. It seemed like Tim was talking to a virtual patient, not the one in the room. Berman (2004) noted the extent to which analysts in training take on their supervisors' biases unconsciously and may apply them indiscriminately, for a variety of motives other than their nonetheless earnest wishes to help their patients.

Our work in the supervision has been to get Tim to feel better about doing nothing, to focus on paying attention and being hopeful about that activity *in itself*, rather than letting his need for certainty or his ambition to satisfy his internalized teachers and colleagues drive him.[3] As we have developed our rapport, things have gotten freer and easier; the patient has come forward in new and very touching ways.

Tim has become more able to tolerate his own discomfort. In addition to the usual experiences of anxiety and uncertainty, his particular unease includes his worries about being a beginning analyst—feeling inferior, idealizing a new professional identity that he has not yet inhabited, fears of doing something wrong, and the like. Although we did not discuss most of these particular issues, my effort was to help create a framework in which Tim's anxieties could have some space for his own attention, rather than being acted upon and thus suppressed. The growing capacity for attention is itself a key factor in how he works differently with his patients, since his way of working against them had rendered him inattentive, even as he thought that he was trying to understand "the right things."

I mean here to illustrate how various anxieties and other internal and institutional realities keep us from engaging with some kinds of confusion as offering desirable potentials, rather than as something to be obviated. Indeterminacy, multiplicity, and unpredictability are all around us. Tolerating, describing, engaging, and even embracing it is at the core of the psychoanalytic aesthetic and therapeutic model; as a discipline, psychoanalysis is founded in the exploration of indeterminacy. Although this is sometimes acknowledged, a reorientation of our own analytic outlook may be in order—for many of us some of the time, and some of us most of the time. We cannot avoid being motivated by the same affinity for predictability and order that captures us and our analysands elsewhere. But it is actually quite liberating to be oriented that *it is our business to be puzzled about what is going on*, to be ready to get lost (Cooper 2010; Steven Cooper, personal communication, 2013).

To the extent that I'm able to do this, I find my own work more enjoyable. Days in the office are a little like traveling, going from town to town with a rough map, knowing that I'll find somewhere to stay most of the time but not knowing exactly where it will be, or whom you will meet or see along the way. The point is to stay interested, to stay aware, to pay attention, and not to get unbearably uncomfortable. When I leave the office on such days, I may feel quite tired, but, oddly, psychologically refreshed, since I've gone to some new places without worrying that I wouldn't get home at night. It might be hard to develop confidence in this kind of position without having had some considerable experience with analyses, but we might see our careers as works in progress toward this. We would do well to support and encourage our colleagues and students in developing and sustaining this pleasure, which is often an acquired one.

Attention as presence

This links directly to the central role of attention as a core analytic virtue. My working assumption these days is that if I pay attention and try to stay involved, that my patients and I are likely to find ourselves doing something useful. Again—this orientation serves as a set point. From this vantage point, paying attention while staying really involved is the immediate goal—an orienting position from which we are constantly derailed but to which we try to return. Freud (1912) referred to something like this in his call for the analyst to suspend everyday preoccupation and the effort to abstract from the analytic situation mindset to maintain "freely floating attention." Bion (1970) specified this in his advice to analysts that we listen "without memory or desire."

The most striking exemplars of this come from several analytic schools, which suggests that this virtue is mostly atheoretical. There are some analysts who just seem like they have emptied their minds of ordinary preoccupation when they listen, able to get in resonance with a new space of attention and possibility. Erik Erikson, Joseph Sandler, Betty Joseph, and of course Emmanuel Ghent come to mind. (See Jessica Benjamin's (2005) homage to Ghent.) These masters have reminded me of the Zen practitioners that I have seen in my occasional and casual encounters with those domains (Baba Ram Dass, Allen Ginsberg, and most notably a monk from Japan who seemed to remove the weight from the room at the San Francisco Zen Center when he walked in. I really could imagine that this guy might be one of those that needed to be held down by chains when he meditated.) Winnicott (1960a, p. 594) noted the link between the analyst's sensitivity and attention when he wrote:

> The analyst who is meeting the needs of a patient . . . needs to be aware of the sensitivity which develops in him or her in response to the patient's immaturity and dependence. This could be thought of as an extension of Freud's description of the analyst as being in a voluntary state of attentiveness.

One might be tempted to think of this kind of attention as exquisitely passive. But it is vital, creative, and energetic, if paradoxically so. An analyst working this way feels like she is doing something, even as it looks like nothing is happening. (I imagine that the analyst's brain would look very active on a functional magnetic resonance image–fMRI.) Dimen (2014, personal communication), blending Corbett's comments with Salamon's, wrote:

> In this reflective state, one "is capable of being in uncertainties, Mysteries, doubts without any irritable reaching after fact & reason," making it possible, desirable, and expectable to bear irresolution, or what you might call "unknowing." Queer theorist Gayle Salamon, commenting on Corbett, expands: unknowing is not not-knowing, but an active state: "to unknow is to revise or undo knowledge" one already has. It is not just to withhold judgment, to "mark . . . the limits of knowledge," but to "engage . . . something beyond that marking of limits." A path to the doing and undoing of the clinical hierarchy between analyst and patient, unknowing affirms that one is "no longer within the regime of knowledge, but . . . engaged in something else too."

The analyst's attention to her own attention

Analysis differs from meditative spiritual practice, of course. Ultimately, it is not oriented toward peace or even clarity, but to the freedom to be found in reality, with all its variations, frustrations, and anxieties. Along similar lines, the analyst cannot be expected to always maintain clear attention, nor to always be without memory or desire; that would be to deny that she is a person. To the extent that Freud's and Bion's prescriptions are useful, they must be understood as ideals, points of reference, with the expectation that these pure positions can never be maintained. Disruptions and distractions from this pure clarity are to be expected; indeed, these are the key touchpoints for the analyst's introspective attention to what is throwing her off, what is coming up, and how her own states of mind may be linked to the patient's. Thus, the interest in the analyst's attention is not only a guide to a way of thinking that is valuable in itself, but also a way of organizing and selecting all the varied, baffling, and often all too numerous array of feelings, images, impressions, perceptions, and the like that occur in the course of a session.

For example, when I find myself distracted with patients, I try to recall (as best as I can) when I became distracted, what was going on at that moment, and what has occupied my attention since then. To a greater extent than I had anticipated, doing this routinely has yielded both productive understandings and a return to relative equanimity and attention. For example, I have sometimes noticed that I have a "song in my head," which is (apparently uncannily) quite related to the patient's material, as when I heard the song "Won't Get Fooled Again," and realized I felt that my patient wasn't being entirely forthcoming about his drug abuse.

One patient recently told me how he was, uncharacteristically, starting to feel confused. Since we had been talking about his father's constant and harsh admonitions, he said that it seemed that his memories were under the floor that he was standing on, leaving him uncertain and empty. Meanwhile, I found myself thinking about the scene from the film *Inglourious Basterds* (Tarantino, 2009), in which a Paris theater explodes into flames, immolating both the top Nazi leaders and many of the American infiltration team and French resisters who arranged the fire. Apparently distracted, I realized that I had begun my "reverie" with an earlier scene in the film, one in which a Gestapo officer exposes and kills a Jewish family hiding under the floorboards of the home of a French farmer who is protecting them. The image of that horrible inferno consuming everyone within the confined theater allowed me to imagine something more about how utterly unmanageable the patient's childhood had been. I could then tell the patient that I wondered whether his memories were even more disturbing and chaotic than he imagined.

This approach also offers a basis for confidence in our abilities and for a confident explanation of some of the *apparent* impracticalities of psychoanalytic method to both patients and therapists in training. I frequently respond to patients who urgently (and sometimes skeptically) ask for specific, practical solutions by explaining that I believe that attending to the feelings and other aspects of what is going on in the midst of a difficult situation is likely to lead to a new and better outcome. This is not to rule out other options, of course, including offering a practical solution, inquiring about the urgency, explaining that the therapeutic process might take some time, describing my own response, offering a specific interpretation of the situation, and so on. Similarly, when supervisees ask, often a bit forlornly, "But what should I do?" after we have come to some understanding of a case, I will often advise that they "just pay attention" to what we have been talking about. (It's like batting in baseball. When you are at the plate, you don't actually plan how you will swing the bat and you definitely shouldn't think about the score: You just try to see the pitch, and if you see the ball well, you will be much more likely to hit it well, and score.)

Psychoanalyses as living systems: Indeterminacy and dynamic flux

Living systems depend on complex and evolving transformations, shifting in response to dynamic environmental conditions. Organizing matter, energy, and information, they relate their internal processes to one another and link them with their environments. To keep going, they have to be flexible, complex, and multi-leveled. (Think about the interplay of human systems from, say, nuclear DNA to the United Nations.) Thriving living systems adapt to their contexts, using and generating information of all sorts. They reorganize themselves and each other at different levels and one another at different levels, rather than simply responding to new events in easily predictable, linear ways. A good example of this is how development proceeds in a family: When the baby is born, everything shifts around—the parents' relationship changes, maybe the mom or the dad stops working, money concerns are different, the grandparents get involved, and all these shifts affect one another. Meanwhile, a baby and her parents influence one another in a wide array of ways to create and sustain the relationships that support the infant's physiological, anatomical, emotional, cognitive, and psychosocial development, all influenced by the cultural and economic contexts. And all of these are typically lived and known as part of a set of overall patterns—of experiences and practices— the identity, personality, the "who she is," of the developing child.

Adaptive systems are both continuous and change over time. When the child is ready for school, all sorts of things shift again: Neuromuscular and psychological systems have changed, the social world is very different, new family arrangements are possible and even required, with one shift again affecting the others: Mom goes back to work, nights are occupied with homework, and so on. This awareness of complexity, instability, *and* continuity within an evolving whole permeates your awareness once you get into thinking this way, even about "ordinary" things.

Psychoanalysts are often exquisitely oriented to the adaptive potentials of uncertainty and chaos, especially when tuned into clinical work. In analysis, there are recurrent rhythms, patterns, and processes; there are also crucial moments of reorganization, where the system shifts and new process "rules" seem to apply. Analysis is fluid, uncertain, shifting, unsteady, and so on: It's "messy"—but it has a form. We can't always say what is going on, but we are not operating without rhyme or reason. Blends of order in chaos are the bread and butter of the complexity theorists. Like the systems theorists, whether in international economics, child development, brain science, atomic physics, or mutual fund management, analysts see meaning and progressive potentials in "messiness."

From a convergent literary-philosophical perspective, Bachelard (1969/1984, pp. xvi–xvii) affirmed the emotional impact emerging from spontaneous creative imagination in the midst of apparently disordered processes:

> Very often, then, it is in the opposite of causality, that is, in reverberation . . . that we find the real measure of a poetic image . . . To say that the poetic image is independent of causality is to make a rather serious statement. But the causes cited by psychologists and psychoanalysts can never really explain the unexpected nature of the new image, any

more than they can explain the attraction it holds for a mind that is foreign to the process of its creation . . . The poet does not confer the past of his image upon me, and yet his image immediately takes root in me.

Nonlinearity, uncertainty, and contemporary analysis

Each analytic pair develops its unique patterns without much explicit planning. From the nonlinear systems perspective, that a process is chaotic does not at all imply that it is not organized. Human social life operates at various levels, in different forms and domains, which assemble into larger systems which have their own forms and qualities, and so on. This is true of each analysis: A brief interaction is part of the rhythm and meaning and feel of the hour as a gestalt, which in turn is part of the sense of the overall analysis, which has a more or less specific dimensionality and feeling at its various moments. How each of these "moments" is viewed may change as the overall process of the analysis evolves, even as they contribute to that evolution.

Thoughtful analysis destabilizes closed but strained systems, so as to amplify the prospects of transformation: This is a very ambitious goal. All our change processes—insight, recognition, new experience, development, developmental provision, and so on—can be understood as new inputs into previously closed systems. If the disequilibration process is properly calibrated, and if there are other tendencies in the system that can be mobilized and amplified, new patterns can emerge and take hold. However, if the disequilibrium is too extreme or too sudden, a system may disintegrate or reorganize in an even more rigid and costly way. Useful psychotherapies usually involve calibrated disequilibria, whether in timing analytic interpretations or when the CBT (cognitive behavioral therapy) therapist tries to set the next behavioral goal at the point at which the patient can tolerate the anxiety entailed in the new steps away from the prevailing symptoms. Some cases become problematic when there is a shocking challenge to an established system, which might then be sorted out with more or less salutary effects by the analyst and patient.

Change in analytic therapy is usually gradual. (This is not to say that there are no "breakthroughs," but these may not be as typical as our literature might lead us to believe.)[4] The nonlinear theorists have shown that systems need a lot of energy to overcome entrenched patterns, so it's not surprising that working at such unstable points goes on for a long time and takes a lot out of us. As things are shaken up, systems tend to resist change, and there may be long intervals when we are hovering between two or more different systems patterns—of affect, internal objects, transference/countertransference, defenses, and so on. Analysts' ability to maintain a thoughtful, attentive state of mind provides a working backdrop for this kind of subtle judgment under uncertain, anxious, and often emotionally turbulent conditions.

Nonlinear dynamic systems theories

The nonlinear dynamic systems models that have emerged from a variety of disciplines are useful in capturing all of this. Here's a brief list of what the nonlinear dynamic systems models stress: complexity; flux and flow; the intertwining of subtle *and* catastrophic change processes; nonlinearity; shifting patterns where things feel the same and yet different all at once; the possibility that small, even accidental, events can lead to large shifts in overall patterns. Developed decades ago, these models have substantial empirical, clinical, and mathematical support, but for our purposes, they are most important because they make our deep, complex, and often implicit working procedures become more available and communicable. Many natural and inanimate systems phenomena follow these patterns, too, as in the oft-cited example of the weather, as I elaborate on in Chapter 18.

The nonlinear dynamic systems theories, then, provide a broad background orientation that highlights the natural values of indeterminacy and dynamic flux and supports analysts' efforts to keep a flexible, free mindset that is resilient in the face of the pressures to foreclose uncertainty: Although they seem abstract at first, these theories capture central and general elements of what analysts and patients *actually do together*—feeling one another out amidst uncertainty, complexity, and continuous flux, all of which lead to both strain and moments of resolution, which then give way to further strain. They are broad, subtle, and complex enough to accommodate the variety and density of the back and forth of the analytic interaction—moment to moment, hour to hour, week by week (Boston Change Process Study Group, 2010; Coburn, 2013; Seligman, 2005; Thelen, 2005; among others). Overall, within this framework, ambiguity and puzzlement are seen as indicators of the transformative potentials of dynamic, two-person psychoanalytic systems: Nonlinear systems perspectives regard uncertainty and chaos as features of systems in flux that may tend to new and more adaptive patterns, even as they also present a risk of maladaptive rigidity. This orientation informs and justifies the analyst's bedrock commitment to attention, interest, and understanding. This dedication can itself facilitate change in inflexible, maladaptive patterns of behavior and experience, and provide the backdrop for other change processes to be effective.

Attention and relational-analytic practice

Psychoanalysis involves two people, at least one of whom usually is in emotional need and pain, is pretty worried and explicitly wants to be helped, and another who has agreed to try to be helpful: The requirements for us are quite different from those of the corollary spiritual practices. The Relational stance today must preserve the simultaneity of engagement, absorption, and attention, all organized in our knowledge of what is really involved in being needed and trying to help. This is of course very demanding. While this may appear obvious, there has been something of a misconception that the analyst's taking action or otherwise being affected by the analytic field is necessarily antagonistic to these commitments.

That we affirmatively admit that we are affected doesn't imply that we don't know what it means to be open, mindful, and observant. The emerging Relational approach is well served to stay rooted in the same commitment to attention and understanding that has appeared in some other analytic orientations, but with the more realistic idea that we have no choice but to be caught up in the patients' influence when we allow ourselves to be so permeable to it. In one sense, the analytic project always settles and unsettles around tensions between a basic awareness of unpredictability, incoherence, and even chaos, on one hand, and the need for something more organized and steady, which is shared by the analyst and patient and also experienced and managed by them in different and separate ways. The elaboration of these differences occurs in a variety of ways, including talk, enactments, private thoughts, and other individual and joint experiences of all sorts, mutual regulation and recognition, frustration and confusion, and on and on. Altogether, if things are going well, these lead toward a growing shared capacity to tolerate uncertainty and anxiety together, with more spaciousness and freedom.

Relational analysts have correctly argued that we understand best by getting involved and that we imagine otherwise at our patients' perils. The

"Relational revolution" offered the liberating destruction of the idealization of the analyst's mind as disembodied. Although this may seem tragic or even heretical for some of our more nostalgic colleagues, we have led the way in bringing reality to bear on the analytic myth. We should stay involved with what we know about the virtues of doing nothing when it supports our paying attention, since paying attention is not doing nothing at all. Our paradoxical interest in getting involved while valuing attention and inaction can be a steady but disequilibrating factor that can facilitate change if things are working out right.

In my final meeting with a very sensitive, classical analytic supervisor, I asked him what he thought about some contemporary theories, the new perspectives of which had been helpful with the traumatized patient whom I had been presenting. He confessed unashamedly that he hadn't read those papers, hadn't even really read Kohut. Then he added a comment worthy of repetition, "But if I've learned one thing in my forty years of analytic practice, it's that if two people get together, and one of them makes a commitment to understand the other, something good will happen" (Herbert Lehmann, personal communication, 1997).

Notes

1 There has been a misconception among critics of Relational analysis that the analyst's taking action or otherwise being affected by the analysand is antagonistic to these virtues: Some of these critics have confounded the "classical" habits of abstinence and nongratification of patients with a superior quality of attention and clarity. I don't believe that this is generally true, and certainly not necessarily so: Relational analysts have highlighted that a central skill for the contemporary analyst in all cases is to get involved while paying attention. Since these elements strain against one another, this can be both paradoxical and difficult. The contemporary relational approach is best rooted in the same commitment to attention and understanding that has appeared in "classical" analytic orientations, with the more realistic idea that there is no choice but to embody these virtues in the midst of our own transformation in the analytic field.

2 For example, differences about self-disclosure often turn on both doctrinal issues and personal characteristics. Some critics of Relational technique don't appreciate that the extent to which the Relational interest in self-disclosure reflects, among other things, a thoughtful (if implicit) way of titrating uncertainty, so as to avoid what some of our most rigid critics do too often—frustrating needs in the name of method rather than searching for the most useful

level of strain. On the other hand, Relational analysts sometimes resort to self-disclosure when a more observational inquiry might be more helpful; at times, these moves are efforts to diffuse anxiety that might be more usefully sustained.

3 Such identifications and ordinary narcissistic striving are often a driving force behind group ideals related to theoretical orientations or the groupthink related to the idealization of analysis as a method.

4 As I have said, many of the most memorable Relational case reports describe dramatic instances of such dissonances. This genre has broken through the reserve of many more conventional clinical papers and thus has been essential in elucidating the value of sorting out and living through breakdowns within the transference-countertransference. However, its appeal may obscure some of the less sensational, mundane everyday back and forth through which analytic dyads negotiate and recalibrate such uncertainties.

Chapter 18

Dynamic systems theories as a basic framework for psychoanalysis

Change processes in development
and therapeutic action

In the last chapter, I proposed that one of the most distinctive and appealing features of psychoanalysis is its focus on mental processes that defy categorization and linear explanation. Analysts tolerate uncertainty, find meaning in apparently disordered and even unruly communication, and embrace the unexpected twists and turns that emerge from intimate attention to the ordinary complexities of everyday life. Nonlinear dynamic systems theories and psychoanalysis share an interest in pattern, the waxing and waning of ambiguity and order, stability and instability over time, the natural value of uncertainty and generative chaos, and the like (Bak, 1996; Prigogine, 1996). Although nonlinear dynamic systems theory may appear esoteric and overly intricate, it can be approached in an intuitive, experience-near way so as to offer a language and imagery that captures many of the basic assumptions that underlie our everyday clinical thinking, interacting, and experiencing. Metaphors employed by systems theory can help us become more precise, spacious, and immediate about basic assumptions that we tend to take for granted, but leave implicit. (See, for example, Gladwell, 2000; Gleick, 1987; Kelso, 1995; Prigogine, 1996; Sardar & Abrams, 1998.)

Dynamic systems theories offer fundamental insights for understanding what goes on in psychoanalyses. Most contemporary analysts now think of analyst and analysand immersed in ongoing, complex patterns of mutual influence; whatever other assumptions they make, they agree that a psychoanalysis is a dyadic and dynamic system. Each psychoanalysis is organized into many of the same basic processes that define other systems. The systems theories provide a window into a new way to think about psychoanalytic metapsychology—a background theory that orients our basic working assumptions. One of the promising features of systems theory is

DOI: 10.4324/9781003607328-24

that it offers a link to the natural sciences without reducing psychological phenomena to a simpler level of explanation. Dynamic systems theories are neither linear nor reductionistic. They do not supplant the psychological-subjective level of analysis that is indispensable to our work and thus do not drag analysis away from its most imaginative virtues.[1]

Dynamic systems theory is fundamentally concerned with the relationships between different elements and processes within organizations of all sorts, whether living or inanimate, as they evolve over time and in their transactions with their larger environments. Emmanuel Ghent (1992, p. xx), whose visionary interest in contemporary music and Buddhism complemented his inspirational role in the emergence of Relational psychoanalysis, wrote:

> [T]he more profound significance of the term relational is that it stresses relation not only between and among external people and things, but also between and among internal personifications and representations. It stresses processes as against reified entities and the relations among processes . . . all the way along the continuum from the physical and physiological, through the neurobiological, ultimately the psychological, and, for some, even the spiritual.

Dynamic systems theories: A brief overview

Over the last several decades, scientists in varied fields have embraced a new mindset: Nonlinear dynamic systems theories study the overall processes by which both living and inanimate systems are ordered. These processes organize everyday phenomena such as the weather, ocean waves, shapes of coastlines, traffic patterns, consumer choices, and the emergence of children's motor abilities. They also shape such fundamental processes as cell respiration, cosmology, and particle physics.

Attention to the changing patterns of systems leads to a nonreductionistic, nonlinear approach, a complex and shifting terrain in which causes and effects cannot be easily parsed—in which effects and causes are, in fact, always being transformed into each other. Systems—organized in multiple levels—reorganize themselves and one another rather than respond in easily predictable, linear ways. Contexts decisively affect outcomes, and the whole is greater than the sum of its parts, because the relationships between the components of each system alter those components.

In Chapter 6, I imagined a young infant who is constitutionally hyper-sensitive to arousal, who would likely do better with a mother who can read his or her cues and approach softly and slowly to avoid disorganizing overstimulation, contrasting here with an intrusive mother, whose exuberance might well be overwhelming. The vulnerability to hyperarousal could not be usefully understood as a variable in itself, as it would be altered differently in each context. Over time, with the responsive mother, the baby might develop an enhanced capacity to organize, whereas with the intrusive mother, sensory input might be even harder to contain. Analyst–patient dyads function in a similar way: A talkative analyst may evoke a transference of being intruded on, and a quieter analyst may evoke the neglectful aspect of the same patient's childhood experience.

Transactional thinking is a key aspect of systems thinking

For a more elaborate illustration we can look to the weather, one of the most commonly cited examples of a nonlinear dynamic system. Weather, of course, reflects an array of physical conditions—temperature, humidity, air movement, the influence of land and ocean masses, and so on. In any given weather system, the various elements form a set of particular relationships, which then organize into larger systems. Moisture in the ocean rises to form clouds; clouds are moved by the wind; they interact with the land as they move over it. Each of these phenomena can be thought of as a subsystem of the overall weather system, and it is how such subsystems are ordered into the larger patterns that ultimately determines the weather in any particular place. You can't predict rain from cloud humidity unless you take many other factors into account, such as air temperature, land temperature, and air pressure. When there is little moisture in the clouds, none of it turns to rain, but with increased humidity and cold, much of it does. This relationship is not linear.

The systems theories back up basic working sensibilities that are taken for granted but are often left implicit. Analysts make decisions all the time on the basis of our implicit recognition that the effect of a single factor or intervention depends on the overall situation. The general principle is the same as for weather: Change in the overall pattern of the system is crucial. Most of the case illustrations throughout the book reflect complex, multi-directional transactions in which the therapists' responses to patients reflected both of their personalities, with mutual influence processes ensuing, such that what and then how these played out in our interactions, and all that followed, was affected by all this.

This kind of system shift is sometimes discussed in terms of *sensitive dependence on initial conditions*, or more popularly, tipping points, and is widely applied to such phenomena as changes in cultural fashion, urban demographics, and illness, as well as weather or traffic (Gladwell, 2000). The often-cited example of the butterfly in Beijing whose fluttering wings lead to a hurricane in Miami illustrates this concept. The butterfly's wings may provide just the extra microdose of air velocity to tip the weather pattern into the new storm system.

Systems routinely amplify tendencies that can shift them in one direction or another. This is illustrated in the example of the hypersensitive baby that I mentioned above, when the mother's caregiving sensitivity amplifies the infant's ability to manage stimulation, which in turn supports further growth in the baby. Adult analysts see similar synergies, as when a progressive development in an analysis leads to a patient becoming more comfortable with intimacy, which may in turn lead to the beginning of a new romantic relationship, providing further support for the analytic progress, and so on. Child therapists are especially sensitive to these kinds of shifts, as they are common, both when cases go well or badly.

In this as well as other ways, *dynamic systems are self-organizing.* Childhood developmental processes are often like this. Once new adaptive capacities and processes are set in motion, they can reinforce themselves as different parts of the system respond to each other and/or the changing environment. New capacities often arise around the same time, and as they emerge together, they coalesce into a new developmental stage: For example, infants late in the first year of life learn to walk, develop a focused attachment with one or two caregivers, and perhaps begin to develop new cognitive capacities. This may set the stage for (or for that matter, be precipitated by) a parent going back to work. Similar system shifts may occur in effective clinical interventions. I saw this when an eight-year-old patient got help with a previously unidentified learning disability, after which the self-doubt and impulsivity for which he had come to therapy improved dramatically along with his school performance. His peer relations also improved somewhat, and his teachers saw him more positively. No homunculus or ghost in the machine is required to direct system change (Kelso, 1995), because the tendency to reorganize is a property of adaptive systems. All these properties of systems have implications for the way in which we think about what makes for change in analyses, to which I turn shortly.

A note on method: Psychoanalysis and the sciences

The dynamic systems theories suggest a different kind of scientific orientation that is more consistent with how analysts and patients actually behave and think. This link thus differs from many others, which have had limited success in documenting psychoanalytic propositions or confirming psychoanalytic techniques by empirical testing. Complexity theory tells us that psychoanalysis is not unscientific just because it cannot be encompassed in a psychotherapy manual. Many of the quantitative sciences, such as physics, biology, and closer to home, psychology (especially developmental psychology), are drawing on the dynamic, complex models because the new approaches can accommodate them and their own linear approaches have been challenged by emerging data that have challenged some of their earlier assumptions and methods: Subatomic physics and medical genetics are among the most conspicuous examples. Such advances are supported by the powerful computing methods that can now be applied to such "big data," as are involved with arrays of variables whose relationships with one another change as the variables themselves change in quantity.

Complexity theories, then, buttress analysis against those who call it unscientific, such as insurers and overzealous advocates of the medical model, as well as those who condemn analysis from the point of view of a correspondence theory of empiricist verification, such as Grunbaum (1984). This is not to say that support from natural science should be our priority or criterion for confidence. Rather than looking to "science" as if it were somehow superior, I take the more hermeneutic approach of looking to various discourses that may be related to analysis, including philosophy, neuroscience, social-critical theory, and more. As I have said in discussing developmental research, there is much to be said for links with innovative scientific methods and findings are useful, but I am even more interested in a metaphorical, analogical, conceptual application.

Looking to dynamic systems theory can help us illuminate and organize what we do and how we talk to one another. Innovative psychoanalysts can now bring analytic thinking closer to the natural sciences without succumbing to positivist reductionism. Nonlinear systems theories offer a perspective that is supported by the sciences but harmonizes with a contemporary constructivist-intersubjectivist perspective that values the shifting and dynamic nature of the experience of reality and truth, especially in the analytic situation. From this point of view, we can consider the possibility that nonlinear dynamic systems theories provide a window toward a new metapsychology for psychoanalysis.[2]

Psychoanalysis as a nonlinear dynamic system

Analyses are dynamic, dyadic relationships, organized by the same dynamic processes as other systems. Each analysis is self-organizing and complex, developing in its own way without much explicit planning about how things should go. Indeed, one of the analyst's basic tasks, in the background though it may be, is to protect such key sources of security as coherence and stability over the complex evolutions and shifts of the analytic process. This is often taken for granted; it's just part of what we do, just like mothers with babies. (See Sandler, 1960, on "the Background of Safety," for a contemporary Freudian discussion.) Many of our crucial concepts, such as holding and containment, address this activity of the analyst. (See Slochower, 1996, for a Relational update of these object relations concepts.) Here again, systems theory calls our attention to important aspects of our everyday work, making them explicit and opening them to better definition. As it does this, it also suggests a pathway to link developmental thinking, especially about infant–parent relationships, with analytic therapeutic action, without relying on simple analogies between infancy and psychopathology, or analytic care and parent–child relationships.

Both parents and therapists make crucial choices under uncertain conditions, unable to predict what will happen next and able only to ascertain the effects of our interventions as they play out in the emerging context that they have, in part, created, and usually implicitly. Many, if not most cases present such ongoing "decision" points. When things go well enough, complex transactional processes in the two-person analytic system lead to a progressive change in the therapeutic process. These various "decisions" are not decisions in the conventional sense, but rather embedded in multiple inextricable processes, including analyst's and patient's personalities, pasts, and economic and cultural situations—both internalized and in the current surround. Analytic decision-making is inevitably an uncertain process, and its predictive potential is limited at best. Some of the harder-to-describe analytic skills such as tact, timing, and intuition rely on conscious and unconscious attention to the emerging patterns of the analytic system. That these different factors and their interrelations are hardly ever in full awareness adds to the overall sense of analytic work as puzzling in some basic way.

Complexity and the analytic sensibility

The dynamic systems languages capture "the feeling of what happens" (Damasio, 1999) in analyses. Although psychoanalysis may be intriguing to most who practice it and many who don't, our languages often fall short of encompassing the immediacy of the essential, everyday experiences that constitute our professional skill and overall identity. The dynamic systems models offer an articulate, scientific basis for the familiar feeling of not knowing what's going on, one that we must tolerate in order to be helpful.

Analysis is full of restless intricacies, ebbs and flows, novel moments amid repetition, with shifting spaces and forms, aligning and realigning in many psychological levels, shapes, and colorations, amidst mixes and matches of stabilities and instabilities, progressions and regressions, repetitions and novelties. Multiple ideas, fantasies, representations, relationship patterns, and feelings all merge, changing and transforming each other over time, and transforming their interrelations as well.

Inevitably, then, psychoanalysts must contend with a recurrent sense of dislocation and relocation. Each analysis is like the weather in a particular location: There are many possible shifts, but not an infinite number. And although you can never quite say when it will change, you know that it will. Our work, sedentary as it is, is frequently exhausting because we keep track, in our bodies as well as our minds, of many factors and their many relations to one another, and these are changing all the time. In a landmark study applying nonlinear dynamic systems theory to infants' motor development, Thelen and Smith (1994, p. xvi) characterized child development as "messy, fluid, and context sensitive." Complex systems theories support this view (whether at the level of cell biochemistry, brain architecture, or international economics). One of the important roles for analytic thinking in the mental health community, and in the culture at large, is to affirm that psychological life is like that too. We are committed to finding meaning in messiness (Boston Change Process Study Group, 2010; Tronick, 2005).

Flexibility as a virtue: Complex systems and situation-specificity in technique

Systems theories do not prescribe analytic technique. But they do illuminate how much questions of technique depend on the particular properties of the analytic system at any given moment; that is, they are situation-specific. Just as the specific patterns that regulate a weather system change with the particular conditions, so do clinical decisions. There are general patterns, and knowing them is very informative, but each analytic dyad is unique.

Constructivism, uncertainty, and complex systems

Werner Heisenberg transformed twentieth century physics, showing that measuring physical phenomena altered them, such that the measurements could not be exact. The brilliant physicist Richard Feynman (1963, p. 138) wrote that Heisenberg's "uncertainty principle 'protects' quantum physics." It may similarly protect psychoanalysis by keeping us in touch with the extent to which the ambiguity in our models reflects basic qualities of what we do and think about in our everyday work. The complex systems theories make clear that it is quite difficult to predict the future of complex systems, and that decisions are frequently, if not inevitably, made with inadequate information. Further, our interventions change the situation into which they are directed. All of this leads to a fuller realization that, although knowing what to do may be very important, to be able to do this with certainty is not in itself a realistic ambition, and being able to not know what to do is a crucial skill.

Complexity and nonlinear causality: Clinical implications

It may be reassuring in clinical work to think in terms of linear causality. But in spite of the impression of "scientific rigor" that it may leave, the linear approach can be quite constraining and does not correspond to the data of the analytic situation, either scientifically or metaphorically. Nevertheless, some analysts do proceed in a reductionistic manner. Too often in case conferences, for example, participants invoke a single factor in history, fantasy, or the like as if one superseded the other, rather than striving for language that captures the overall sense of what is going on in the patient's mind and in the analytic setting. Along similar lines, some analysts almost automatically translate patients' references to extra-analytic relationships as reflecting transferences or needs. To some extent, all this reflects an inevitable aspect of analytic cultures—the dynamics of the small groups in which therapists talk and the large groups in which our languages are shaped. But we should not underestimate the effect of the absence of a vivid, unifying language that allows for movement between different levels and points toward the larger patterns that hold them together. Analytic practice, in fact, demands that we tolerate uncertainty; if we cannot, or if our language discourages such tolerance, a narrow and constraining focus may limit the expansive potentials of the analytic setup. The following case example is illustrative.

Clinical illustration: Jared

Jared sought analysis for help with anxious inhibitions that kept him from pursuing professional and romantic goals. His apparently active and interested style was suffused with an underlying pattern of submissiveness, at first articulated in the hope that I would give him an explanation that would cure him. Passive defiance and a covert mistrust of authority, paradoxically, supported this defense and kept his conflictual self-negation stable.

During his adolescence, Jared had seen an analyst who kept relating his oscillating rebellions and depressions to his reactions to his parents' divorce when he was four. When Jared came into analysis with me, he was precociously identified with this reductionistic approach; he could engage in intellectual detective work aimed at finding the causes of his problems without actually letting himself becoming deeply involved with me or the analytic dynamic. This style both concealed and expressed the very apprehension and defiance that the interpretations were supposed to correct.

It would have been tempting to reduce Jared's style as a patient to his own character defenses, especially his tendency to intellectualize and oversimplify his own experience. But I suspect that the earlier analyst had relied too heavily on a linear explanation. Perhaps the reduction of Jared's current experience into linear, hierarchical causes supported something defensive—and deadening—in his personality. In addition, as this approach fell short of a more complex and authentic recognition of his experience, it confirmed Jared's fear that his complex and conflict-ridden experience would be overlooked as it had been after the divorce, when his parents dismissed his questions with unresponsive clichés. It felt like he was an outsider to the very process that was supposed to help him. He had compensated with an ambivalent idealizing pseudosubmission to his father which was now repeated in the analysis, hiding a competitive and often negative pseudosubmission now embodied in Jared's view that analysis would work by providing him with a single idea that would bring him relief. This complex set of transactions—between past and present, intrapsychic reality and external actuality, intra-analytic process and everyday life—is best captured by the systems theories.

Some might object that this vignette offers little that is new, but instead contrasts the previous analyst's crude overreliance on genetic interpretation with what "good analysts" would do. I don't disagree. But reductionism rears its head even in the best analyses, and a rough example such as this one illustrates, in the breach, how a complex systems approach can protect us, as Feynman said, against narrow readings of both structural and relationalist models. Systems theories explicate what good therapists already do. "Both-and" thinking is one of the best things about the psychoanalytic method, is more consistent with systems thinking than an "either-or" approach, and is more congenial to most patients.

Further, when translated into the clinical situation, the systems languages can often provide direct ways of speaking to patients. It can be useful to talk explicitly about the "costs and benefits" of patients' personality styles and how they are inflexible or repetitive. I sometimes talk with patients locked into transferences about how they are "unavailable to new information" (invoking here some of the ideas about transference and metacognition from Chapter 13). Such terms are in fact more ordinary for many patients than some of our customary, but sometimes more esoteric, terms for developmental narratives, impulses, defenses, and the like.

Psychopathology, therapeutic action, and systems change

Systems theories help us think about the therapeutic action of psychoanalysis. How do people get so stuck when they seem capable of "doing better?" How do analyses have such powerful effects, changing lifelong patterns even when many of the patient's life situations reinforce those patterns?

Psychopathology: Rigidity and equilibria in psychological systems

The problems that bring people to analytic therapy can be thought of as reflecting closed, inflexible systems.[3] The systems theorists describe how adaptive systems can grow by becoming more *inclusive*, restructuring so as to encompass new energy and information from the environment. But rather than including and responding to new information and novel opportunities, closed systems are repetitive, inflexible, and unable to adapt to changing environments. This inflexibility means that new experiences can hardly be taken as anything other than repetitions of the past or external representations of the inner world. Patterns are repeated, because few others are recognized as available.

Paradoxically, psychic fragility leads to rigid systems, even though such rigidity increases the possibility of breakdown. The self-amplifying properties of dynamic systems can go toward either more or less "costly" adaptations: Closed systems exclude possible new solutions that might work better. Psychological styles amplify certain ways of feeling and relating while dampening others, as when an anxious African-American child's protests in class lead the teacher to see him as a "bad boy" and exacerbate her race-driven caricature of him as "violent," which increases his push-back and confirms her problematic projection. This can play out in a wide array of life situations—professional trajectories, intimate relationships, and many more. This is a reformulation of Freud's repetition compulsion idea in terms of the self-organizing properties of systems.

Such thinking is implicit, indeed, in much analytic thinking, though it has not been common for it to be cast in systems language. Fairbairn's (1958, p. 380) description of the place of closed systems in the analytic patient's resistance to change, however, is a dramatic exception:

> I have now come to regard as *the greatest of all sources of resistance— viz. the maintenance of the patient's internal world as a closed system.* In terms of the theory of the mental constitution which I have proposed, the maintenance of such a closed system involves the perpetuation of the relationships between the various ego structures and their respective internal objects, as well as between one another; and, since the nature of these relationships is the ultimate source of both symptoms and deviations in character, *it becomes still another aim*

of psychoanalytic treatment to effect breaches of the closed system which constitutes the patient's inner world, and thus to make this world accessible to the influence of outer reality.

(Italics in original)

Louise

Many people take such maladaptive styles for granted even when those styles are quite costly to them, and the analyst who challenges these may be roundly rebuffed. It is well-known that many patients take offers of help or intimacy as threats, because of their memories and fantasies of mistreatment, abandonment, and guilt. One of my patients, Louise, had been sexually abused as a child. She had tremendous difficulty settling into treatment and responded suspiciously to anything that could be taken to confirm the view that I was actually exploiting her. When she found herself at a dinner party with a man who appeared kind and genuinely interested in her, she became anxious and dissociative and had to leave. Her experience of the past overrode her current situations, and she was unavailable to the new opportunities for adaptation that were available to her.

Attractor states and the resistance to change

Attractor states are the overall patterns that organize a system under particular conditions; they often look like a trough when graphed as equations. Once an attractor pattern is in place, a fair amount of new energy is required to disrupt and reorganize the situation. For instance, as long as most businesses use Windows software, Microsoft will dominate the corporate software market and will be able to resist even vigorous challenge. It will take a major shift in those patterns to change the entire situation, since there needs to be uniformity for commerce to proceed.

Patients sometimes respond with incredulity to the suggestion that talking about feelings can make a difference, because they have lived in a psychological and interpersonal world where emotional reflection is precluded. They "know" that communicating authentically will turn out badly or really doesn't matter anyway. I have sometimes found it useful to let patients know that I understand that they can't imagine that things could possibly be different, as when I told one patient that "you couldn't believe that you could get angry with me and that I would still care about you."

Disequilibration as a therapeutic force: Tact, timing, and shaking things up

On the other hand, when people seek analytic therapy, their systems are usually already under some strain; that is, they are moving toward disequilibrium. A life event—such as a personal loss, a relationship failure, a professional setback—may have challenged an established but overly rigid system. For example, many of us become concerned about not having met a life goal that has become a developmental imperative as we get older—say, marriage or professional advancement in our thirties or forties. Such dissonances between actual situations and the developmental pressures exemplify an emerging disequilibrium. Alternatively, an interpersonal relationship such as marriage, parenting, or a business partnership may become strained; here the disequilibrium is between the individual and the social environment. In both children and adults, shifts between developmental phases often work similarly; these can set the stage for new openings as well as constricting rigidities. A six-year-old girl starting first grade who can't pay attention without moving around may have been well-accommodated by both her parents and her kindergarten teacher, but when she is expected to sit in her seat in first grade, new difficulties ensue and the underlying difficulty may surface, if there is one.

Thinking in terms of disequilibria can help to formulate specific interventions. In early sessions, for example, it may help to explicitly describe such dissonances, saying something like, "You have come to feel that your usual styles don't work anymore as you become more concerned about making a place for yourself in your organization." Again, this is ordinary technique, but the systems theory model directly accounts for it.

Psychoanalysis creates, alters, and amplifies disequilibrations. All the change processes that we tend to consider—insight, recognition, new experience, development, developmental provision, and more—can be conceptualized as new inputs into previously closed systems. In general, such inputs can lead to, or amplify, the disruption of already established but maladaptive patterns and facilitate the emergence of more adaptive ones. If the disequilibration process is properly calibrated, and if there are other tendencies in the system that can be mobilized and amplified, new patterns can emerge and take hold. If the disequilibrium is too extreme or too sudden, however, a system may disintegrate, or it may reorganize in an even more rigid and costly way.

Working at such unstable points can be full of strain. Even as things are shaking up, systems resist change: They must have persisted because they have been adaptive, even if costly. Skilled therapists know this intuitively and titrate their interventions accordingly when anxieties and other affects are intense, but they do it mostly implicitly. Parents do much the same, much of the time. The attractor state theory's idea that change requires lots of energy offers an account of how working with patients (or children) at turbulent, transitional moments can be so tiring. Systems theory helps make the routine explicit.

Darrell

Here is an oversimplified but illustrative example. Darrell was a twenty-three-year-old gay man who had been chronically traumatized as a child. His mother had frequent, dramatic outbursts, sometimes angry, sometimes desperately sobbing. His parents' marriage was violent, and his father would break down and turn to the boy for solace, moaning about how humiliated his wife had made him feel. Darrell's father was sexually stimulating, walking around the house naked for hours and drying himself after showers while the boy was in the bathroom, tacitly encouraging him to watch. (Darrell suspected that his father was expressing his own homosexual feelings, of which he might have hardly been aware.) Before coming to therapy, Darrell had adapted to the painful inner residues of these experiences by maintaining a superficially charming exterior at work and in a series of similarly shallow social relationships, while organizing his sexual life in ritualized episodes with rigid role playing.

Darrell sought treatment as he was establishing a stable, intimate relationship with a man who was also habitually sexually submissive. He was concerned that his established sex patterns would threaten that newly valued arrangement, because they could not both play the same role. Over the first years of treatment, Darrell and I developed an enthusiastic rapport. Slowly and often with great anxiety, he could see how the past was both repeated and defended against in the present situation. He became more able to assert himself at work without losing his overall social skill, and his sexual life became less stereotypic and compelled.

We could say that Darrell entered therapy with his established coping system in disequilibrium from the strain of the new relationship, progressive though it was. The analytic work further disrupted this pattern through several different pathways—the collaborative therapeutic relationship, the insights linking the past with the characterological defense, the new experience of seeing that anxieties can be understood rather than just covered up and acted on, and so on. Meanwhile, the new potentials for less compelled, more flexible thinking and relating were freed and supported by the same factors that had caused the disequilibration in the first place—the new partner, the direct effects of the treatment, and the additional fact that Darrell's emerging versatility at the office was rewarded by his supervisors and colleagues.

Amplification and dampening as change processes: Synergies in therapeutic action

Darrell's therapy illustrates also how the opening of a closed system can alter the balance of personality trends—amplifying dormant potentials or subsystems that may be more flexible or open, while dampening or interrupting others that are more repetitive and closed off. Shifts in the internal world may be picked up in the external world, feed back into the internal world, and so on. Changes in one domain, such as work, can affect other areas, such as intimate relationships.

In a parallel account, infancy researchers have described the self-righting tendencies of early caregiving systems in which small adaptive inputs are amplified in positive feedback loops to make substantial differences (Sameroff & Emde, 1989; Seligman, 1994). For example, a mother recovering from a postpartum depression may find her baby eagerly responding to her emerging interest, bringing the mother rather quickly into a new, more delighted mode of interactive regulation. This may accelerate her recovery from the depression—with her mood improved, and with more positive internal representations reactivated and amplified, leading to more positive affect and pleasure in parenting. Things can change very quickly under such circumstances. In analysis, too, such tendencies exist: Analyzing transference may disrupt established characterological patterns that lead to new extra-analytic interpersonal relationships, which can in turn amplify the analysand's sense that there are alternatives to the established expectations. Sometimes the process may go in the opposite direction, with extra-analytic events leading the way.

Child therapists are especially familiar with such shifts, involved as they are with the life events, developmental pushes, and concrete interventions that shift the course of a child's development. There are special moments in child psychotherapies when the whole sense of the developmental system changes, when many different factors are changing at the same time—for instance, a child is doing better at school and making new friends; the parents are getting along better and their work life is improving. Further developments with Jared, the young man with the "linear analyst," illustrate this in more detail. (See Chapter 1.)

Jared

As Jared's analysis proceeded, he offered more details about how his anxious inhibitions were keeping him from pursuing desired professional and romantic goals. At work, for example, he was competent but cautious. In particular, his fear of being criticized or disappointed by older men in authority kept him from taking on tasks that were essential for success. In the course of his treatment, he became able to see how competitive he actually felt with these men, and that his imagined intimidation at their hands preserved an idealized image of his own father, who was a very successful man, but emotionally shallow and difficult in ways that Jared knew far better than his father's many admirers. As he became more forthright about his father's limitations, he could display his competence more openly and, eventually, became freer with his own aggression. Mixed with this aggression, the working relationship with me was cooperative and reflective even in the negative transference, which tended to amplify the effects of the insights about the past. In addition to being more active at work, Jared ended an ambivalent relationship with a woman, eventually marrying someone else to whom he was strongly attracted. These developments, in turn, enhanced the effects of the analysis.

But it was harder for Jared to stay with the longings that his father's departure had left unfulfilled, and in parallel, to acknowledge how emotionally dependent he was on the analysis. The birth of his first child had a dramatic effect on this particular equilibrium, by introducing new possibilities for a loving, intimate relationship with his daughter and, eventually, his wife. This amplified his awareness of how disappointed he was in his father. When he found himself so compelled by the new baby, he realized with more intensity and immediacy how wide the gap was between what he had longed for in childhood and what he had experienced. Reviewing these issues in analysis prior to the birth had potentiated his readiness to fall in love with his baby daughter, and this new love enhanced the analytic process. Jared also became more tolerant of the dependent transference.

Intertwined processes such as these are common in analytic work. But again, their form is in many respects better articulated by the nonlinear systems theories than by conventional psychoanalytic theory alone.

Optimal novelty: Balancing new experience and repetition

Both developmentalists and analysts emphasize the value of working at the right distance from the analysand's expectations, needs, and desires. The nonlinear systems theories capture this in their discussion of the "emergent properties" of systems. Kohut (1977) proposed that optimal frustration stimulated the development of new psychic structure—as opposed to not enough frustration, which would protect the current stasis, or too much frustration, which could lead to disintegration. Bacal (1985) expanded this idea into the concept of optimal responsiveness. Insight-oriented analysts have generally advised that interpretations stay close enough to the current defensive structure so as not to overwhelm it with previously warded-off ideas, but not so close as to leave those structures untouched.

These principles run parallel to a general developmental orientation. Vygotsky's (1962) conceptualization of the "zone of proximal development," an area distant enough from the current competences to present a challenge, but close enough to support the sense of new abilities and structures, applies to good analytic work. This corresponds to the general psychological finding that the best learning takes place under conditions of optimal novelty. These dynamics can often be observed microanalytically, whether infant–parent or patient–therapist interactions. (See Chapter 14 for the vignette in which Jamal Jr.'s father places the candy wrapper at just the point at which it was *previously* out of the baby's reach, and the infant strains and finally creeps over to grasp it.)

As in human developmental process, changes evolve over extended periods of time, emerging at certain moments and then receding as treatments settle into (and fall out of) new equilibria. Analytic therapists, even more than other psychotherapists, work to offer a relationship that is tailored to the patient, attending carefully to the particular emerging circumstances of every case, usually in substantial detail. Many of our technical decisions involve finding the right way to introduce something new into a more or less closed system while respecting its constraints—which, after all, define the range of meanings and points of contact with the patient.

Darrell

For example, Darrell (who had been traumatized by his mother's dramatic outbursts and his father's inappropriate sexual stimulation) became more anxious as his stereotypic sex life changed, and he recovered more memories and became angrier at his parents. He managed his anxiety in the sessions by praising the analytic process and me, enthusiastically letting me know how important the new insights were. Underlying this was a repetition of the earlier style of submissive and exhibitionistic management of his objects, as he pseudocompliantly treated me as someone to be entertained with his stories of new insights gained, but avoided the deeper feelings and recognition of how afraid he was that something would somehow go awry. Although I became aware of this enacted transference–countertransference pattern, I was initially restrained about challenging it, feeling that he needed to rely on it. In other words, this part of his system should not yet be disequilibrated. Instead, I tried to unobtrusively emphasize the possibility that he could talk more spontaneously about distressed feelings without having them fully packaged, rather than always coming up with a new idea.

Turning points, tipping points, breakthroughs: Sensitivity to initial conditions

We might say that much routine analytic work involves building more complex, inclusive structures over time. Change in psychoanalysis is incremental and uneven, and it often becomes apparent only over extended time periods. (Colleagues in case consultation groups who hear one another's cases every few months may be more likely to see shifts than the therapists themselves.) At the same time, though, there is a distinctive recognition of breakthroughs—those crucial, transformative moments where something leaps forward and the analysis shifts. Such moments are regarded by analysts of all theoretical perspectives as remarkable, but there is little explicit agreement about how they occur. They are often regarded by nonanalysts with suspicion and as among the least scientific of analytic phenomena. But the dynamic systems idea of sensitive dependence on initial conditions—the theory of tipping points—provides an account of how apparently circumscribed events in analyses can potentiate change processes that are fundamental to living systems. With this theory in mind, we need not think of ourselves as engaged in some esoteric and private process that cannot be communicated to those who have not been immersed in it.

The wide range of potential applications of the idea of tipping points (see Gladwell, 2000) is illustrated in an example from European history: the assassination of Archduke Ferdinand that sparked World War I. At a moment when the European geopolitical system was in flux, the shooting of the Archduke set in motion a process that radically transformed the politics of the twentieth century. Although something else might have started a war, that war might have turned out differently. It's possible to imagine that if there had been no incendiary event, things would have taken a quite different course.

Analysts of various persuasions all describe tipping points, albeit in different ways. Freud's (Breuer & Freud, 1895) earliest cases set the style for this trend: His one-time interpretations of the sexual origins of his patients' hysterical paralyses immediately relieved their symptoms. Since then, many drive-defense analysts have described crucial interpretations that change a patient's awareness and lead to dramatic symptom relief (e.g., Erikson, 1950/1963; Fraiberg et al., 1975). From a quite different conceptual perspective, Betty Joseph (2000), a leading contemporary Kleinian, describes an analysis in which she and the analysand went along in a rather pleasant and apparently productive mode, but with something somehow missing. Joseph describes the fundamental turning point in the treatment that came with her recognition that the patient's agreeableness was keeping real analytic work from going forward. In yet a different voice, Symington (1983), a Middle Group analyst, describes how particular "acts of freedom" by the analyst—spontaneous and unpremeditated gestures—can change the course of an analysis.

Such moments are commonly reported in the intersubjective-relational literature, too. Jody Davies (2004) describes a turning point when a previously contemptuous patient brings her a warm concoction that her own mother had offered her during childhood illnesses, during a week when Davies herself was quite under the weather. The Boston Change Process Study Group (2010) has stressed the importance of those "moments of meeting" that transform the patient's self-organization and promote the "dyadic expansion of consciousness" (Tronick et al., 1998, p. 290).

Such tipping points can also lead to quite painful and unfortunate outcomes, as in the following situation.

Janine and her infant

Sometimes a system tips in a less progressive direction. This is well-illustrated by the case of Janine, a twenty-year-old, single Salvadoran immigrant. Beaten as a child, she had a history of drug abuse and explosive outbursts. She had become HIV positive and eventually homeless. But when she became pregnant, she organized herself to make use of a number of interpersonal and bureaucratic supports, including a concerned aunt and a zealous community worker. Housing was found, and her infant-parent therapist felt that she might indeed become a competent and nurturant mother. Pregnancy amplified Janine's potentials for finding and sustaining protection and support; there was some hope that the various types of assistance could continue to support those potentials, and that the arrival of the infant would amplify them even further.

Because her HIV status was so complicated, the baby's birth took place at an elite university birth center, a hotel-like place set up to compete for high-end business. Janine felt quite out of place there; cultural and class differences led to tensions and even suspicions between her and the nursing staff; these tensions might well have been less pronounced at a community hospital. In this situation, she lost some of her emerging but fragile self-confidence and ability to regulate her self-protective, confrontational rough-edged reactivity, which in turn led her to be more likely to fulfill the staff's negative expectations.

In this emerging context, a particular event set a decisive process into motion, one that was to lead to the termination of Janine's parental rights: This was a tipping point. On one occasion, Janine reacted quite angrily to a nurse who seemed, at least to the therapist hearing the report, to be insensitive, provocative, and perhaps biased against immigrants, if not Latinas. Although Janine was very tender with her baby after birth, the child protective agency followed a hospital social worker's recommendation that the baby be removed. Traumatized, Janine became hopeless and angry. During the limited visitations with her son that took place over the following weeks, Janine was quite rough and unempathic. Eventually, parental rights were terminated. The events of the hospital stay amplified the destructive and isolative patterns in Janine's personality, which reflected both her history and the current situation.

Janine's efforts to become a competent parent involved a delicate dynamic, which was very sensitive to the relatively small inputs of the hospital environment and the specific interaction with the abrasive nurse. In this case, the dynamic processes that may seem so abstract when presented as theoretical generalities were manifested in the almost unbearably poignant pathways by which an everyday tragedy unfolded.

Parts and wholes: Fractals and self-similarity

The nonlinear dynamic systems theory conceptualization of "fractals" can illuminate two central analytic assumptions that are not usually articulated: that we can make inferences about a patient's psychology based on recurring features of an analysis, and that intervening in an analysis can have important effects outside it. We generalize and intervene confidently about transferences of dyadic object relations or impulse-defense patterns to describe and change character style and core conflicts. For example, when a patient expressed her worries about having gotten angry at a colleague, I was disposed to comment on her conflicts with me. Developmental phase theory relies on similar patterning. The Freudian conceptualization idea of "orality" extends the incorporative form of eating to configure the metaphoric image of the "digestion" of external relationships so as to transform them into internal objects that can be relied upon. Klein (1946) took this further to discuss the "expulsion" of bad objects by the infant.

In fractal theory, complexity theorists have elaborated something analogous. Fractal systems are characterized by the principle of self-similarity: that "any subsystem . . . is equivalent to the whole system" (Sardar & Abrams, 1998, p. 35). The contours of the edges of a snowflake—say, a protrusion with the three points at its tip—are reproduced in varying recursions so that the tip of each of those points itself has three points, and so on.

Other examples include how the fanning out of a tree or the airways in the lungs, reproduce the general form of the system. The basic form reiterates at the various levels of the system. Here, systems theories support one of our basic inferential procedures as following established scientific paradigms. We routinely treat the analytic situation as a fractal system: The analytic relationship is a fractal of the patient's overall dynamics; transference is a fractal of these; and so on. And we rely on the assumption that what happens in the analysis can lead to changes in the patient's overall way of living.

Streamlining complexity: Psychoanalysis as a not-so-complex system

Although I have so far concentrated on the elaborate complexity of the analytic dyad, there is another side to the story. Compared to most other relationships of similar intensity, the analytic relationship is a relatively controlled and contained system. Many of the usual irregularities and uncertainties of everyday life are screened out of the process, built as it is on a few well-defined dimensions: The timing, location, and duration are reliable and predictable; the contact is circumscribed; the basic exchange is defined in terms of a payment for time and professional asymmetries with regard to responsibility; and so on. Simplifying the system focuses attention on those features that are most salient for the analysis, such as feelings, fantasies, relationship patterns, and defenses.

This is the backdrop for what makes analyses work. Each analysis is just complex enough to bring key issues into play, but simple enough to avoid the myriad ways that those issues are obscured in ordinary social interactions. In those immensely complex arenas, psychological patterns can be easily kept away from awareness; instead, they are acted on and repeated as other persons and institutions actualize and confirm internal realities, blurring their roots in the analysand's particular personality.

Nonlinear dynamic systems theories and developmental psychodynamics: Toward a general psychoanalytic metaframework

Throughout its history, psychoanalysis has struggled with controversies about whether they all share common assumptions, and if so, what these might be (e.g., Wallerstein, 1991).

A model that emphasizes shifting patterns of complexity, patterns that organize and reorganize over time and at different levels of psychic process, may bring some clarity and some flexibility to this discussion. In addition, the move toward a complexity-based orientation would reflect the state of the theory. That is, the organized chaos in analytic theory could be seen as a reflection of the multifaceted nature of the analytic field of study, rather than as a symptom or an impediment—the view that our theories are not unified because our subject matter is complex.

The link with a robust developmental approach has been very productive in bringing the nonlinear dynamic systems theory model to the broader analytic field. Erikson's strong rereading of Freud's psychosexual-structural model anticipated the systems thinking, as well as the intersubjective approach, as Rebecca Shahmoon Shanok and I (1996) have argued.

Building a new theory around systems-organizing principles such as integration, regulation, and mutuality, Erikson opened analysis to an array of new ideas from developmental psychology and other social sciences, including history, anthropology, and political science.

As I wrote in Chapters 3 and 4, a developmental perspective pushes the psychoanalytic field toward embracing complexity (Sally Provence, personal communication, 1983); looking at children in their actual worlds calls upon us to see bigger and "thicker" pictures. (See Geertz, 1973, for an elaboration of his very useful idea of "thick description.") The infant research analyst-developmentalists were more explicit in bringing systems theory insights from developmental psychology and neuroscience to the analytic arena. Sander's (2002) work was especially innovative in this regard (see Chapter 19); recently, D. N. Stern (2010; see Chapter 16) and Schore (2012) are among the many who have advanced this project further. This synergized with the new intersubjective-relational model of a bidirectional two-person system, overdetermined by characteristics of both analysand and analyst, which also synergized with a hermeneutic-constructivist epistemology. A different set of dimensions of the analytic field were thus highlighted, among them ambiguity, complexity, epistemological uncertainty, multiperspectivism, and an interest in co-construction and evolving process. Although these qualities had not been ignored in the previous analytic literature, here they were treated as virtues rather than as regrettable impediments or (worse) the outcome of flawed thinking, poor technique, or the analyst's personal problems. Instead of being marginalized, these matters were now elevated to the center of clinical theorizing.

Psychoanalysis seeks to change the patterns that order and coordinate life processes, primarily at the level of psychological and interpersonal systems, often in very complex ways. Therefore, we must expect to find ourselves regularly at the boundary of order and chaos. This is the nature of systems, whether animate or inanimate, and in that context, our analytic experiences make a basic kind of sense.

Notes

1   Many analysts have contributed to the ongoing effort to apply nonlinear dynamic systems theories to analysis. Sander's (2002) efforts have been distinctive in their innovative and comprehensive scope. (See Chapter 19.) Among the many

others deserving mention are Bacal and Herzog (2003), Beebe and Lachmann (2002), Charles (2002), Coburn (2002), Galatzer-Levy (2002), Ghent (2002), Harris (2005), Miller (2004), Schore (1994), Shane and Coburn (2002), and Stolorow (1997).

2 Freud's (1895) "Project for a Scientific Psychology" offers surprising resonances to this.

3 Rose Gupta was helpful in clarifying this conceptualization.

Chapter 19

Searching for core principles

Louis Sander's synthesis of the biological, psychological, and relational factors and contemporary developmental psychodynamics

Louis Sander rethought the psychoanalytic approach to psychic structure, motivation, and therapeutic action, synthesizing infant observation research, nonlinear dynamic systems theories, and current biology, physics, and other "hard" sciences. From this vantage point, he opened a window for a broad and inclusive relational metapsychology of the highest order, updating Freud's project of linking psychoanalysis with scientific paradigms. Sander emphasized the dynamic relationships between elements in systems, innovating in both method and content. This chapter offers an account of Sander's broad and deep integration of psychoanalysis and developmental research.

Sander was one of the most ambitious, comprehensive, and profound psychoanalytic theorists of our time. Yet his work is not widely known outside the world of developmental psychoanalysis. Among those cognoscenti, Sander is still revered as an intellectual godfather: He began looking at babies with crystal clarity before any of the original crop of infant observers did, influenced them all, and has retained his status as their inspiration. Exploring the theoretical implications of those observations, he proposed an exceptionally bold synthesis that brought systems theories from physics, neuroscience, and general biology to bear on the basic questions of psychic structure and motivation.

Sander is one of our great, if sometimes neglected, innovators. One of the first analysts to have undertaken systematic infant observation research, his framework for early development stands as one of the essential conceptualizations in our field. His coordination of psychoanalysis with neuroscientific and biological theorizing may be the foremost effort to update Freud's project of rooting psychoanalysis in biology. Sander's work refuted those who justify outmoded pseudobiological concepts, such

DOI: 10.4324/9781003607328-25

as "the drives," by claiming that they preserve the role of the body and of biological science in psychoanalysis. Sander gives us access to modern biological meta-paradigms that are as timely for us today as the mechanistic paradigms of Helmholtz were for Freud and his contemporaries.

When I organized a symposium in homage to Sander, the admiration for Sander was extraordinary. The most distinguished colleagues were ready to drop everything to join. The innovative theorist Arnold Modell's reaction was typical: Caught between patients, he said, "Anything for Lou. Just tell me when to show up." Berry Brazelton (unsuccessfully) worked for weeks to rearrange his schedule, while Jessica Benjamin succeeded. Edward Tronick, one of the first to apply the concept of mutual regulation in developmental observation, produced an innovative contribution to the psychoanalytic theory of moods; he named his central observational concept after Sander. When the symposium was to be published, Stephen Mitchell went out of his way to add his own essay. Here, I consider why Sander is so revered.

Integrating developmental observation with theoretical imagination

Sander died in 2012, at the age of 94, while living on the same property in California's Napa County on which he spent his childhood. From there, he remained involved with the infant mental health and infancy research communities until shortly before his death, marking his seventh decade in those fields. He began to observe babies and their parents in the 1950s, when many clinicians still thought so little of the neonatal mind that they believed that newborns were blind. His methods were original and highly creative, as was his acute vision. For example, in one of his early experiments (Sander, 1988), he asked the mothers of some seven-day-old infants to wear a ski mask during nursing and found that these neonates reacted with dismay at a very specific moment in the feeding process. This finding showed not only that infants had already developed interpersonal expectancies, but also that neonates had an organized internal world, with a protorepresentational system that interacted with the mother's care with much more complexity than researchers in all the fields studying infants had yet imagined. Unlike much academic research, Sander's work was both ingenious and naturalistic. In a later experiment, described later in the chapter, he compared the effects of feeding on demand with scheduled feeding, in a pioneering study of the dynamic effects on psychic structure of these first caregiving transactions.

Sander's work also has immediate clinical and personal resonances. No less a psychoanalytic theorist than Jessica Benjamin (2002) has written movingly about the difference that Sander's findings would have made for her with her first baby, had the so-called experts understood what Sander was beginning to reveal. He discovered things that mattered, even as he proceeded as a careful developmental researcher. Sander brought a rare capacity to look at the essential aspects of what was there to be seen, at the same time that he could engage the deepest theoretical dimensions. In another paper, for example, he (2002) began by describing the group behavior of fireflies to show how the self-organizing properties of biological systems—at whatever level—are part of psychoanalytic clinical work.

Toward a grand theory: Biology, dynamic systems theories, and psychoanalytic metapsychology

Sander's work evolved from specific studies of particular moments of early infant development to implement what was always his core theoretical project: the integration of several domains of knowledge about life to find basic principles that apply to the psychoanalytic study of development and psychotherapy. With exceptional breadth, he drew on infant research, contemporary neuroscience, nonlinear dynamic systems theories, and theoretical biology, with its links to those broader systems theories.

The specifics of this evolution are worth elaborating. In Sander's (1988) paper on the effects of different feeding arrangements in the first weeks, he shows how the most concrete details of infant care give form to psychological structures, patterning along the same principles that regulate biological systems of increasing complexity, from cells to dyadic interpersonal systems. Sander thus construes psychic structure as a matter of the individual organism's capacity to coordinate its needs and interests with the environment's responses, all taking on particular rhythms in time and space, full of affect and growing layers of meaning. As with the best infant research, the quotidian details and the most abstract concerns come together, providing a theory of deep psychic structure that is rooted in what can be observed. Sander thus provided a conceptual basis drawn from close observation of infant care that anticipated more recent empirical findings about the effects of infant-parent relationships on later childhood and adulthood. (See Chapter 9.) As an inspiration and member of the Boston Change Process Study Group, Sander was in the forefront of the application of this method to clinical psychoanalysis, showing how the careful attention to the details of patient–therapist interaction yields access to the deeper levels of psychic life.

A quote from Sander's summary (2002, p. 24) of this research demonstrates how he moves from the most mundane moments of infant care to the core questions of contemporary psychoanalysis:

> My own (Sander, 1975) research encounter with biological systems . . . began with a 24-hour bassinet monitor. With pressure-sensitive pads on which newborn infants lay in their bassinets, it was possible to record heart rate, respiratory rate, and movement patterns continuously as they occurred in real time around the clock. The monitor also recorded automatically the timing of caregiver presence or absence at the cribside, infant crying, infant time in and timeout of the bassinet, and so forth . . .
>
> Over the first 10 days of life, for example, we compared samples of neonates fed on "infant-demand" with samples of neonates fed every four hours by the clock, regardless of their state. The usual rhythm of the neonate brings an awakening roughly every four hours around the clock. However, the demand-fed sample began to show the emergence, in days three or four, of one or two longer sleep periods per 24 hours . . . In other words, the sleep-awake rhythms of the neonates in the demand-fed sample now began to synchronize with the diurnal 24-hour day of the caregiver. Thus a quality of coherence in the new infant-caregiver system emerged as the timing of the caregivers' initiative to feed began to synchronize with the timing of the infants' rhythm of state and hunger . . .
>
> The neonates fed every four hours around the clock regardless of their state, however, showed no such change; they did not develop a new day-night organization but remained awake and crying as often and as long in the nightly 12 hours as in the daytime 12 hours.
>
> We can see here the role of infant "agency" to self-regulate in the resolution of the dynamic tension between neonate and caregiver by the joining of the directionality between them . . . The infant becomes a system within a larger system, held together by the capability of biorhythms to phase-shift, increase or decrease period length, moving in or out of synchrony with other rhythms.

Sander and the core questions

Abstract as it may sound, this theorizing goes directly to the compelling immediacy of what babies and mothers do with each other. On the side of parents who follow their infants' leads as soon and as much as reasonable, Sander shows that mutual regulation builds the capacity for self-regulation: Tough love doesn't make babies stronger. He saw that an infant is a person from the very beginning, and he used both ingenious empirical studies and innovative theorizing in making this plain. By understanding that feeling is the royal road to significance, Sander, always a fine scientist, went directly to where the affective and bodily action is. Sander developed a biopsychosocial, relational model of the development of psychic structure: From the moment of birth, if not before, personality forms as the infant actively engages the human environment. Following the pathways given by the properties of biological systems, she influences that environment as she is shaped by it, to create something uniquely human and simultaneously specific for each person. In Sander's hands, as in Freud's, Erikson's, and Winnicott's, the encounter between what is true of life in general and what is unique to each human life becomes the ground for psychoanalytic theorizing of the highest order.

Sander generated one of the first detailed models of the developmental phases that occur within the first three years of life, which served as a model for several that followed; he also led a developmental-longitudinal study, the data of which have only begun to be exploited. Sander's work animated the emerging generation of such analytic infant researchers as Stern, Brazelton, Greenspan, Beebe, and Emde and continues to inspire colleagues. Allan Schore (1999, personal communication) freely credits Sander's syntheses as a basic inspiration for his own path-breaking work.

Sander, science, and psychoanalytic theories

Sander's work is among the most visionary applications of contemporary natural scientific models to analysis, including such core concepts as organization, integration, activity, specificity, rhythmicity, and recognition. (In this way, he reflects the influence of the Ego Psychological project, updating, extending, and sophisticating it.) His creative applications of nonlinear dynamic systems models leads to an understanding of life processes as intrinsically motivated, as it were, to find stable but flexible forms, in constant exchange with their environments; these forms take specific shapes and rhythms as internal and external relationships organize the matter and energy that constitute them. For example, a contemporary biologist, Ingber (1998) coined the term *tensegrity* to describe how cell material is organized in flexible but stable forms that allow the organism to interact responsively with its surround without losing its own physical and functional identity. Neuroscientists, at a higher level of abstraction but with a similar sense of form, depict the developing organization of the brain as assemblies of neurons, associating to form functional systems that are organized coherently so as to give rise to such mental phenomena as memory, and ultimately, consciousness. (See, for example, Damasio, 1999; and Edelman & Tononi, 2000.) The physical, physiological, and psychological are conceived as interrelated and mutually influencing, as part of the unified systems of life process.

Sander's extraordinary move, then, was to apply these developments to the questions that most concern psychoanalysts and developmental psychologists: self-experience, recognition, meaning-making, interpersonal relations, how people change. Just as his theorizing about early caregiving interaction both guides and frees our approach to the ordinary details of what babies and mothers actually do, his elegant concepts provide the metapsychology for the emerging set of clinical concepts that locate the patient–analyst interaction as a dynamic system at the center of the change process. Sander's own work on psychotherapy process synergized with the growing emphasis on agency, reorganization, the multileveled recognition process, and meaning-making in specific individual-environment interactions.

Sander, then, demonstrates that today's science is on the side of contemporary innovations within psychoanalysis. This clarification should not be surprising, since innovations in various scientific disciplines might well be expected to influence one another. But psychoanalysis has not generally kept pace with new developments in biology, neuroscience, and physics, although the effort to seek such coherence was crucial for Freud: as Modell (2002, p. 55) noted in discussing Sander's work, "the biology that Freud employed is now 100 years out of date." Various factors have contributed to this lag. Translation and integration of nonanalytic findings have become more difficult, as knowledge in other fields has exploded. In addition, traditional analysts may have been deterred by the possibility that new biological and neuroscientific findings would undermine Freud's original metapsychological assumptions and, more broadly, challenge the overall idealization of him. Orthodox Freudians sometimes make a specious claim that it is drive theory that maintains the presence of the biological in psychoanalysis: For them, it is as if the only way that biology can be asserted into psychoanalysis is by affirming instinct theory.

Sander's synthesis opens the door to twenty-first-century science without reductionism of any kind. Dynamic systems theories are explicitly anti-reductionistic. Even as Sander invokes some of the same physical terms as Freud did, he reworks their implications in the light of new scientific models and current psychoanalytic theorizing. For example, Sander revises Freud's conception of how the organism's energy activates mental life: He supplants the now outmoded image of a pulsionlike biological force with a biochemically informed model of energy structured in biological systems through molecules organized through the hierarchies of biophysical structure, beginning with cells and ultimately into the level of personalities and interpersonal systems. Here, the social and the biological are understood as mutually constructed and hence inextricable, rather than as if there were some "bedrock" biological dimension that functioned as a "first cause." Once liberated from the Freudian orthodoxy, the term *energy* is free to work in an experience-near form. (We all know what it means to talk about our personal energy and colloquially link it to our biopsychosocial functioning, as in, "My energy is low today; I'm coming down with a flu," or "New York is a high-energy city.") In addition, there is nothing in Sander's orientation that closes it off to social and cultural factors. The inclusive spirit of his work parallels its method and its subject—the engaged integration of self-development with the fullest possible awareness of the world around.

Sander and the psychoanalytic orientations

Sander's overall interest in synthesis, both as a method and as a principle of the mind, reflects the influence of the grand Ego Psychological theorists so prominent during his beginning years as a psychoanalyst—Erik Erikson (1950/1963) and Hartmann, Kris, and Loewenstein (Hartmann, 1956). Sander (1994, personal communication) told me that his work was an effort to apply and refine the Eriksonian framework to infancy;

his emphasis on adaptation, mutual regulation, and the integration of the biological, individual, and social in the framework of everyday actuality thoroughly embodies Erikson's (1950/1963, 1959) approach. (See also Sander, 1995.) Many of today's Ego Psychologists have emphasized the gap between theory and clinical practice, but Sander remained committed to their dialogue. His priority has been, most of all, to keep the integrative discussion going and to keep it current.

In this, as in other ways, he has much in common with the contemporary American intersubjectivist-relationalists. Sander's emphasis on relationships places him squarely in line with the contemporary rejection of the primacy of endogenous and solipsistic motivations. He is basically interested in systems, and many of his specific concepts, such as recognition, agency, and "moments of meeting," directly parallel those of the Relationalists. He thus stands with the other infant researchers, whose work has both spearheaded and been buttressed by the overall relational innovation.

Sander may thus be understood as exploring the possibilities for a "relational metapsychology," rooted in dynamic systems theories and linked to current developments in the natural sciences: Implicitly, he broadened the connotations of the "relational" to include not just the relationships between people and their internal representations, but also the various kinds of relationships, ranging from the sociocultural through the microscopic chemical and physical ones, that organize life itself. He suggests that these various levels of relations are themselves interrelated, their patterns becoming essential to the texture and feeling of what it is to be human, at the levels of both the species and of each individual. (See the quote from Ghent, 1992, in Chapter 18.)

Sander declared that his own goal of integrating knowledge from different disciplines parallels one of the crucial tasks of life itself—"putting it together." Finally, Sander's project was to explore:

the spectrum of ways we experience our own self-awareness within our awareness of our surround. This [exploration] suggests a way the ever-developing brain and its experiential engagement with the world would be able to join in an organizing process, permitting the emergence of new levels of wholeness, as one's experience of recognition expanded, leading to an increasingly inclusive coherence in one's own self-organizing self, within one's awareness of what is going on in one's world around. It is just the facilitation of such an organizing process that is the goal of therapeutic process.

(2002, p. 39)

What concerns psychoanalysts is just as essentially "biological" as what happens at the cellular level, and therapeutic process is a form of life process. Biology is not destiny; it is another way to learn about who we are.

References

Ainsworth, M. (1978). *Patterns of attachment: A psychological study of the strange situation*. Mahwah, NJ: Lawrence Erlbaum Associates.

Althusser, L. (1971). *Essays on ideology*. London: Verso.

Alvarez, A. (1992). *Live company: Psychoanalytic psychotherapy with autistic, borderline, deprived and abused children*. New York: Routledge.

Alvarez, A. (2012). *The thinking heart: Three levels of psychoanalytic therapy with disturbed children*. New York: Routledge.

Ammaniti, M. and Trentini, C. (2009). How new knowledge about parenting reveals the neurobiological implications of intersubjectivity: A conceptual synthesis of recent research. *Psychoanalytic Dialogues, 19*, 537–555.

Arlow, J. A. (1986). Psychoanalysis and time. *Journal of the American Psychoanalytic Association, 34*, 507–528.

Aron, L. (1990). One-person and two-person psychologies and the method of psychoanalysis. *Psychoanalytic Psychology, 7*, 475–485.

Aron, L. (1996). *A meeting of minds: Mutuality in psychoanalysis*. Hillsdale, NJ: Analytic Press.

Aron, L. and Anderson, F. S. (1998). *Relational perspectives on the body*. Hillsdale, NJ: Analytic Press.

Aron, L. and Harris, A. (Eds.). (1993). *The legacy of Sandor Ferenczi*. Hillsdale, NJ: Analytic Press.

Aron, L. and Starr, K. (2013). *A psychotherapy for the people: Toward a progressive psychoanalysis*. New York: Routledge.

Atwood, G. E. and Stolorow, R. D. (1984). *Structures of subjectivity: Explorations in psychoanalytic phenomenology*. Hillsdale, NJ: Analytic Press.

Bacal, H. A. (1985). Optimal responsiveness and the therapeutic process. In A. Goldberg (Ed.), *Progress in self psychology* (Vol. 1, pp. 202–227). Hillsdale, NJ: Analytic Press.

Bacal, H. A. and Herzog, B. (2003). Specificity theory and optimal responsiveness: An outline. *Psychoanalytic Psychology, 20*, 635–648.

Bachelard, G. (1984). *The poetics of space*. Boston, MA: Beacon Press (original work published 1969).

Bak, P. (1996). *How nature works: The science of self-organized criticality*. New York: Copernicus Books.

Balint, M. (1968). *The basic fault: Therapeutic aspects of regression*. Evanston, IL: Northwestern University Press.

Baranger, M. and Baranger, W. (2008). The analytic situation as a dynamic field. *International Journal of Psychoanalysis, 89*, 795–826.

Bass, A. (2014). Three pleas for a measure of uncertainty, reverie, and private contemplation in the chaotic, interactive, nonlinear dynamic field of inter-personal/intersubjective relational psychoanalysis. *Psychoanalytic Dialogues, 24*, 663–675.

Bass, A. (2015). The dialogue of unconsciouses, mutual analysis and the uses of the self in contemporary relational psychoanalysis. *Psychoanalytic Dialogues, 25*, 2–17.

Bateman, A. and Fonagy, P. (2009). Randomized controlled trial of outpatient mentalization-based treatment versus structured clinical management for border-line personality disorder. *American Journal of Psychiatry, 166*, 1355–1364.

Beebe, B. (2004). Symposium on intersubjectivity in infant research and its implications for adult treatment, IV. Faces-in-relation: A case study. *Psychoanalytic Dialogues, 14*, 1–51.

Beebe, B., Cohen, P., Lachmann, F. and Yothers, D. (2017). *The mother-infant interaction picture book: Origins of attachment*. New York: Norton.

Beebe, B., Jaffe, J., Markese, S., Buck, K., Chen, H., Cohen, P., Bahrick, L., Andrews, H. and Feldstein, S. (2010). The origins of 12-month attachment: A microanalysis of 4-month mother-infant attachment. *Attachment and Human Development, 12*, 3–141.

Beebe, B., Knoblauch, S., Rustin, J. and Sorter, D. (2005). *Forms of inter-subjectivity in infant research and adult treatment*. New York: Other Press.

Beebe, B. and Lachmann, F. M. (1988). The contribution of mother-infant mutual influence to the origins of self- and object-representations. *Psychoanalytic Psychology, 5*, 305–337.

Beebe, B. and Lachmann, F. M. (2002). *Infant research and adult treatment*. Hillsdale, NJ: Analytic Press.

Beebe, B., Lachmann, F. M., Markese, S. and Bahrick, L. (2012a). On the origins of disorganized attachment and internal working models: Paper I. A dyadic systems approach. *Psychoanalytic Dialogues, 22*, 253–272.

Beebe, B., Lachmann, F. M., Markese, S., Buck, K. A., Bahrick, L. E., Chen, H. and Jaffe, J. (2012b). On the origins of disorganized attachment and internal working models: Paper II. An empirical microanalysis of 4-month mother-infant interaction. *Psychoanalytic Dialogues, 22*, 352–374.

Benjamin, J. (1988). *The bonds of love: Psychoanalysis, feminism and the problem of domination*. New York: Pantheon.

Benjamin, J. (1995). *Like subjects, love objects: Essays on recognition and sexual difference*. New Haven, CT: Yale University Press.

Benjamin, J. (2002). The rhythm of recognition: Comments on the work of Louis Sander. *Psychoanalytic Dialogues, 12*, 43–53.

Benjamin, J. (2004). Beyond doer and done to: An intersubjective view of thirdness. *Psychoanalytic Quarterly, 73*, 5–46.

Benjamin, J. (2005). From many into one: Attention, energy, and the containing of multitudes. *Psychoanalytic Dialogues, 15*, 185–202.

Benjamin, W. (1968). *Illuminations: Essays and reflections*. New York: Schocken Books.

Berman, E. (2004). *Impossible training: A relational view of psychoanalytic education*. Hillsdale, NJ: Analytic Press.

Bernheimer, C. and Kahane, C. (Eds.). (1990). *In Dora's case: Freud-hysteria-feminism*. New York: Columbia University Press.

Bick, E. (1968). Notes on infant observation in psycho-analytic training. *International Journal of Psychoanalysis, 49*, 558–566.

Bion, W. R. (1962). The psycho-analytic study of thinking. *International Journal of Psychoanalysis, 43*, 306–310.

Bion, W. R. (1965). *Transformations*. London: Maresfield.

Bion, W. R. (1967). Notes on memory and desire. *The Psychoanalytic Forum, 2*, 3.

Bion, W. R. (1970). *Attention and interpretation: A scientific approach to insight in psycho-analysis and groups*. London: Tavistock.

Black, M. J. (2003). Enactment: Analytic musings on energy, language, and personal growth. *Psychoanalytic Dialogues, 13*, 633–655.

Blanck, R. and Blanck, G. (1994). *Ego psychology: Theory and practice*. New York: Columbia University Press.

Bleger, J. (1967). Psycho-analysis of the psycho-analytic frame. *International Journal of Psychoanalysis, 48*, 511–519.

Bloom, H. (1997). *The anxiety of influence: A theory of poetry* (2nd ed.). New York: Oxford University Press.

Bollas, C. (1987). *The shadow of the object: Psychoanalysis of the unthought known*. London: Free Association Press.

Boston Change Process Study Group. (2010). *Change in psychotherapy: A unifying paradigm*. New York: W.W. Norton.

Bowlby, J. (1969). *Attachment and loss, vol. 1: Attachment*. New York: Basic Books.

Bowlby, J. (1973). *Attachment and loss, vol.2: Separation, anxiety and anger*. New York: Basic Books.

Bowlby, J. (1980). *Attachment and loss, vol. 3: Loss*. New York: Basic Books.

Bowlby, J. (1988). *A secure base: Parent-child attachment and healthy human development*. New York: Basic Books.

Brandt, K., Perry, B. D., Seligman, S. and Tronick, E. (Eds.). (2014). *Infant and early childhood mental health: Core concepts and clinical practice*. Washington, DC: American Psychiatric Publishing.

Brazelton, T. B. and Cramer, B. G. (1990). *The earliest relationship: Parents, infants and the drama of early attachment*. Reading, MA: Addison-Wesley.

Brazelton, T. B., Koslowski, B. and Main, M. (1974). The origins of reciprocity: The early mother-infant interaction. In M. Lewis and L. A. Rosenblum (Eds.), *The effect of the infant on its caregiver* (pp. 49–76). New York: John Wiley & Sons.

Breuer, J. and Freud, S. (1895). Studies on hysteria. In J. Strachey (Ed. and Trans.), *The standard edition of the complete psychological works of Sigmund Freud* (Vol. 2, pp. 1–309). London: Hogarth Press.

Britton, R. (1992). Keeping things in mind. In R. Anderson (Ed.), *Clinical lectures on Klein and Bion* (pp. 102–113). London: Routledge.

Britton, R. (1999). *Belief and imagination: Explorations in psychoanalysis*. London: Routledge.

Bromberg, P. M. (1998). *Standing in the spaces: Essays on clinical process, trauma, and dissociation*. Hillsdale, NJ: Analytic Press.

Bromberg, P. M. (2011). *The shadow of the tsunami and the growth of the relational mind*. New York: Routledge.

Caper, R. (1997). A mind of one's own. *International Journal of Psychoanalysis*, *78*, 265–278.

Carlton, L. and Shane, E. (2014). Gerald Edelman's project: How Gerald Edelman's theory of consciousness completes Darwin's theory of evolution and provides a basis for a brain-based psychoanalytic perspective. *Psychoanalytic Inquiry*, *34*, 847–863.

Caruth, C. (Ed.). (1995). *Trauma: Explorations in memory*. Baltimore, MD: Johns Hopkins University Press.

Charles, M. (2002). *Patterns: Essential building blocks of experience*. Hillsdale, NJ: Analytic Press.

Chodorow, N. (1978). *The reproduction of mothering: Psychoanalysis and the sociology of gender*. Berkeley, CA: University of California Press.

Chodorow, N. (1999). *The power of feelings: Personal meaning in psychoanalysis, gender, and culture*. New Haven, CT: Yale University Press.

Civitarese, G. (2005). Fire at the theatre: (Un)reality of/in the transference and interpretation. *International Journal of Psychoanalysis*, *86*, 1299–1316.

Civitarese, G. and Ferro, A. (2012). The secret of faces: Commentary on paper by Rachael Peltz. *Psychoanalytic Dialogues*, *22*, 296–304.

Clarkin, J. F., Yeomans, F. E. and Kernberg, O. F. (2006). *Psychotherapy for borderline conditions: Focusing on object relations*. Washington, DC: American Psychiatric Association.

Clyman, R. B. (1991). The procedural organization of emotions: A contribution from cognitive science to the theory of therapeutic action. *Journal of the American Psychoanalytic Association*, *39*, 349–382.

Coburn, W. J. (2002). A world of systems: The role of systemic patterns of experience in the therapeutic process. *Psychoanalytic Inquiry*, *22*, 655–677.

Coburn, W. J. (2013). *Psychoanalytic complexity: Attitudes that matter in psychoanalysis and psychotherapy*. London: Routledge.

Cooper, S. H. (2010). *A disturbance in the field: Essays in transference-countertransference engagement*. New York: Routledge.

Cooper, S. H. (2014). The things we carry: Finding/creating the object and the analyst's self-reflecting participation. *Psychoanalytic Dialogues*, *25*, 615–620.

Cooper, S. H., Corbett, K. and Seligman, S. (2014). Clinical reflection and ritual as forms of participation and interaction: Reply to Bass and Stern. *Psychoanalytic Dialogues*, *24*, 684–690.

Corbett, K. (2009). *Boyhoods: Rethinking masculinities*. New Haven, CT: Yale University Press.

Corbett, K. (2014). The analyst's private space: Spontaneity, ritual, psychotherapeutic action, and self-care. *Psychoanalytic Dialogues*, *25*, 637–647.

Cozolino, L. (2010). *The neuroscience of psychotherapy: Healing the social brain* (2nd ed.). New York: W.W. Norton.

Crane, T. (1995). Intentionality. In T. Honderich (Ed.), *The Oxford companion to philosophy* (pp. 412–413). Oxford: Oxford University Press.

Crastnopol, M. (2015). *Micro-trauma: A psychoanalytic understanding of cumulative psychic injury*. New York: Routledge.

Damasio, A. (1999). *The feeling of what happens: Body and emotion in the consciousness*. New York: Harcourt Brace and Company.

Darwin, C., Ekman, P. and Prodger P. (1998). *The expression of the emotions in man and animals* (3rd ed.). London: Harper Collins. (Original work published 1872)

Davies, J. M. (2004). Whose bad objects are we anyway? Repetition and our elusive love affair with evil. *Psychoanalytic Dialogues*, *14*, 711–732.

Davies, J. M. and Frawley, M. G. (1994). *Treating the adult survivor of childhood sexual abuse: A psychoanalytic perspective*. New York: Basic Books.

Davis, L. (2016). Eleven pleasures of translating. *New York Review of Books*, December 8. www.nybooks.com/articles/2016/12/08/eleven-pleasures-of-translating/

Demos, E. V. (1988). Affect and the development of the self: A new frontier. In A. Goldberg (Ed.), *Frontiers in self psychology: Progress in self psychology* (Vol. 3, pp. 27–54). Hillsdale, NJ: Analytic Press.

DiCorcia, J. A. and Tronick, E. (2011). Quotidian resilience: Exploring mechanisms that drive resilience from a perspective of everyday stress and coping. *Neuroscience & Biobehavioral Reviews*, *35*(7), 1593–1602.

Dimen, M. and Goldner, V. (1999). *Gender in psychoanalytic space: Between clinic and culture*. New York: Other Press.

Dollard, J. and Miller, N. E. (1950). *Personality and psychotherapy: An analysis in terms of learning, thinking, and culture*. New York: McGraw Hill.

Dozier, M., Stovall-McClough, K. C., and Albus, K. E. (2008). Attachment and psychopathology in adulthood. In J. Cassidy & P. R. Shaver (Eds.), *Handbook of attachment: Theory, research, and clinical applications* (2nd ed., pp. 718–744). The Guilford Press.

Dupont, J. (Ed.). (1995). *The clinical diary of Sándor Ferenczi* (M. Balint and N. Z. Jackson, Trans.). Cambridge MA: Harvard University Press.

Edelman, G. and Tononi, G. (2000). Reentry and the dynamic core: Neural correlates of conscious experience. In T. Metzinger (Ed.), *Neural correlates of consciousness: Empirical and conceptual questions* (pp. 139–151). Cambridge, MA: MIT Press.

Edgcumbe, R. and Burgner, M. (1972). Some problems in the conceptualization of early object relationships—Part I: The concepts of need satisfaction and need-satisfying relationships. *Psychoanalytic Study of the Child*, *27*, 283–314.

Ehrenberg, D. B. (1992). *The intimate edge: Extending the reach of psychoanalytic interaction*. New York: W. W. Norton.

Ekman, P. and Friesen, W. V. (1969). The repertoire of nonverbal behavior: Categories, origins, usage, and coding. *Semiotica*, *1*, 49–98.

Elise, D. (1997). Primary femininity, bisexuality and the female ego ideal: A re-examination of female developmental theory. *Psychoanalytic Quarterly*, *66*, 489–517.

Ellis, B. J., Boyce, W. T., Belsky, J., Bakermans-Kranenburg, M. J. and Van Ijzendoorn, M. H. (2011). Differential susceptibility to the environment: An evolutionary-neurodevelopmental theory. *Development and Psychopathology*, *23*, 7–28.

Emde, R. N. (1983). The prerepresentational self and its affective core. *Psychoanalytic Study of the Child*, *38*, 165–192.

Emde, R. N. (1988a). Development terminable and interminable: I. Innate and motivational factors from infancy. *International Journal of Psychoanalysis*, *69*, 23–42.

Emde, R. N. (1988b). Development terminable and interminable: II. Recent psychoanalytic theory and therapeutic considerations. *International Journal of Psychoanalysis*, *69*, 283–296.

Emde, R. N., Biringen, Z., Clyman, R. B. and Oppenheim, D. (1991). The moral self of infancy: Affective core and procedural knowledge. *Developmental Review*, *11*, 251–270.

Emde, R. N. and Sorce, J. E. (1983). The rewards of infancy: Emotional availability and maternal referencing. In J. D. Call, E. Galenson and R. Tyson (Eds.), *Frontiers of infant psychiatry* (Vol. 1, pp. 17–30). New York: Basic Books.

Erikson, E. H. (1958). *Young man Luther*. New York: W.W. Norton.

Erikson, E. H. (1959). *Identity and the life cycle*. New York: International Universities Press.

Erikson, E. H. (1963). *Childhood and society*. New York: W.W. Norton. (Original work published 1950)

Erikson, E. H. (1964). *Insight and responsibility: Lectures on the ethical implications of psychoanalytic insight*. New York: W.W. Norton.

Erikson, E. H. (1968). *Identity: Youth and crisis*. New York: W.W. Norton.

Erikson, E. H. (1969). *Gandhi's truth*. New York: W.W. Norton.

Faimberg, H. (1988). The telescoping of generations: Genealogy of certain identifications. *Contemporary Psychoanalysis*, *24*, 99–117.

Fairbairn, W. R. D. (1952). *An object relations theory of personality*. New York: Basic Books.

Fairbairn, W. R. D. (1958). On the nature and aims of psychoanalytical treatment. *International Journal of Psychoanalysis*, *39*, 374–385.

Fast, I. (1985). *Event theory: A Piaget-Freud integration*. Hillsdale, NJ: Lawrence Erlbaum Associates.

Ferenczi, S. (1949a). Notes and fragments (1930–32). *International Journal of Psychoanalysis*, *30*, 231–242.

Ferenczi, S. (1949b). Confusion of tongues between the adults and the child (The language of tenderness and of passion). *International Journal of Psychoanalysis*, *30*, 225–230.

Ferro, A. (2002). *In the analyst's consulting room*. London: Routledge.

Feynman, R. P. (1963). *Six easy pieces*. Cambridge, MA: Perseus Books.

Fonagy, P. (2001). *Attachment theory and psychoanalysis*. New York: The Other Press.

Fonagy, P. and Bateman, A. (2008). Mentalization-based treatment of borderline personality disorder. In E. L. Jurist, A. Slade and S. Bergner (Eds.), *Mind to mind: Infant research, neuroscience and psychoanalysis* (pp. 139–165). New York: The Other Press.

Fonagy, P. and Target, M. (1996). Playing with reality: I. Theory of mind and the normal development of psychic reality. *International Journal of Psychoanalysis*, *77*, 217–234.

Fonagy, P., Gergely, G., Jurist, E. and Target, M. (2002). *Affect regulation, mentalization and the development of the self*. New York: The Other Press.

Fonagy, P., Gergely, G. and Target, M. (2008). Psychoanalytic constructs and attachment theory and research. In J. Cassidy and P. R. Shaver (Eds.), *Handbook of attachment: Theory, research, and clinical applications* (2nd ed., pp. 783–810). New York: Guilford Press.

Fonagy, P., Steele, M., Steele, H., Leigh, T., Kennedy, R., Mattoon, G. and Target, M. (1995). Attachment, the reflective self, and borderline states: The predictive specificity of the Adult Attachment Interview and pathological emotional development. In S. Goldberg, R. Muir and J. Kerr (Eds.), *Attachment theory: Social, developmental and clinical perspectives* (pp. 233–277). Hillsdale, NJ: Analytic Press.

Fosha, D. (2000). *The transforming power of affect: A model of accelerated change*. New York: Basic Books.

Foucault, M. (1978). *The history of sexuality, vol. 1: An introduction*. New York: Vintage.

Fraiberg, S. (1982). Pathological defenses in infancy. *Psychoanalytic Quarterly*, *51*, 612–635.

Fraiberg, S. (Ed.) (1980). *Clinical studies in infant mental health: The first year of life*. New York: Basic Books.

Fraiberg, S., Adelson, E. and Shapiro, V. (1975). Ghosts in the nursery: A psychoanalytic approach to the problem of impaired infant-mother relationships. *Journal of the American Academy of Child Psychiatry*, *14*, 387–422.

Freud, A. (1936). *The ego and the mechanisms of defense*. New York: International Universities Press.

Freud, A. (1963). The concept of developmental lines. *Psychoanalytic Study of the Child*, *18*, 245–265.

Freud, A. (1965). *Normality and pathology in childhood: Assessments of development*. Philadelphia, PA: University of Pennsylvania Press.

Freud, A. and Burlingham, D. T. (1943). *War and children*. New York: Medical War Books.

Freud, S. (1895). Project for a scientific psychology. In J. Strachey (Ed. and Trans.), *The standard edition of the complete psychological works of Sigmund Freud* (Vol. 1, pp. 283–294). London: Hogarth Press.

Freud, S. (1905a). Fragment of an analysis of a case of hysteria. In J. Strachey (Ed. and Trans.), *The standard edition of the complete psychological works of Sigmund Freud* (Vol. 7, pp. 1–222). London: Hogarth Press.

Freud, S. (1905b). Three essays on the theory of sexuality. In J. Strachey (Ed. and Trans.), *The standard edition of the complete psychological works of Sigmund Freud* (Vol. 7, pp. 225–245). London: Hogarth Press.

Freud, S. (1909). Analysis of a phobia in a five-year-old boy. In J. Strachey (Ed. and Trans.), *The standard edition of the complete psychological works of Sigmund Freud* (Vol. 10, pp. 1–149). London: Hogarth Press.

Freud, S. (1911). Formulations regarding the two principles of mental functioning. In J. Strachey (Ed. and Trans.), *The standard edition of the complete psychological works of Sigmund Freud* (Vol. 12, pp. 213–226). London: Hogarth Press.

Freud, S. (1912). Recommendations to physicians practicing psycho-analysis. In J. Strachey (Ed. and Trans.), *The standard edition of the complete psychological works of Sigmund Freud* (Vol. 12, pp. 111–112). London: Hogarth Press.

Freud, S. (1913). Totem and taboo: Some points of agreement between the mental lives of savages and neurotics. In J. Strachey (Ed. and Trans.), *The standard edition of the complete psychological works of Sigmund Freud* (Vol. 8, pp. 1–162). London: Hogarth Press.

Freud, S. (1914a). On narcissism: An introduction. In J. Strachey (Ed. and Trans.), *The standard edition of the complete psychological works of Sigmund Freud* (Vol. 14, pp. 73–102). London: Hogarth Press.

Freud, S. (1914b). Remembering, repeating and working through. In J. Strachey (Ed. and Trans.), *The standard edition of the complete psychological works of Sigmund Freud* (Vol. 12, pp. 145–156). London: Hogarth Press.

Freud, S. (1917a). Mourning and melancholia. In J. Strachey (Ed. and Trans.), *The standard edition of the complete psychological works of Sigmund Freud* (Vol. 14, pp. 243–258). London: Hogarth Press.

Freud, S. (1917b). Fixation to traumas: The unconscious. In J. Strachey (Ed. and Trans.), *The standard edition of the complete psychological works of Sigmund Freud* (Vol. 16, pp. 272–285). London: Hogarth Press.

Freud, S. (1917c). Some thoughts on development and regression—Aetiology. In J. Strachey (Ed. and Trans.), *The standard edition of the complete psychological works of Sigmund Freud* (Vol. 16, pp. 339–357). London: Hogarth Press.

Freud, S. (1917d). The paths to the formation of symptoms. In J. Strachey (Ed. and Trans.), *The standard edition of the complete psychological works of Sigmund Freud* (Vol. 16, pp. 358–376). London: Hogarth Press.

Freud, S. (1920). Beyond the pleasure principle. In J. Strachey (Ed. and Trans.), *The standard edition of the complete psychological works of Sigmund Freud* (Vol. 18, pp. 1–63). London: Hogarth Press.

Freud, S. (1923). The ego and the id. In J. Strachey (Ed. and Trans.), *The standard edition of the complete psychological works of Sigmund Freud* (Vol. 20, pp. 75–176). London: Hogarth Press.

Freud, S. (1926). Inhibitions, symptoms and anxiety. In J. Strachey (Ed. and Trans.), *The standard edition of the complete psychological works of Sigmund Freud* (Vol. 19, pp. 1–66). London: Hogarth Press.

Freud, S. (1927). The future of an illusion. In J. Strachey (Ed. and Trans.), *The standard edition of the complete psychological works of Sigmund Freud* (Vol. 21, pp.1–56). London: Hogarth Press.

Freud, S. (1930). Civilization and its discontents. In J. Strachey (Ed. and Trans.), *The standard edition of the complete psychological works of Sigmund Freud* (Vol. 21, pp. 57–146). London: Hogarth Press.

Freud, S. (1933a). Sándor Ferenczi. *International Journal of Psychoanalysis, 14,* 297–299.

Freud, S. (1933b). Why war? In J. Strachey (Ed. and Trans.), *The standard edition of the complete psychological works of Sigmund Freud* (Vol. 22, pp. 195–216). London: Hogarth Press.

Freud, S. (1938). Splitting of the ego in the process of defence. In J. Strachey (Ed. and Trans.), *The standard edition of the complete psychological works of Sigmund Freud* (Vol. 23, pp. 271–278). London: Hogarth Press.

Fromm, E. (1999). *Escape from freedom.* New York: Henry Holt. (Original work published 1941)

Gabbard, G., Miller, L. and Martinez, M. (2008). A neurobiological perspective on mentalizing and internal object relations in traumatized borderline patients. In E. L. Jurist, A. Slade and S. Bergner (Eds.), *Mind to mind: Infant research, neuroscience, and psychoanalysis* (pp. 202–224). New York: Other Press.

Galassi, J. (2012). The great Montale in English. *New York Review of Books,* November 8. www.nybooks.com/articles/2012/11/08/great-montale-english/

Galatzer-Levy, R. M. (2002). Emergence. *Psychoanalytic Inquiry, 22,* 727–798.

Gallese, V. (2009). Mirror neurons, embodied simulation, and the neural basis of social identification. *Psychoanalytic Dialogues, 19,* 519–536.

Gay, P. (1988). *Freud: A life for our time.* New York: W. W. Norton.

Geertz, C. (1973). *The interpretation of cultures.* New York: Basic Books.

Geissman, C. and Geissman, P. (1998). *A history of child psychoanalysis.* London: Routledge.

Ghent, E. (1992). Foreword. In N. J. Skolnick and S. C. Warshaw (Eds.), *Relational perspectives in psychoanalysis* (pp. xiii–xviii). Hillsdale, NJ: Analytic Press.

Ghent, E. (2002). Wish, need, drive: Motive in the light of dynamic systems theory and Edelman's selectionist theory. *Psychoanalytic Dialogues, 12,* 763–808.

Gilmore, K. J. and Meersand, P. (2014). *Normal child and adolescent development: A psychodynamic primer.* Washington, DC: American Psychiatric Publishing.

Gladwell, M. (2000). *The tipping point: How little things can make a big difference.* Boston, MA: Little, Brown.

Gleick, J. (1987). *Chaos: Making a new science.* New York: Penguin.

Goldner, V. (2014). Romantic bonds, binds, and ruptures: Couples on the brink. *Psychoanalytic Dialogues, 24,* 402–418.

Green, A. (1999). *The fabric of affect in psychoanalytic discourse* (A. Sheridan, Trans.). London: Routledge. (Original work published 1973)

Green, A. (2000). Science and science fiction in infant research. In J. Sandler, A. M. Sandler and R. Davies (Eds.), *Clinical and observational psychoanalytic research: Roots of a controversy* (pp. 41–72). London: Karnac Books.

Greenberg, J. and Mitchell, S. (1983). *Object relations in psychoanalytic theory.* Cambridge, MA: Harvard University Press.

Greenberg, L. S. and Johnson, S. M. (1988). *Emotionally focused therapy for couples*. New York: Guilford Press.

Greenson, R. R. (1967). *The technique and practice of psychoanalysis* (vol. 1). New York: International Universities Press.

Greenspan, S. I. (1979). *Intelligence and adaptation: An integration of psychoanalytic and Piagetian developmental psychology*. New York: International Universities Press.

Greenspan, S. I. (1981). *Psychopathology and adaptation in infancy and early childhood*. New York: International Universities Press.

Greenspan, S. I. and Pollock, G. H. (Eds.). (1989). *The course of life* (Vol. 1). Madison, CT: International Universities Press.

Grigsby, J. and Schneiders, J. L. (1991). Neuroscience, modularity and personality theory: Conceptual foundations of a model of complex human functioning. *Psychiatry, 54*, 21–38.

Grotstein, J. S. (1994). Projective identification reappraised: Part I. *Contemporary Psychoanalysis, 30*, 708–746.

Grotstein, J. S. (1995). Projective identification reappraised: Part II. *Contemporary Psychoanalysis, 31*, 479–511.

Group for the Advancement of Psychiatry (GAP). (1966). *Psychopathological disorders in childhood: Theoretical considerations and a proposed classification*. New York: Group for the Advancement of Psychiatry.

Grunbaum, A. (1984). *Foundations of psychoanalysis: A philosophical critique*. Berkeley, CA: University of California Press.

Guralnik, O. and Simeon, D. (2010). Depersonalization: Standing in the spaces between recognition and interpellation. *Psychoanalytic Dialogues, 20*, 400–416.

Halberstam, J. (2005). Queer temporalities and postmodern geographies. In *In a queer time and place: Transgender bodies, subcultural lives* (pp. 1–20). New York: New York University Press.

Harris, A. E. (1991). Gender as contradiction. *Psychoanalytic Dialogues, 1*, 197–224.

Harris, A. E. (2005). *Gender as soft assembly*. Hillsdale, NJ: Analytic Press.

Harris, A. E. (2012). *Psychoanalysis and political culture*. Paper presented at the Annual Meeting of the International Association of Relational Psychoanalysis and Psychotherapy, New York.

Harris, A. E. (2015). "Language is there to bewilder itself and others": Theoretical and clinical contributions of Sabina Spielrein. *Journal of the American Psychoanalytic Association, 63*, 727–767.

Harrison, A. M. (2003). Change in psychoanalysis: Getting from A to B. *Journal of the American Psychoanalytic Association, 51*, 221–257.

Harrison, A. M. (2005). Herd the animals into the barn: A parent consultation model of child evaluation. *Psychoanalytic Study of Child, 60*, 128–157.

Harrison, A. M. and Tronick, E. Z. (2007). Now we have a playground: Emerging new ideas of therapeutic action. *Journal of the American Psychoanalytic Association, 55*, 853–874.

Hartman, S. (2011). Darren and Stephen: Erotic interludes in political transference. In M. Dimen (Ed.), *With culture in mind: Psychoanalytic stories* (pp. 19–23). New York: Routledge.

Hartmann, H. (1956). *Essays on ego psychology.* New York: International Universities Press.

Hartmann, H. (1958). *Ego psychology and the problem of adaptation.* New York: International Universities Press.

Heckman, J. (2008). *Schools, skills, and synapses.* http://ftp.iza.org/dp3515.pdf

Hegel, G. W. F. (1977). *Phenomenology of spirit.* Oxford: Oxford University Press.

Heidegger, M. (1962). *Being and time.* Oxford: Blackwell.

Heimann, P. (1950). On counter-transference. *International Journal of Psychoanalysis, 31*, 81–84.

Heller, M. and Haynal, V. (1997). The doctor's face: A mirror of his patient's suicidal projects. In J. Guimon (Ed.), *The body in psychotherapy* (pp. 46–51). Basel: Karger.

Herman, J. L. (1992). *Trauma and recovery.* New York: Basic Books.

Hesse, E. and Main, M. (2000). Disorganized infant, child, and adult attachment: Collapse in behavioral and attentional strategies. *Journal of the American Psychoanalytic Association, 48*, 1097–1128.

Hofer, M. A. (2014). The emerging synthesis of development and evolution: A new biology for psychoanalysis. *Neuropsychoanalysis: An Interdisciplinary Journal for Psychoanalysis and the Neurosciences, 16*(1), 3–22.

Hoffman, I. Z. (1998). *Ritual and spontaneity in the psychoanalytic process: A dialectical-constructivist view.* Hillsdale, NJ: Analytic Press.

Hollander, E. and Berlin, H. A. (2008). Neuropsychiatric aspects of aggression and impulse control disorders. In S. C. Yudofsky and R. E. Hales (Eds.), *The American Psychiatric Association textbook of neuropsychiatry and behavioral neurosciences* (pp. 535–565). Washington, DC: American Psychiatric Association Press.

Horney, K. (1935). The problem of feminine masochism. *Psychoanalytic Review, 22*, 241–257.

Hug-Hellmuth, H. (1921). On the technique of child-analysis. *International Journal of Psychoanalysis, 2*, 287–305.

Iacoboni, M. (2008). *Mirroring people: The new science of how we connect with others.* New York: Farrar, Straus and Giroux.

Ingber, D. E. (1998). The architecture of life: A universal set of building rules seems to guide the design of organic structures—from simple carbon compounds to complex cells and tissues. *Scientific American, 278,* 48–58.

Isaacs, S. (1948). The nature and function of phantasy. *International Journal of Psychoanalysis, 29,* 73–97.

Jacoby, R. (1975). *Social amnesia.* Boston, MA: Beacon Press.

Jaffe, J., Beebe, B., Feldstein, S., Crown, C. and Jasnow, M. (2001). Rhythms of dialogue in early infancy. *Monographs of the Society for Research in Child Development, 66,* 1–132.

Joseph, B. (1985). Transference: The total situation. *International Journal of Psychoanalysis, 66,* 447–454.

Joseph, B. (1988). Transference: The total situation. In E. B. Spillius (Ed.), *Melanie Klein today: Developments in theory and practice: Vol. 2: Mainly clinical* (pp. 52–60). London: Routledge.

Joseph, B. (2000). Agreeableness as an obstacle. *International Journal of Psychoanalysis, 81,* 641–649.

Jurist, E. L., Slade, A. and Bergner, S. (Eds.). (2008). *Mind to mind: Infant research, neuroscience and psychoanalysis.* New York: Other Press.

Kelso, J. A. S. (1995). *Dynamic patterns: The self-organization of brain and behavior.* Cambridge, MA: MIT Press.

Kerman, J. (1994). *Write all these down: Essays on music.* Berkeley, CA: University of California Press.

Kernberg, O. F. (1976). *Object relations theory and clinical psychoanalysis.* New York: Jason Aronson.

Klein, M. (1932). *The psycho-analysis of children.* London: Hogarth Press.

Klein, M. (1935). A contribution to the psychogenesis of manic-depressive states. *The International Journal of Psychoanalysis, 16,* 145–174.

Klein, M. (1940). Mourning and its relation to manic-depressive states. *International Journal of Psychoanalysis, 21,* 125–153.

Klein, M. (1946). Notes on some schizoid mechanisms. In J. Riviere (Ed.), *Developments in psychoanalysis* (pp. 292–320). London: Hogarth Press.

Klein, M. (1952). Some theoretical conclusions regarding the emotional life of the infant. In M. Klein, P. Heimann, S. Isaacs and J. Riviere (Eds.), *Developments in psychoanalysis* (pp. 198–236). London: Karnac Books.

Klein, M. (1961). *Narrative of a child analysis: The conduct of the psycho-analysis of children as seen in the treatment of a ten-year-old boy.* London: Hogarth Press and the Institute of Psycho-Analysis.

Klein, M. (1975). *Envy and gratitude and other works, 1946–1963* (M. R. Khan, Ed.). London: Hogarth Press.

Knoblauch, S. (2000). *The musical edge of therapeutic dialogue.* Hillsdale, NJ: Analytic Press.

Knoblauch, S. (2005). Body rhythms and the unconscious: Expanding clinical attention with the polyrhythmic weave. *Psychoanalytic Dialogues*, *15*, 807–827.

Kohut, H. (1977). *The restoration of the self.* New York: International Universities Press.

Kojève, A. (1969). *Introduction to the reading of Hegel.* New York: Basic Books.

Kristeva, J. (1989). *Black sun* (L. S. Roudiez, Trans.). New York: Columbia University Press.

Kuhn, T. S. (1970). *The structure of scientific revolutions* (2nd ed.). Chicago, IL: University of Chicago Press.

Kwawer, J. S. (n.d.). *Origins, theory, and practice: 1943–present.* www.wawhite. org/index.php?page=our-history

Lacan, J. (1949). The mirror stage as formative of the function of the I as revealed in psychoanalytic experience. In *Écrits: A selection* (pp. 1–6). New York: W.W. Norton.

Lacan, J. (1953). Some reflections on the ego. *International Journal of Psychoanalysis*, *34*, 11–17.

LaCapra, D. (2001). *Writing history, writing trauma.* Baltimore, MD: Johns Hopkins University Press.

Lachmann, F. M. (2001). Some contributions of empirical infant research to adult psychoanalysis: What have we learned? How can we apply it? *Psychoanalytic Dialogues*, *11*, 167–185.

Laing, R. D. (1961). *The self and others.* London: Tavistock.

Laing, R. D. (1971). *Knots.* New York: Pantheon.

Laplanche, J. (1999). *Essays on otherness.* London: Routledge.

Levi-Strauss, C.-L. (1971). *The elementary structures of kinship.* Boston, MA: Beacon Press. (Original work published 1949)

Lichtenberg, J. D. (1983). *Psychoanalysis and infant research.* Hillsdale, NJ: Analytic Press.

Lichtenberg, J. D. (1989). *Psychoanalysis and motivation.* Hillsdale, NJ: Analytic Press.

Lidz, T. (1983). *The person: His and her development throughout the life cycle.* New York: Basic Books. (Original work published 1968)

Lieberman, A. F., Ippen, C. G. and Van Horn, P. (2005). *Don't hit my mommy! A manual for child-parent psychotherapy with young children exposed to violence and other trauma* (2nd ed.). Washington, DC: Zero to Three.

Likierman, M. (2002). *Melanie Klein: Her work in context.* London: Continuum International.

Linehan, M. M., Kanter, J. W. and Comtois, K. A. (1999). Dialectical behavior therapy for borderline personality disorder: Efficacy, specificity, and cost effectiveness. In D. S. Janowsky (Ed.), *Psychotherapy indications and outcomes* (pp. 93–118). Washington, DC: American Psychiatric Association.

Loewald, H. W. (1960). On the therapeutic action of psychoanalysis. *International Journal of Psychoanalysis, 41*, 16–33.

Loewald, H. W. (1979). The waning of the Oedipus complex. *Journal of the American Psychoanalytic Association, 27*, 751–775.

Loewald, H. W. (1980). The experience of time. In *Papers on psychoanalysis* (pp. 138–146). New Haven, CT: Yale University Press.

Lyons-Ruth, K. (2006). The interface between attachment and intersubjectivity: Perspective from the longitudinal study of disorganized attachment. *Psychoanalytic Inquiry, 26*, 595–616.

Lyons-Ruth, K. and the Boston Change Process Study Group (1998). Implicit relational knowing: Its role in development and psychoanalytic treatment. *Infant Mental Health Journal, 19*, 282–289.

Mahler, M. S. (1972). On the first three subphases of the separation-individuation process. *International Journal of Psychoanalysis, 53*, 333–338.

Mahler, M. S., Pine, F. and Bergman, A. (1975). *The psychological birth of the human infant*. New York: Basic Books.

Main, M. (1995). Discourse, prediction and studies in attachment: Implications for psychoanalysis. In T. Shapiro and R. N. Emde (Eds.), *Research in psychoanalysis: Process, development, outcome* (pp. 209–245). Madison, CT: International Universities Press.

Main, M. (2000). The organized categories of infant, child, and adult attachment: Flexible vs. inflexible attention under attachment related stress. *Journal of the American Psychoanalytic Association, 48*, 1055–1097.

Main, M. and Solomon, J. (1990). Procedures for identifying infants as disorganized/disoriented during the Ainsworth Strange Situation. In M. T. Greenberg, D. Cicchetti and E. M. Cummings (Eds.), *Attachment in the preschool years: Theory, research and investigation* (pp. 121–160). Chicago, IL: University of Chicago Press.

Main, M., Hesse, E. and Kaplan, N. (2005). Predictability of attachment behaviors and representational process at 1, 6, and 19 years of age. In K. Grossman, K. Grossman and E. Waters (Eds.), *The Berkeley longitudinal study* (pp. 245–304). New York: Guilford Press.

Main, M., Kaplan, N. and Cassidy, J. (1985). Security in infancy, childhood and adulthood: A move to the level of representation. In I. Bretherton and E. Waters (Eds.), *Growing points of attachment theory and research* (pp. 66–104). Chicago, IL: University of Chicago Press.

Makari, G. (2008). *Revolution in mind: The creation of psychoanalysis*. New York: Harper Collins.

Marcuse, H. (1955). *Eros and civilization*. New York: Vintage.

Mayes, L., Fonagy, P. and Target, M. (2007). *Developmental science and psychoanalysis: An integration*. London: Karnac Books.

Meltzer, D. (1978). *The Kleinian development*. London: Karnac Books.

Meltzoff, A. N. and Moore, M. K. (1977). Imitation of facial and manual gestures by human neonates. *Science, 198*, 75–78.

Merleau-Ponty, M. (2004). *Basic writings* (T. Baldwin, Ed.). London: Routledge.

Merleau-Ponty, M. (2012). *Phenomenology of perception* (D. Landes, Trans.). London: Routledge. (Original work published 1945)

Miller, M. L. (2004). Dynamic systems and the therapeutic action of the analyst: II. Clinical application and illustrations. *Psychoanalytic Psychologist, 21*, 54–69.

Mitchell, J. (1975). *Psychoanalysis and feminism*. London: Allen Lane.

Mitchell, J. (2000). *Mad men and medusas: Reclaiming hysteria*. New York: Basic Books.

Mitchell, S. A. (1988). *Relational concepts in psychoanalysis: An integration*. Cambridge, MA: Harvard University Press.

Mitchell, S. A. (1993). *Hope and dread in psychoanalysis*. New York: Basic Books.

Mitchell, S. A. (1997). *Influence and autonomy in psychoanalysis*. Hillsdale, NJ: Analytic Press.

Mitchell, S. A. (2000). *Relationality: From attachment to intersubjectivity*. Hillsdale, NJ: Analytic Press.

Mitchell, S. A. and Black, M. J. (1995). *Freud and beyond: A history of modern psychoanalytic thought*. New York: Basic Books.

Modell, A. H. (1990). *Other times, other realities: Toward a theory of psychoanalytic treatment*. Cambridge, MA: Harvard University Press.

Modell, A. H. (2002). An appreciation of the contribution of Louis Sander. *Psychoanalytic Dialogues, 12*, 55–63.

National Research Council and Institute of Medicine. (2000). *From neurons to neighbourhoods: The science of early childhood development*. Washington, DC: National Academy Press.

Ogden, P., Minton, K. and Pain, C. (2006). *Trauma and the body: A sensorimotor approach to psychotherapy*. New York: W. W. Norton.

Ogden, T. H. (1982). *Projective identification and psychotherapeutic technique*. Northvale, NJ: Jason Aronson.

Ogden, T. H. (1986). *The matrix of the mind*. Northvale, NJ: Jason Aronson.

Ogden, T. H. (1992). The dialectically constituted/decentered subject of psychoanalysis, I: The Freudian subject. *International Journal of Psychoanalysis, 73*, 517–526.

Ogden, T. H. (1994a). *Subjects of analysis*. Northvale, NJ: Jason Aronson.

Ogden, T. H. (1994b). The analytic third: Working with intersubjective clinical facts. *International Journal of Psychoanalysis, 75*, 3–20.

Ogden, T. H. (2007). On talking as dreaming. *International Journal of Psychoanalysis, 88*, 575–589.

Palombo, J., Bendiscen, H. K. and Koch, B. J. (2009). *Guide to psychoanalytic developmental theories*. New York: Springer.

Panksepp, J. and Biven, L. (2012). *The archaeology of mind: Neuroevolutionary origins of human emotions*. New York: W.W. Norton.

Parsons, T. (1964). *Social structure and personality*. New York: Free Press.

Perry, B. D. (2007). *The boy who was raised as a dog: And other stories from a child psychiatrist's notebook*. New York: Basic Books.

Perry, B. D., Pollard, R. A., Blakely, T. L., Baker, W. L. and Vigilante, D. (1995). Childhood trauma, the neurobiology of adaptation, and "use-dependent" development of the brain: How states become traits. *Infant Mental Health Journal, 16*, 271–291.

Phillips, A. (1988). *Winnicott*. Cambridge, MA: Harvard University Press.

Pine, F. (1985). *Developmental theory and clinical process*. New Haven, CT: Yale University Press.

Pizer, B. (2003). When the crunch is a (k)not. *Psychoanalytic Dialogues, 13*, 171–192.

Pizer, S. (1992). The negotiation of paradox in the analytic process. *Psychoanalytic Dialogues, 2*, 215–240.

Plomin, R., Loehlin, J. C. and DeFries, H. C. (1985). Genetic and environmental components of "environmental influences." *Developmental Psychology, 21*, 391–402.

Polan, H. J. and Hofer, M. A. (2008). Psychobiological origins of infant attachment and its role in development. In J. Cassidy and P. R. Shaver (Eds.), *Handbook of attachment: Theory, research, and clinical applications* (2nd ed., pp. 158–172). New York: Guilford Press.

Porges, S. W. (2011). *The polyvagal theory: Neurophysiological foundations of emotions, attachment, communication, self-regulation*. New York: W. W. Norton.

Prigogine, I. (1996). *The end of certainty: Time, chaos and the new laws of nature*. New York: Free Press.

Proust, M. (2002). *Swann's way* (L. Davis, Trans.). New York: Penguin.

Rapaport, D. (1959). *A historical survey of psychoanalytic ego psychology*. New York: International Universities Press.

Rayner, E. (1990). *The independent mind in British psychoanalysis*. London: Free Association.

Reich, W. (1933). *Character analysis* (3rd ed.). New York: Noonday Press. (Original work published 1927)

Renn, P. (2012). *The silent past and the invisible present: Memory, trauma, and representation in psychotherapy*. New York: Routledge.

Ricoeur, P. (1988). *Time and narrative* (vol. 3). Chicago, IL: University of Chicago Press.

Ringstrom, P. A. (2001). Cultivating the improvisational in psychoanalytic treatment. *Psychoanalytic Dialogues, 11*, 727–754.

Rizzolatti, G. and Craighero, L. (2004). The mirror neuron system. *Annual Review of Neuroscience, 27*, 169–192.

Rizzolatti, G., Fadiga, L., Gallese, V. and Fogassi, L. (1996). Premotor cortex and the recognition of motor actions. *Cognitive Brain Research, 3*, 131–141.

Rosenfeld, H. A. (1971). A clinical approach to the psychoanalytic theory of the life and death instincts: An investigation into the aggressive aspects of narcissism. *International Journal of Psychoanalysis, 52*, 169–178.

Roth, J. (1987). *Hotel savoy* (J. Hoare, Trans.). New York: Overlook Press. (Original work published 1924)

Roth, J. (2011). *The Radetsky march* (J. Neugroschel, Trans.). New York: Penguin. (Original work published 1932)

Rozmarin, E. (2012). Introduction: The bonds of love at 25. *Studies in Gender and Sexuality, 13*, 237–239.

Said, E. (1978). *Orientalism*. New York: Pantheon.

Saketopoulou, A. (2014). Mourning the body as bedrock: Developmental considerations in treating transsexual patients analytically. *Journal of the American Psychoanalytic Association, 62*, 773–806.

Salo, F. and Paul, C. (2017). Understanding the sexuality of infants within caregiving relationships in the first year. *Psychoanalytic Dialogues, 27*, 320–337.

Sameroff, A. J. (1983). Developmental systems: Context and evolution. In P. Mussen (Ed.), *Handbook of child psychology* (Vol. 1, pp. 237–294). New York: Wiley.

Sameroff, A. J. and Chandler, M. J. (1975). Reproductive risk and the continuum of caretaking casualty. In F. D. Horowitz (Ed.), *Review of child development research* (Vol. 4, pp. 187–244). Chicago, IL: University of Chicago Press.

Sameroff, A. J. and Emde, R. N. (1989). *Relationship disturbances in early childhood: A developmental approach*. New York: Basic Books.

Sander, L. W. (1975). Infant and caretaking environment: Investigation and conceptualization of adaptive behavior in a system of increasing complexity. In E. J. Anthony (Ed.), *Explorations in child psychiatry* (pp. 129–166). New York: Plenum Press.

Sander, L. W. (1988). The event-structure of regulation in the neonate-caregiver system as a biological background for early organization of psychic structure.

In A. Goldberg (Ed.), *Frontiers of self psychology: Progress in self psychology* (Vol. 3, pp. 64–77). Hillsdale, NJ: Analytic Press.

Sander, L. W. (1995). Identity and the experience of specificity in a process of recognition: Commentary on Seligman and Shanok. *Psychoanalytic Dialogues, 5*, 579–593.

Sander, L. W. (2002). Thinking differently: Principles of process in living systems and the specificity of being known. *Psychoanalytic Dialogues, 2*, 11–42.

Sander, L. W. (2008). *Living systems, evolving consciousness, and the emerging person: A selection of papers from the life work of Louis Sander* (G. Amadei and I. Bianchi, Eds.). New York: Analytic Press.

Sandler, J. (1960). The background of safety. *International Journal of Psychoanalysis, 41*, 352–365.

Sandler, J. (1987). The concept of projective identification. In J. Sandler (Ed.), *Projection, identification, projective identification* (pp. 13–26). New York: International Universities Press.

Sandler, J., Dare, C., Dreher, A. U. and Holder, A. (1991). *The patient and the analyst: The basis of the psychoanalytic process*. London: Karnac Books.

Sandler, J. and Rosenblatt, B. (1962). The concept of the representational world. *Psychoanalytic Study of the Child, 17*, 128–145.

Sardar, Z. and Abrams, I. (1998). *Introducing chaos*. New York: Totem Books.

Schachtel, E. G. (1959). *Metamorphosis: On the conflict of human development and the psychology of creativity*. New York: Basic Books.

Schafer, R. (1968). *Aspects of internalization*. New York: International Universities Press.

Schafer, R. (1983). *The analytic attitude*. New York: Basic Books.

Schore, A. N. (1994). *Affect regulation and origin of the self*. Hillsdale, NJ: Lawrence Erlbaum Associates.

Schore, A. N. (2003a). *Affect dysregulation and the disorders of the self*. New York: W.W. Norton.

Schore, A. N. (2003b). *Affect regulation and the repair of the self*. New York: W.W. Norton.

Schore, A. N. (2012). *The science of the art of psychotherapy*. New York: W.W. Norton.

Schorske, C. (1981). *Fin-de-siecle Vienna: Politics and culture*. New York: Vintage.

Schweder, R. A. (Ed.). (2009). *The child: An encyclopedic companion*. Chicago, IL: University of Chicago Press.

Segal, H. (1957). Notes on symbol formation. *International Journal of Psychoanalysis, 38*, 391–397.

Seligman, S. (1994). Applying psychoanalysis in an unconventional context: Adapting infant-parent psychotherapy to a changing population. *Psychoanalytic Study of the Child, 49*, 481–510.

Seligman, S. (1996). Commentary on "The irrelevance of infant observation for psychoanalysis," by Peter Wolff. *Journal of the American Psychoanalytic Association, 44,* 430–446.

Seligman, S. (1997). Historical legacies and contemporary innovation: Introduction to symposium on child analysis, part I. *Psychoanalytic Dialogues, 7,* 707–723.

Seligman, S. (1999). Integrating Kleinian theory and intersubjective infant research: Observing projective identification. *Psychoanalytic Dialogues, 9,* 129–159.

Seligman, S. (2000). Clinical implications of attachment theory. *Journal of the American Psychoanalytic Association, 48,* 1189–1196.

Seligman, S. (2003). The developmental perspective in relational psychoanalysis. *Contemporary Psychoanalysis, 39*(3), 477–508.

Seligman, S. (2005). Dynamic systems theories as a metaframework for psychoanalysis. *Psychoanalytic Dialogues, 15,* 285–319.

Seligman, S. (2006). The analyst's theoretical persuasion and the construction of a conscientious analysis: Commentary on a paper by Meira Likierman. *Psychoanalytic Dialogues, 16,* 397–405.

Seligman, S. (2010). The sensibility of baseball. *Contemporary Psychoanalysis, 46,* 562–577.

Seligman, S. (2011). Review of Daniel Stern's *Forms of vitality*: Exploring dynamic experience in psychology, the arts, psychotherapy, and development. *Journal of the American Psychoanalytic Association, 59,* 859–868.

Seligman, S. (2012a). *Relational psychoanalysis: New Left origins.* Paper presented at the annual meeting of the International Association of Relational Psychoanalysis and Psychotherapy, New York.

Seligman, S. (2012b). The baby out of the bathwater: Microseconds, psychic structure, and psychotherapy. *Psychoanalytic Dialogues, 22,* 499–509.

Seligman, S. (2013). Baseball time. *Raritan: A Quarterly Review, 32,* 54–68.

Seligman, S. (2014a). Paying attention and feeling puzzled: The analytic mindset as an agent of therapeutic change. *Psychoanalytic Dialogues, 25,* 648–662.

Seligman, S. (2014b). Attachment, intersubjectivity, and mentalization within the experience of the child, the parent, and the provider. In K. Brandt, B. D. Perry, S. Seligman and E. Tronick (Eds.), *Infant and early childhood mental health: Core concepts and clinical practice* (pp. 309–322). Washington, DC: American Psychiatric Publishing.

Seligman, S. (2016). Disorders of temporality and the subjective experience of time: Unresponsive objects and the vacuity of the future. *Psychoanalytic Dialogues, 26,* 1–19.

Seligman, S. (2018). Illusion as a basic psychic principle: Winnicott, Freud, Oedipus, and Trump. *Journal of the American Psychoanalytic Association, 66,* 263–288.

Seligman, S. (2021). Reconstructing the depressive position: Creativity and style in Winnicott's "Concern" paper. *Journal of the American Psychoanalytic Association, 69*, 491–512.

Seligman, S. and Bader, M. (1991). The doctorate of mental health program in its social-political context. In R. S. Wallerstein (Ed.), *The doctorate in mental health: An experiment in mental health professional education* (pp. 179–194). Lanham, MD: University Press of America.

Seligman, S. and Harrison, A. M. (2011). Infant research and adult psychotherapy. In G. O. Gabbard, B. E. Litowitz and P. Williams (Eds.), *American Psychiatric Association textbook of psychoanalysis* (2nd ed., pp. 239–252). Washington, DC: American Psychiatric Publishing.

Seligman, S. and Shanok, R. S. (1995). Subjectivity, complexity, and the social world: Erikson's identity concept and contemporary relational theories. *Psychoanalytic Dialogues, 5*, 537–565.

Seligman, S. and Shanok, R. S. (1996). Erikson, our contemporary: His anticipation of an intersubjective perspective. *Psychoanalysis and Contemporary Thought, 19*, 339–365.

Shane, E. and Coburn, W. J. (Eds.). (2002). *Contemporary dynamic systems theories: Innovative contributions to psychoanalysis*. Hillsdale, NJ: Analytic Press.

Shane, M., Shane, E. and Gales, M. (1997). *Intimate attachments: Toward a new self psychology*. New York: Guilford Press.

Shaw, T. (2013). Nietzsche: The lightning fire. *The New York Review of Books*. www.nybooks.com/articles/2013/10/24/nietzsche-lightning-fire

Shonkoff, J. P., Boyce, W. T. and McEwen, B. S. (2009). Neuroscience, molecular biology, and the childhood roots of health disparities: Building a new framework for health promotion and disease promotion. *Journal of the American Medical Association, 301*(21), 2252–2259.

Siegel, D. J. (2015). *The developing mind: How relationships and the brain interact to shape who we are* (2nd ed.). New York: Guilford Press.

Slade, A. (2008). Attachment theory and research: Implications for the theory and practice of individual psychotherapy with adults. In J. Cassidy and P. R. Shaver (Eds.), *Handbook of attachment: Theory, research and clinical applications* (2nd ed., pp. 762–782). New York: Guilford Press.

Slade, A. (2014). Imagining fear: Attachment, threat, and psychic experience. *Psychoanalytic Dialogues, 24*, 253–266.

Slavin, J. (2016). "I have been trying to get them to respond to me": Sexuality and agency in psychoanalysis. *Contemporary Psychoanalysis, 52*, 1–20.

Slavin, M. and Kriegman, D. (1992). *The adaptive design of the human psyche: Psychoanalysis, evolutionary biology, and the therapeutic process*. New York: Guilford Press.

Sletvold, J. (2014). *The embodied analyst: From Freud and Reich to relationality.* London: Routledge.

Slochower, J. (1996). *Holding and psychoanalysis: A relational perspective.* Hillsdale, NJ: Analytic Press.

Snyder, T. (2010). *Bloodlands: Europe between Hitler and Stalin.* New York: Basic Books.

Spillius, E. B. (1988). *Melanie Klein today: Developments in theory and practice, Vol. 1: Mainly theory.* London: Routledge.

Spillius, E. B., Milton, J., Garvey, P., Couve, C. and Steiner, D. (2011). *The new dictionary of Kleinian thought.* London: Routledge.

Spitz, R. A. (1965). *The first year of life: A psychoanalytic study of normal and deviant development of object relations.* New York: International Universities Press.

Steiner, J. (1987). The interplay between pathological organizations and the paranoid-schizoid and depressive positions. *International Journal of Psychoanalysis, 63,* 241–251.

Steiner, J. (1993). *Psychic retreats: Pathological organizations in psychotic, neurotic, and borderline patients.* London: Routledge.

Stern, D. B. (1989). The analyst's unformulated experience of the patient. *Contemporary Psychoanalysis, 25,* 1–33.

Stern, D. N. (1971). A microanalysis of mother-infant interaction. *Journal of the American Academy of Child Psychiatry, 10,* 501–517.

Stern, D. N. (1977). *The first relationship: Infant and mother.* Cambridge, MA: Harvard University Press.

Stern, D. N. (1985). *The interpersonal world of the infant.* New York: Basic Books.

Stern, D. N. (1990). *Diary of a baby.* New York: Basic Books.

Stern, D. N. (1995). *The motherhood constellation: A unified view of parent-infant psychotherapy.* New York: Basic Books.

Stern, D. N. (2004). *The present moment in psychotherapy and everyday life.* New York: W.W. Norton.

Stern, D. N. (2010). *Forms of vitality: Exploring dynamic experience in psychology, the arts, psychotherapy and development.* Oxford: Oxford University Press.

Stern, D. N., Sander, L. W., Nahum, J. P., Harrison, A. M., Lyons-Ruth, K., Morgan, A. C., Bruschweiler-Stern, N. and Tronick, E. Z. (1998). Non-interpretive mechanisms in psychoanalytic therapy: The "something more" than interpretation. *International Journal of Psychoanalysis, 79,* 903–921.

Stolorow, R. D. (1997). Dynamic, dyadic, intersubjective systems: An evolving paradigm for psychoanalysis. *Psychoanalytic Psychology, 14,* 337–346.

Stolorow, R. D. and Atwood, G. E. (1992). Three realms of the unconscious. In *Contexts of being: The intersubjective foundations of psychological life* (pp. 29–40). Hillsdale, NJ: Analytic Press.

Stolorow, R. D., Atwood, G. E. and Brandchaft, B. (Eds.). (1994). *The intersubjective perspective*. Northvale, NJ: Jason Aronson.

Stolorow, R. D., Atwood, G. E. and Orange, D. M. (2002). *Worlds of experience: Interweaving philosophical and clinical dimensions in psychoanalysis*. New York: Basic Books.

Stolorow, R. D., Brandchaft, B. and Atwood, G. E. (1987). *Psychoanalytic treatment*. Hillsdale, NJ: Analytic Press.

Stone, L. (1954). The widening scope of indications for psychoanalysis. *Journal of the American Psychoanalytic Association, 2*, 567–594.

Sullivan, H. S. (1953). *The interpersonal theory of psychiatry*. New York: W. W. Norton.

Symington, N. (1983). The analyst's act of freedom as agent of therapeutic change. *International Review of Psychoanalysis, 10*, 283–291.

Tarantino, Q. (Director) (2009). *Inglorious basterds* [motion picture]. United States: Universal Pictures.

Thelen, E. (2005). Dynamic systems theory and the complexity of change. *Psychoanalytic Dialogues, 15*, 255–284.

Thelen, E. and Smith, L. B. (1994). *A dynamic systems approach to the development of cognition and action*. Cambridge, MA: MIT Press.

Tomasello, M. (1999). *The cultural origins of human cognition*. Cambridge, MA: Harvard University Press.

Tomkins, S. S. (1962). *Affect, imagery, consciousness: Vol. I. The positive affects*. New York: Springer.

Tomkins, S. S. (1963). *Affect, imagery, consciousness: Vol. II. The negative affects*. New York: Springer.

Tortora, S. (2005). *The dancing dialogue: Using the communicative power of movement with young children*. Baltimore, MD: Brookes.

Trevarthen, C. (1980). The foundations of intersubjectivity: Development of interpersonal and cooperative understanding in infants. In D. R. Olson (Ed.), *The social foundation of language and thought: Essays in honor of Jerome Bruner* (pp. 316–341). New York: Norton.

Trevarthen, C. (1993). The self born in intersubjectivity: The psychology of an infant communicating. In U. Neisser (Ed.), *The perceived self: Ecological and interpersonal sources of self-knowledge* (pp. 121–172). New York: Cambridge University Press.

Trevarthen, C. (2009). The intersubjective psychobiology of human meaning: Learning of culture depends on interest for cooperative practical work and affectation for the joyful art of good company. *Psychoanalytic Dialogues, 19*, 507–518.

Tronick, E. Z. (1998). Dyadically expanded states of consciousness and the process of therapeutic change. *Infant Mental Health Journal, 19*, 290–299.

Tronick, E. Z. (2005). Why is connection with others so critical? The formation of dyadic states of consciousness and the expansion of individual states of consciousness: Coherence governed selection and the co-creation of meaning out of messy meaning making. In J. Nadel and D. Muir (Eds.), *Emotional development: Recent research advances* (pp. 293–316). New York: Oxford University Press.

Tronick, E. Z. (2007). *The neurobehavioral and social-emotional development of infants and children*. New York: W. W. Norton.

Tronick, E. Z., Brunschweiler-Stern, N., Harrison, A. M., Lyons-Ruth, K., Morgan, A. C., Nahum, J. P. and Stern, D. N. (1998). Dyadically expanded states of consciousness and the process of therapeutic change. *Infant Mental Health Journal, 19*, 290–299.

Tustin, F. (1981). *Autistic states in children*. London: Routledge and Kegan Paul.

Tyson, P. and Tyson, R. L. (1990). *Psychoanalytic theories of development: An integration*. New Haven, CT: Yale University Press.

Van Der Kolk, B. A. (2014). *The body keeps the score: Brain, mind, and body in the healing of trauma*. New York: The Penguin Group.

Van Der Kolk, B. A. and Fisler, R. E. (1994). Childhood abuse and neglect and loss of self-regulation. *Bulletin of the Menninger Clinic, 58*, 145–168.

van IJzendoorn, M. H. (1995). Adult attachment representations, parental responsiveness, and infant attachment: A meta-analysis on the predictive validity of the Adult Attachment Interview. *Psychological Bulletin, 117*, 387–403.

Vygotsky, L. (1962). *Thought and language*. Cambridge, MA: MIT Press.

Wallerstein, R. S. (1980). Psychoanalysis and academic psychiatry—bridges. *Psychoanalytic Study of the Child, 35*, 419–448.

Wallerstein, R. S. (1991). *The common ground of psychoanalysis*. Northvale, NJ: Jason Aronson.

Wallerstein, R. S. (1998). *Lay analysis: Life inside the controversy*. Hillsdale, NJ: Analytic Press.

Wallin, D. J. (2007). *Attachment in psychotherapy*. New York: Guilford Press.

Weinstein, F. and Platt, G. (1969). *The wish to be free: Society, psyche, and value change*. Berkeley, CA: University of California Press.

Winnicott, D. W. (1947). Hate in the countertransference. In *Through paediatrics to psychoanalysis* (pp. 142–156). London: Hogarth Press.

Winnicott, D. W. (1949). Mind and its relation to the psyche-soma. In *Through paediatrics to psychoanalysis* (pp. 243–254). London: Hogarth Press.

Winnicott, D. W. (1951). Transitional objects and transitional phenomena. In *Playing and reality* (pp. 1–25). New York: Basic Books.

Winnicott, D. W. (1956). Primary maternal preoccupation. In *Through paediatrics to psychoanalysis* (pp. 300–305). London: Hogarth Press.

Winnicott, D. W. (1958a). The capacity to be alone. *International Journal of Psychoanalysis*, *39*, 416–420.

Winnicott, D. W. (1958b). *Through paediatrics to psychoanalysis*. London: Hogarth Press.

Winnicott, D. W. (1960a). The theory of parent-infant relationship. *International Journal of Psychoanalysis*, *41*, 585–595.

Winnicott, D. W. (1960b). Ego distortions in terms of true and false self. In *The maturational processes and the facilitating environment* (pp. 140–152). New York: International Universities Press.

Winnicott, D. W. (1962). A personal view of the Kleinian contribution. In *The maturational processes and the facilitating environment* (pp. 166–170). New York: International Universities Press.

Winnicott, D. W. (1963). Fear of breakdown. In C. Winnicott, R. Shepherd and M. Davis (Eds.), *Psycho-analytic explorations* (pp. 87–95). Cambridge, MA: Harvard University Press.

Winnicott, D. W. (1965a). *The maturational processes and the facilitating environment*. New York: International Universities Press.

Winnicott, D. W. (1965b). The capacity for concern. In *The maturational processes and the facilitating environment* (pp. 73–82). New York: International Universities Press.

Winnicott, D. W. (1970). *Playing and reality*. New York: Basic Books.

Winnicott, D. W. (1974). Fear of breakdown. *International Review of Psychoanalysis*, *1*, 103–107.

Winnicott, D. W. (1967). The location of cultural experience. *International Journal of Psychoanalysis*, *48*, 368–372.

Winograd, B. (2014). Black psychoanalysts speak [video]. *PEP Video Grants*, *1*(1).

Wollheim, R. (1993). *The mind and its depths*. Cambridge, MA: Harvard University Press.

Zborowski, M. and Herzog, E. (1952). *Life is with people: The Jewish little-town of Eastern Europe*. New York: International Universities Press.

Index

innate adaptive motivation 46
innate destructive instinct 177–178
instinct-energy model 39, 40, 142, 200
instincts 14n1, 28, 37, 41–42, 44n1,
49, 54, 57, 103, 159, 191; aggressive
6, 21; asocial 21, 28; bodily based
27, 53, 123, 145, 180; death 53,
65n12, 165, 179; destructive 52,
61, 177–179; drives 26, 41, 45–46,
92; gratification 25, 141; impulses
47; innate destructive 177–178;
instinct-energy model 39, 40, 142,
200; libidinal (life) 6, 52, 179, 231;
motivations 36, 60, 150; needs
51; opposing 53; primeval 65n12;
primitive 4, 6, 8, 35n7, 45–46;
psychic reality 55; psychosexual
stage model with 145; sexual 21,
35n4, 61; vicissitudes 125
instinct theory 81, 87, 200, 282; body
and (human) objects in 38–39;
classical 178; dislocating 141;
irrationalist 43; oriented criticisms
123–124; psychoanalytic 192–194;
rejection of 141–142, 178
interdisciplinarity 73–74
internal working models 112, 127,
131, 132, 154, 163, 177–178
interpersonal motivation 51
interpersonal neurobiology 97
interpersonal psychoanalysis 83–85, 87
intersubjective motivation system 149,
152, 232
intersubjectivity 4–5, 19, 57, 88,
94, 98–99, 104, 108, 146n3,
147–149, 161, 164, 179, 184,
186–187, 190, 192, 195, 207–209,
213, 217, 221–222, 283; affect
and 90–92; child development 4;
emergence of 165; foundations of
150–151; motivation 149, 152, 232;
recognition 98; two-person approach
104–105; vital 199
intrinsic motivation 281

irrationalist instinct theory 43
Isaacs, S. 193

Jaffe, J. 127, 129, 135, 138–139
Joseph, B. 270

Kernberg, O. 17, 80
Klein, M. 3, 15, 17, 147–148, 171,
193; anxiety 47, 179; bad objects
61, 117, 272; death instincts 179;
depressive position 54, 159, 164;
infantile primitive mind 51; infant–
parent observation and 190–191;
metapsychology 191–193; object
relations (see object relations);
paranoid-schizoid position 53–54,
159, 168, 171, 191; phantasy 10–11,
14n1, 53, 132, 159, 178, 180–181,
184, 186, 190–193; primary process
181; thinking and 159–160
Kohut, H. 17, 80, 82, 85, 144, 165,
250, 268
Kris, K. 81, 282

Lacan, J. 9
Lachmann, F. M. 95
Levi-Strauss, C.-L. 41
libidinal (life) instinct 6, 52, 179, 231
Lichtenberg, J. 121
Loewald, H. 80, 203, 205, 207, 213
Loewenstein, R. 64, 81, 282
Lyons-Ruth, K. 113

Mahler, M. 17, 80, 144, 164
Main, M. 97, 197
maternal authority 143
maternal care 41, 52, 58, 61, 141
maternal subjectivity, into
developmental theory 143–144
mediation 2, 130, 167, 177
Meltzoff, A. N. 89
memories 26, 30, 47, 75, 89, 106,
114, 136, 154, 173, 203–204, 206,
214–215, 229, 281; actual 162;

For Product Safety Concerns and Information please contact our EU
representative GPSR@taylorandfrancis.com
Taylor & Francis Verlag GmbH, Kaufingerstraße 24, 80331 München, Germany

www.ingramcontent.com/pod-product-compliance
Lightning Source LLC
Chambersburg PA
CBHW050627280326
41932CB00015B/2556

9 7 8 1 0 3 2 9 9 8 4 8 0